TABLE OF CONTENTS

ETHICAL VALUES FOR HUMAN CIVILITY

IMPERATIVES FOR PEACE

WILLIE JAMES WEBB

ETHICAL VALUES FOR HUMAN CIVILITY
IMPERATIVES FOR PEACE

WILLIE JAMES WEBB
(THEOLOGICAL ETHICIST)

CHAPTER 1
INTRODUCTION
THE PRACTICE OF PUBLIC THEOLOGY

The practice of public theology is the manifestation of the revelation of God's will, commandments, ways, methods, wisdom, and works in the social and public arenas of society. The practice of "public theology" is the open disclosure of God's ordained mission for humanity. It is the implementation of the foundational principles and sound doctrines of biblical knowledge and the Gospel of Jesus Christ for the uplift of humanity. It must be emphasized that these foundational principles and sound doctrines are based on Biblical knowledge and the Gospel of Jesus Christ.

The knowledge, understanding, and practice of public theology are very significant and even urgent at this present time in the 21st Century. The barriers, restrictions, and limitations of God's Biblical Word and the Gospel of Jesus Christ in the American culture have left serious and critical ethical, moral, and spiritual deficits. The Judeo-Christian values of the United States have been the glue and social cohesion that have held the United States together through slavery, the Revolutionary War, the Civil War, the 1932 Depression, World War II, and other major domestic and international conflicts. Tragically, those traditional values have been corroded and diluted in America through educational restrictions, immigration, religious privatization and growing secularization.

There are periods in the history of Christianity and the Church where the Church and Christian believers retreated from the public domain, public square, and general society.

Without going into lengthy detail about these retreats of Christian believers from general society. There are notable periods in history when Christian believers withdrew and retreated into monasteries, convents, and local private churches and places of worship. However, it must be noted that during the Middle Ages and Dark Ages, humanity did not have the phenomenal technological capabilities that exist in the 21"-Century. The stakes, the hazards, and the capabilities are astronomically and exponentially higher due to 21st Century technology. So, public theology needs to get more involved in this unstable moral decline and increase in the power of technology. This is the worst time in history for Christian believers to retreat from the public square. The public theologians must be the moral compass, the vanguard of truth, responsible stewards, guardian angels, vigilant watchmen, and humanitarian rescuers for civilization.

Currently, in the 21st Century in America, most Christian activities are geared toward private priestly religion and worship on Sunday and other days Along with this trend of private religious practice and worship, secular forces and even federal laws are requiring religion, particularly Christianity, to be absent or silent in public. This perilous trend is robbing and depriving the American culture of its fundamental ethical, moral, and spiritual survival values.

The message of God and the mission of Christ are designed for all people, in both private and in public life. During this critical cultural crisis time, the validated knowledge about God in the Bible and the Risen Savior in Jesus Christ must be taught, practiced, and proclaimed with evangelical zeal, the prophetic voice, and spiritual Holy Ghost power. This biblical illiteracy, idolatrous, and atheistic culture have created in America the most confused, chaotic, and potentially most disastrous culture in the history of the country. It is insane that "A Nation under God," with a Declaration that "All men are created equal" and are endowed by their Creator with certain "inalienable Rights-life, liberty and the pursuit of happiness," could descend to such depraved depths. THE BIBLICAL KNOWLEDGE ABOUT GOD IS FOR ALL PEOPLE AND FOR ALL GENERATIONS FOR ALL TIME. GOD IS SOVEREIGN WITH ABSOLUTE POWER, AUTHORITY, AND INFINITE JURISDICTION. The barriers, restrictions, limitations, and the exclusive privatization of God's message and love for mankind must be removed in America and the world. HUMANITY'S TOTAL DEPENDENCE IS ON GOD.

It is the challenge and duty of public theology to lead the way in removing the barriers, restrictions, and limitations of Biblical knowledge and the love of Christ that exist in the public domain. Private religion and Biblical knowledge must be expanded and included in the public domain and public square of American culture and the world. THERE ARE NO OFF LIMITS TO GOD. IT IS EVIL TO SEPARATE PEOPLE AND ESPECIALLY CHILDREN FROM THE KNOWLEDGE AND THE LOVE OF GOD.

Public theology is the manifestation of the revelation of God's Will, Commandments, Ways, Methods, Wisdom and Works in all the social and public arenas of society. The practice of "public theology" is the open disclosure of God's ordained mission for humanity. The foundational principles and sound doctrines for the practice of public theology are based on Biblical knowledge and the Gospel of Jesus Christ.

How can the will of God be known? The Will of God is found in abundance in God's creation. God's creation is an expression of his will. The Book of Genesis indicates God's favor after each of the six days of God's creation. God declared his creation as being good and very good. It is sacrilegious and ludicrous for a human to attempt to change and improve on God's creation. God's creation is a declaration of God's Will. The Holy Bible is a declaration of God's Will. The Bible is a complete book and an authority within itself. The Bible speaks for itself and prohibits any subtractions or additions. It is the literary composite of God's Will. Jesus Christ is the Word of God made flesh in the history of mankind. Jesus Christ is the undeviating Will of God. God's Will and nature are revealed in the minds, hearts, spirits, souls and bodies of human beings. God's Will is revealed in the social, economic, educational, religious, and cultural institutions of mankind. God's Will is expressed in just and righteous nations. God's will is found explicitly in the way, the truth, and the life in Jesus Christ.

The practice of public theology is to be obedient to God's Will in the execution of God's will in the lives of every person, agency, and institution on the earth. The will of God makes all things work together for good and peace. It is significant that God created the man and the woman in God's image and likeness (Genesis 1:26-27). It is also significant to note that the first thing that God did for the man and the woman was give his blessings and commandments to them. God blessed them and said, "Be fruitful, and multiply, and replenish the earth, subdue it: and have dominion over the fish of the sea, and over the fowl of the air, and over a living thing that moveth upon the earth" (Genesis 1:28).

It is worth noting that God's first commandment to man and woman included public theology There was no provision for a private religion or place of worship. The man and the woman were blessed and given responsibility on the horizontal level for taking care of the earth and having dominion over all life on the earth, the sky, and the seas.

God did not set geographical limitations for the first man and woman on the earth. God gave them the authority to replenish, subdue, and have dominion. Fast forwarding from antiquity to the 21st Century, it appears that the Church has imposed limitations upon itself. It also appears that the secular state or government has imposed limitations on the people of God. In this 21st Century, there is much talk and observance of the idea of "separation of Church and State." It also appears that the secular state or government sets limitations and draws the lines of demarcation. It also appears that the supreme authority for making the laws for the nation of America has been vested in the Supreme Court of the United States. It is not at all clear as to how the U. S. Supreme Court arrives at its decisions. It is determined by the majority vote of nine jurists. There have been many 5 to 4 decisions. The ultimate ruling authority for Supreme Court decision-making is not clear. These decisions seem to be arbitrary, random, opinionated, and even politically biased. Much more can be said about the validity of American administrative and judicial decisions. It is clear that decision-making is far removed from the Bible and the authority of God. Tragically, the privatized society has eliminated God and the Bible from the public's decision-making authority.

The retreat and acquiescence of God's Church (people) into private religion, combined with secular government authority, have removed the Bible and God's authority from public policy making and governance in the United States of America. This reversal and shift of authority from the people of God to the people of the secular world has invited the ungodly and anti-God people into the public square of public policy making and enforcement. Many people in government make public policy who have no knowledge of the Bible or God's will. Anti-God public policies and practices are wreaking havoc on America's and the planet's survival values and lives. The history of America makes it clear where the Nation went wrong by neglecting and abandoning the ordinances, statutes, laws, commandments, and love of God. The history of the American Church makes it clear where the Church went wrong by becoming silent, privatized, and acquiescent to the world. The Church must revisit the blessings and the commandments given to the first man and the first woman to be fruitful and multiply, replenish the earth, subdue it, and have dominion.

The conscientious practice of public theology is a viable vehicle to revive private religion and biblical knowledge and expand them into the public arenas of society. The salvation message of God must be preached, taught, and practiced with commitment, diligence, and power. It must arouse the complacent churches. It must permeate the schools and the halls of academia without ceasing. Biblical knowledge and the love of Christ must be sown into the minds, hearts, agencies, institutions, and culture as an urgent priority. The nature of man was made to be nurtured by the spirit and love of God. Man cannot get along well without God. Without God, minds become deranged; hearts become wicked; souls become lost; relationships become hostile; purposes become confused; cultures become corrupted; nations become destabilized; and Humanity and civilizations are destroyed. The first commandment to the first man and first woman (Genesis 1:28) is still in effect. It is perilous for humanity to ignore or neglect the commandments of God throughout the Bible.

The habitation of the earth is fraught with constant manmade dangers and natural disasters. For this reason, man must be watchful, faithful, responsible, and resourceful. Man does not have the luxury of being slothful, childish, irresponsible, and wasteful of the gifts and resources of God. Man (humankind) cannot afford to be ignorant, foolish, and incompetent with all the looming dangers and disasters of hurricanes, tornadoes, floods, lightning bolts, droughts, earthquakes, volcanic eruptions, forest fires, falling trees, poisonous plants, dangerous animals, famines, diseases, wickedness, and evil. Man must be diligent in obeying Genesis 1:28 and the other commandments, including the knowledge, wisdom, and love of God. Man must grow up and take full advantage of God's bountiful generosity.

These omnibus dangers and disasters cannot be subdued through restricted, private, priestly religion. The earth cannot be replenished through restricted, private, selfish religion. The people of God cannot effectively exercise dominion through self-imposed restricted, and withdrawn religion in a private place of retreat and defeat. True religion requires good, faithful and responsible stewardship on the part of man.

God has put man and woman in charge of the earth as faithful stewards having dominion (Genesis 1:28). The generous and loving God has equipped both men and women with his image and likeness. God made man and woman special with autonomous, creative, and innovative abilities to carry out the commandments: to "be fruitful," to "multiply," to "replenish the earth," to "subdue it," and to "have dominion."

The carrying out and execution of the blessings and commandments of God require biblical knowledge and a variety of pastoral, ministerial, administrative, counseling, case management, and clinical skills. The execution of this theological practice is fraught with many risks, hazards, and dangers. The parish priestly pulpit ministry is less complicated than the practice of public theology in the public domain. The parish ministry is more simple, routine, and ritualistic. For these reasons, the private worship ministry is more prescribed, controlled, restricted, and predictable. The parish ministry provides a haven of solemnity, comfort, and safety. This private, safe haven of quietness and comfort can diminish the incentive for practicing public theology outside of the walls of this comfortable, safe haven.

The public theology mission field ministry is more exposed in the open public arena and thus more vulnerable to unknown and unpredictable variables. Therefore, the public theologian must learn a more diverse combination of social, political, economic, and community resource development skills. Whatever variety of knowledge and skills the public theologian may acquire, the biblical theological foundation must remain as the authoritative supporting foundation and guiding force.

To be an effective public theologian, the theologian must be able to navigate a complex web of legal, ethical, moral, political, social, personal, and community issues. Therefore, the practice of public theology can be considered the skilled, efficient, ethical, and benevolent provision of God's resources and services for human beings and for the public good based on biblical authority. Public theology embraces the biblical concept that the mission of human life is to bless and uplift humanity, provide for its salvation needs, and glorify God with the gifts and resources of God.

The loving and merciful God has provided man with four distinct domains of knowledge to determine what is true and how this true knowledge can be used to fulfill God's will and God's commandments to man. These four knowledge domains are not arbitrary. They are definitive and can be tested. God has given man the sensibilities to perceive these four domains of knowledge and use them to bless humanity and solve problems. The word s a 11 is used frequently in the Bible. It is used as a preservative or flavoring substance in the Bible. Jesus uses the word, SALT in the Bible. He even indicated that his disciples are "the salt of the earth." (Matthew 5:13). Based on this brief biblical reference, liberty is taken to use SALT as an acronym to highlight these four domains of knowledge that God gives to man to evaluate and test the truth and also to use to solve problems and carry out God's commandments. The S represents SCIENCE; the A in salt represents ART; the L in salt represents LAW; and the T in salt represents THEOLOGY. Therefore, the four domains of knowledge to rest and evaluate for truth are SCIENCE, ART, LAW, and THEOLOGY. The rationality of truth can be discerned and determined through the cognitive and sensibilities of the mind. These four domains of knowledge are vital for the practice of public theology. God has provided man with a rational mind and an intuitive spirit to recognize and discern that which is true and what is false. SALT: science, art, law, and theology are the domains of knowledge and tools for the recognition of truth to be used to practice public theology to transform and create a world and a civilization that reflects God's Kingdom on earth.

The Christian Association of Public Theologians and the Christian Institute of Public Theology were incorporated in the State of Georgia in 2002 in Atlanta to more fully utilize the gifts and resources of God to help mankind be more humane and civil in reflecting the image and glory of God in the building of God's Kingdom in Atlanta, America, and the earth. God has blessed these corporations to utilize more fully God's gifts of science, art, law, and theology to solve human problems and continue the unfinished work of building God's Kingdom on earth. These two corporations, known as CAPT and CIPT, are on the front lines of the battle for God's Kingdom.

This book provides the foundations, biblical authority, relevant principles, and guidance for the practice of public theology. The aim is to make the practice of public theology sensible and practical with the minimum amount of academic rhetorical theories and discourse. The explanations, illustrations, and outlines are designed to be practical for replication and implementation. The practice of public theology involves ideas and principles that can be transmitted and put into effect to educate and impact positive change for the good of society. The ideas, truths, and biblical principles shared in this book are in response to the serious cultural crisis that humanity faces. These ideas, truths, and principles are designed for action. They are biblical answers for our acute problems. They are urgent recommendations for action plans that can be done and must be done. These are ideas for actions and implementation for societal reformation and transformation.

It is an urgent call to implement the survival values that God has shared with humanity. These survival values are designed to confront evil and wickedness with love and goodness; to confront ignorance and foolishness with knowledge and wisdom; to confront injustice and crime with righteousness, justice, and mercy; to confront insanity and hatred with civility and sobriety; to confront darkness and death with abundant life and the light of the world. God has provided his people with a workable plan to defeat the forces of evil and darkness. The practice of public theology provides the ideas, values, principles, and methodologies to implement the plan given by God to defeat the evil and wicked forces in God's world and in our lives.

This appeal to get involved and engaged in this spiritual warfare goes out to every God-fearing person, including ministers, professionals, teachers, families, churches, schools, businesses, governments, and nations. We must not fail ourselves, our children, our families, our communities, past generations, our cities, states, and nations. We must not fail our God and the sacrifice of Jesus Christ on Calvary's Cross. The generous God has placed us in charge of the earth and given us dominion over all other creatures. He has given us the knowledge of science, art, law, and theology. He has given us the bounty of the earth. He has given us the Bible, which contains inexhaustible knowledge about life and living. He has given us his Son as our Savior. He has established for us a household of faith. He has prepared for us a new heaven and a new earth. He offers us eternal life where there will be no more sorrows, no more tears, no more pain, and no more death. Will you answer the call to be a soldier in this spiritual warfare?

Willie James Webb

W. J WEBB MA, MS, MDIV
(THEOLOGICAL ETHICIST)
The Demonic Agenda
Evil Obsessions Against the People of God
The Public Theologian

	THEIR POSITIONS	THEIR OCCUPATIONS
1.	Anti-God	Worshippers of Idols
2.	Anti-Christ	Haters of God's Will
3.	Anti-Love	Unbridled Hatred
4.	Anti-Truth	Deceptive Liars
5.	Anti-Goodness	Advocates of Evil
6.	Anti-Knowledge	Imposition of Ignorance
7.	Anti-Justice	Perpetrators of Evil
8.	Anti-Righteousness	Majors in Wickedness
9.	Anti-Cross	Hatred of Christ's Victory
10.	Anti-Liberty	Violators of Human & Civil Rights
11.	Anti-Democracy	Uncivil Contempt for Human Equality
12.	Anti-Life	Pathological Human Destructiveness

GOD'S PEOPLE CAN AND MUST DEFEAT THIS DEMONIC AGENDA BY EXTINGUISHING THE "Anti" prefixes preceding THE GOD GIVEN VALUES WITH THE PRO-PREFIXES AFFIRMING THESE PRECIOUS GOD GIVEN VALUES OF HUMAN SURVIVAL FOR HUMANKIND. BECOME THE DILIGENT PROLIFERS THAT GOD CREATED YOU TO BE IN THE ABUNDANT AND ETERNAL LIFE IN JESUS CHRIST!!!

The Public Theologian

CONFORMITY TO THIS WORLD DESTROYS SURVIVAL VALUES
The Need for Mind Renewal and Transformation
(The Christian Institute of Public Theology)

1. Where is the truth that has been lost in information and knowledge?
2. Where is the wisdom that has been lost in understanding and reason?
3. Where is the love that has been lost in affection and fellowship?
4. Where is the compassion that has been lost in passion and relationships?
5. Where is the humaneness that has been lost in humanity?
6. Where is the civility that has been lost in civilization?
7. Where is the wholeness that is lost in separation and division?
8. Where is the beauty that has been lost in the essence of art?
9. Where is the hope that has been lost in future expectations?
10. Where is the love that is revealed and expressed in Jesus Christ?
11. Where is the hope that has been lost in life's journey for the future?
12. Where is the beauty that has been lost in the expression of the soul?
13. Where is the joy that has been lost in the fellowship of living?
14. Where is the belief that has been lost in life, abundant and eternal life?

15. Where is the expectation that has been lost in the vindication of justice?
16. Where is the faith that has been lost in the promises of God?
17. Where is the courage that has been lost to live a victorious life?
18. Where is the bravery that has been lost to confront the enemies of life?
19. Where is the boldness that has been lost in standing for a righteous cause?
20. Where are the minds that have lost the hunger for knowledge?
21. Where are the souls that have lost the thirst and yearning for truth?
22. Where are the north stars, the pillars of clouds, pillars of fire and the moral compass?
23. Where is the psychology, sociology, theology, and Christology lost in technology?
24. Where are the prophetic voices of truth, justice, freedom & love, lost in silence?

For to be carnally minded is death; but to be spiritually minded is life and peace. Because the carnal mind is enmity against God (Romans 8:7). So, then they that are in the flesh cannot please God (Romans 8:8).

For who has known the mind of the Lord, that he may instruct him? But we have the mind of Christ (Corinthians 2:16). Let this mind be in you which was also in Christ Jesus (Philippians 2:5). Thou wilt keep him in perfect peace, whose mind is stayed on thee (Isaiah 26:3).

There is neither Jew nor Greek, there is neither bond nor free, there is neither male nor female: for ye are all one in Christ Jesus (Galatians 3:28).

Getting Out of the Flesh (Diverse Identities) is Critical for corporate Human Wholeness.

THE SPIRIT OF GOD AND BIBLICAL KNOWLEDGE ARE CRITICAL FOR HUMAN SURVIVAL VALUES

EXPANDING PRIVATE RELIGION TO PUBLIC THEOLOGY
REVEREND W. J. WEBB
MDIV, MS, MA, CCS,CPE

Why does the influence of the Church and clergy seem to be ineffective in decreasing the growing American division and moral and ethical decadence in society and the Nation? Is it because the Church and clergy are self-restricted in their private religion? When observing the number of people who attend churches, synagogues, temples, shrines, mosques, and other places of worship, it is impressive. There has been a decline in church attendance, but the number of people who attend are impressive. However, it appears that this massive church attendance is not translating into the corresponding positive unifying moral and ethical social force for human justice and mutual respect that it should.

When the input into an enterprise does not match up to the output, it is reasonable to examine the disparity. When considering the rich worship and enlightening educational experiences and services, we conclude that good and worthwhile things are going on. However, this goodness of the Church and religion are not being transmitted to the vast numbers of needy recipients. Upon close examination, it appears that the Church and other educational and worship institutions are participating in and even indulging in private religion. Participation in private religion has numerous significant advantages. However, exclusive private religion is unaffordable and superfluous in a world with a growing danger of public chaos. This escalation of public chaos is a danger to the Church and all other institutions.

There has always been a place in the Church for private religion and individual salvation. There have been great revivalists and evangelists who specialize in winning souls for Christ. This is a good religious practice. It is biblical and foundational for spiritual transformation and personal regeneration. Being born again and becoming a new creature in Christ is the most dramatic work of God in a person's life. Therefore, private religion must remain a basic tenet of religion. The challenge is to use this foundation in the outside mission field of public theology. The Biblical Scriptures are replete with private religion and public theology. Somehow, they have been separated. The American and world crises compel the full utilization of private religion and public theology.

The practice of private religion and the exclusion of public theology often leads to self-righteousness, spiritual pride and personal exclusiveness characterized by the attitude of, "I and we, are better than you and them." Romans 10:2-3 describes how self-righteousness Is different from the righteousness of God. This self-righteousness is illustrated by the priest and Levite (Luke 10:31) who passed by a victimized man left half dead on the Jericho Road. It is also illustrated by the pharisee and publican (Luke 18:11) who went up unto the temple to pray. The pharisee bragged on himself and looked down upon the publican. The publican acknowledged that he was a sinner and went down to his house justified rather than the self-righteous pharisee. The private priestly function of religion can become self-righteous, prideful and devoid of public concerns.

The pitfall of private religion is that it becomes the model for true religion and the complete fulfillment of religious duties and obligations. When private religious worshippers meet their Church responsibilities, most are satisfied that they have met their total religious obligations and duties. However, the social, public, and community responsibilities are often omitted without any consciousness or feeling of responsibility Many morally upright people live their lives with no sense of duty or responsibility to the public or social welfare. They feel that it is someone else's job and God's to confront social injustice, corruption, and evil in society. It is this concept of individual salvation and private religion that blinds religious people from seeing or perceiving any responsibility for fighting against evil and building a just society and God's Kingdom on earth.

It was my good fortune to attend the Billy Graham Crusade during the summer of 1957 at Madison Square Garden and Yankee Stadium. I was a strong adherent to individual salvation and private religion even before attending the summer-long Crusade in New York City. I was very hyped about individual salvation and private religion when I entered Morehouse College in the fall of 1957. I learned about the social gospel and public theology at Morehouse College, primarily from the late Reverend Lucus Tobin, a religion professor. There was a great opportunity to learn a lot about religion because President Benjamin E. Mass required the daily chapel attendance of all Morehouse students. Also in 1957, the Morehouse School of Religion was located on the campus of Morehouse College.

Reverend Tobin frequently emphasized the importance of caring for a man's body, families, communities, institutions, and governments, which comprise the totality of human life experiences in society. Reverend Tobin introduced many of the public theologians and social gospel movement theologians. Among them were Walter Rauschenbush, Reinhold Niiebuhr, and Paul Tillich. These men were social gospel leaders who labored at the intersection of religion, politics, and public policy. The social gospel is an outgrowth of public theology as opposed to private religion as practiced in most churches. Public theology broadens private religion beyond its limited private arena within the church walls. Public theology, under the jurisdiction and authority of God, is concerned with the totality of human life as individuals, groups, and society.

Paul Tillich gives us something serious to think about in the following statement: "Man's capacity for justice makes democracy possible, but man's inclination to injustice makes democracy necessary." If this noble and necessary experiment of democracy in America is to work, the churches and the clergy must drastically extend their private religion into public theological practices. Martin Luther King, Jr. and others rose to the occasion.

Reverend W. J. Webb is the CEO of The Christian Association of Public Theologians and the Author of THE WAY OUT OF DARKNESS-Vital Public Theology.

CAPT, INC P.O. BOX 3148 ATLANTA, GA 30302

GOALS AND THEMES FOR PUBLIC THEOLOGY

Theological Approaches for Cultural Transformation
Foundations for Biblical Exposition
(Christian Institute of Public Theology)

1.	Biblical Truth Dissemination	25.	The University of Justice
2.	Artistic Creations	26.	Righteousness of God
3.	Exemplification of Love	27.	Refinement of Humanity
4.	Earth Replenishment	28.	Valid Universal Principles
5.	Ethical Actions	29.	God's Spirit and Truth
6.	Environmental Protection	30.	Man Made in God's Image
7.	Environmental Safety	31.	Purpose of Human Life
8.	Ethical Actions	32.	Universal Biblical Truths
9.	Ethical Reformation	33.	The Bible and Human Nature
10.	Esthetics of Beauty	34.	Biblical Salvation Knowledge
11.	Equity in Justice	35.	The Spiritual Domain
12.	Cultured Sociality	36.	Cultural Transformation
13.	Civilized Expressions	37.	Kingdom of Righteousness

14.	Characterization of Goodness	38.	The Nature of Love
15.	Health and Wholeness	39.	The Gift of Life
16.	Humanitarian Innovations	40.	The Gift of Jesus Christ
17.	Cultural Refinement	41.	The Household of Faith
18.	Decency and Order	42.	Universal Christian Values
19.	Revelations of Excellence	43.	The Armor of God
20.	Reality of Truth	44.	Transcending Power
21.	Spiritual Discernment	45.	God's Ultimate Authority
22.	Redemptive Human	46.	God's Sovereign
23.	Humanization of Technology	47.	New Creature in Christ
24.	God's Ethical Standards for Humanity	48.	Salvation in Jesus Christ

LET US BEGIN THIS NOBLE MISSION OF GOD

The enumerated goals and themes above apply to all humanity on earth. They represent the love of God for humanity and the gift of God to save humanity. God offers these goals and themes to partner with mankind and to enlighten humanity; to enrich, sustain, enhance, and show the way to abundant life and eternal salvation through Jesus Christ. These goals for humanity and themes for love and living have the potential to build God's Kingdom on earth, where all mankind can live as brothers and sisters. The Bible is the blueprint for life and human survival. These goals and themes for a living can heal sick nations, transform corrupt cultures, and establish God's Kingdom of Righteousness on the earth. LET US WORK TOWARDS THESE GOALS AND SPREAD THIS GOOD NEWS OF GOD THROUGHOUT THE EARTH!

SPIRITUAL TRANSFORMATION
ETHICAL CULTURAL REFORMATION
BIBLICAL TRUTH DISSEMINATION

To stop the corruptive and destructive moral decay, the above urgently needed revolutionary initiatives must be implemented through a serious, organized effort by the methodologies and services enumerated below throughout the American culture This unprecedentedly aggressive and deteriorating cultural corruption is unsustainable. All sane and responsible American citizens must get actively involved in this spiritual, ethical, and biblical knowledge revolution to save America and the world.

GUIDING THEMES OF UNIVERSAL HUMAN VALUES

1. Accept and teach historically and scientifically validated human survival values.
2. Extol the excellence of the value of love.
3. Practice and teach justice and equity for all people, as required by the Creator.
4. Embrace the theological and spiritual domains of knowledge.
5. Overcome self-righteousness and embrace the righteousness of God.
6. Allow and instruct that all things be done with decency and order.
7. Follow the theologically validated moral compass as the way of righteousness.
8. Embrace sound health and wholeness for all people and nations.

UNIVERSAL STANDARDS FOR CIVILIZED LIVING

1. Follow the Great Commandment: "Love God and your neighbor as yourself."
2. Be guided by love, righteousness, justice, peace, goodwill, and mercy.
3. Be fruitful, multiply, and train up children in the way they should go.
4. Sustain loving, responsible, healthy, knowledgeable, ethical, and nurturing families.
5. Replenish the earth, subdue it, have dominion over it, and be responsible, productive stewards.

6. Cultivate environmental protection, health, beauty, and technological safety and security.
7. Initiate and innovate humanitarian artistic creations to advance life and civilization.
8. Sustain a government of the people, by the people, and for the people, with protected unalienable rights.
9. Let there be "One Nation Under God, with Liberty and Justice for All."
10. "Let every soul be subject to the higher powers. For there is no power but that of God."

EDUCATIONAL ASSIMILATION OF METHODOLOGIES AND PRACTICES

1. Teach and practice character education.
2. Claim successful human and spiritual identities.
3. Develop life skills and skills for successful living.
4. Openness to the engagement of truth.
5. Elevate cultural enrichment.
6. Live up to standards of ethical and moral behavior.
7. Practice the most elevated civilized personal and corporate expressions.

EDUCATIONAL ASSIMILATION OF METHODOLOGIES AND PRACTICES (CONTINUED)

8. Provide redemptive services. (Life enhancement services)
9. Major in Cultural Refinement and Esthetic Beauty.
10. Develop personal pride, self-worth, and artistic appreciation.

11. Gain appreciation for human dignity, business ethics, and professionalism.
12. Develop uncompromising honesty and personal integrity.
13. Motivation for optimum development of talents, gifts, and human potential.
14. Learn and subscribe to humanitarian codes of ethics to express love and mercy.
15. Learn and practice reverence for God and respect for the sacredness of human life.
16. Seek knowledge, wisdom, and understanding as the blind seek light.
17. Continue to seek until you find out who you are and your purpose in life.
18. Learn to live your life to the fullest despite deficits and oppositions.
19. Exercise the courage to embrace the eternal values of GOODNESS, TRUTH AND BEAUTY as created by GOD.
20. These acronyms of the Bible may be helpful and insightful:

B-asic I-nformation B-efore L-eaving E-arth   Bible
B-e I-nformed B-y L-ove E-ternal   Bible
B-lessed I-ntelligence B-y L-ove E-ternal   Bible
B-asic I-nformation B-efore L-ife E-nds   Bible

THE BIBLE IS THE INEXHAUSTIBLE RULE BOOK FOR LIVING FOR EVERY PERSON, FAMILY, GENERATION AND NATION; LIVING, DEAD AND YET TO BE BORN. THE FOREMOST PRIORITY OF EVERY PERSON, GENERATION AND NATION IS TO LEARN THE

RULES, LAWS, LOVE AND SALVATION OF GOD AS RECORDED IN THE HOLY BIBLE AND WORD OF GOD.

Truth Educational Institutions
The Christian Institute of Public Theology
The Christian Association of Public Theologians
The Christian Art Academy
The Audio-Visual School of Truth
The Educational Mall
Foundations of Truth Centers

The Christian Institute of Public Theology
Atlanta, GA 30311

FOUNDATION BAPTIST COMMUNITY CHURCH
Atlanta, GA.
Guides for Effective Bible Study

Devotional Period: Musical Selections) - Prayer - Scripture Reading (By Devotion Leader) Greetings, Acknowledgments - Introductions -Testimonial Expressions (Bible Teacher)

Purpose and Objectives of the Bible Study Fellowship

The purpose of the Bible Study Fellowship class is to learn about the Word of God and the teachings of the Bible through the Scriptural texts contained in the Old Testament and the New Testament through scheduled, systematic study procedures led by a qualified, credentialed, professed believer in Jesus Christ.

Objectives:

1. Increase biblical literacy and spiritual enlightenment about God's biblical revelations.
2. Help individuals find faith, develop faith, multiply faith, and apply faith in Jesus Christ.
3. Study to be approved of God and competent to witness and teach God's Word of truth.
4. Develop and enlighten a fellowship of committed believers in Jesus Christ.
5. Learn about God's love for mankind and His salvation gift in Jesus Christ
6. Learn about the greatest ethical, moral, and spiritual values known to mankind.

7. Learn about the greatest classical literature and the greatest story ever told in history.
8. Learn about the 39 books of the Old Testament & the 27 books of the New Testament
9. Learn about the most fascinating characters of the Bible: Adam & Eve, the patriarchs, Abraham, Isaac, Jacob (Joseph & other sons), Moses, Samson & Delilah, Ruth, Samuel, David, Solomon, the prophets of Israel, Jesus the Christ and his disciples, Paul, & Revelation.
10. Learn about great events of the Bible: Creation, The Flood, Tower of Babel, Egyptian Bondage, Crossing Red Sea, Samson & Delilah, David Slays Goliath, Daniel in the Lion's Den, Hebrews in Fiery Furnace, Birth of Christ Miracles, Crucifixion, Resurrection, Ascension, Pentecost Conversion of Saul, John the Revelator
11. Guidance for educational enlightenment, spiritual growth, and successful community living.
12. Develop a biblical knowledge, wisdom, and understanding foundation competent to share the Good News of God's Salvation for mankind.

An Understanding of the Following Words and Concepts is Helpful for Clergy and Laity to Understand Our Present Culture Crisis in this Twenty-First Century in America:

Absolutism	Atheism Authority	Conservative
Accommodation		Concentration
Acculturation	Bureaucracy	Creationism
Activism		Cultism
Advocate	Capitalism	Cultural Diversity
Agnosticism	Celebration	Custom

Alienation	Confusion	
Annihilation	Conflict	Darwinism
Arbitrary	Conform	Delusional
Arrogance – Art	Communism	Denial
Asceticism	Competition	Demoralization
Assimilation	Compensation	Despotism
Desegregation		Justice
Deterioration	Heresy	
Dementia	Hierarchy	Legalism
Dignity	Humanism	Liberal
Disorder		Liberation
DSM-IV	Ideology	
	Identification	Materialism
Ecumenism	Idolatry	Mentor
Egoism Elitism	Idols	Migration
Elevate Escapism		Mobility
Ethnocentrism	Immigration	Monotheism
Ethics Evolution	Indignation	Monogamy
Exclusive	Infiltration	Morality
Extremism	Injustice	
Existentialism	Indoctrinate	Nature
	Influence	Nation
Fanaticism	Inclusive	Nihilism
Fatalism	Integration	Nurture
Fellowship	International	
Fellowship Fraud	Intervention	Objectivity
Forfeiture	Illusion	Oblivious
	Isolation	Occult
Globalism	Invalidate	Obsolete
Greed		

The Christian Institute of Public Theology Inc.

THE CHRISTIAN INSTITUTE OF PUBLIC THEOLOGY

Testing the Spirits Through the Functions of Religion

"BELOVED, BELIEVE NOT EVERY SPIRIT, BUT TRY THE SPIRITS WHETHER THEY ARE OF GOD: BECAUSE MANY FALSE PROPHETS ARE GONE OUT INTO THE WORLD." (1 John 4:1)

There are two primary functions of religion. They are the PRIESTLEY FUNCTION and the PROPHETIC FUNCTION.

1. The Priestley Function communicates to God with reverence, repentance, praise, honor, adoration, glorification, petitions of gratitude, blessings, guidance, strength, and prayers of thanksgiving. The petitions are on behalf of myself and others. It is a spiritual journey to the blessings and mercies of God. The spiritual flow is communicated Up to God. Meditations, music, prayers, and worship are priestly functions. The act of sincere worship with its splendorous rituals and ceremonies is often a powerful spiritual force that provides healing, inspiration, and consolation.

    Despite the magnificence of the priestly function of religion, it must be balanced with the other functions of religion The priestly function comes from man and is directed to God. This one-way flow of the spirit from man to God has the potential to eliminate man's responsibility to partner in his own salvation. It can lead men to believe that God will fix everything for them without their participation. This gives insight into why churches and religions become private and irrelevant to the problems and raging crises of the world. The extension and expansion of private religion beyond the walls of the Church is an introduction to public theology and the Prophetic Function of religion.

2. The Prophetic Function of religion represents the spiritual flow of the communication Coming down from God to man through the Prophet of God. The Prophetic Function of religion is God speaking to man. Religion's prophetic function is to be God's voice and message to man. It represents God's Will, Warnings, Commandments, Intentions, Mandates, Revelations, Anointing, Prophecy, Empowerment, Assurances, Promises, Gifts, and fulfillment. The Prophetic Function of religion is God speaking to man. God speaks to man through prophets, kings, angels, designated messengers, and his creation. His only begotten son, Jesus Christ.

It must be recognized that tension exists between the Priestly Function of religion and The Prophetic Function of religion. The Priestly Function is more acceptable and safer for man. Because God's commandments, will, and ways conflict with the world, there is ongoing chronic resistance to religion's prophetic function. The Priestly is more private and isolated from the outside world. The Prophetic Function demands JUSTICE, RIGHTEOUSNESS, LOVE, OBEDIENCE TO GOD, TRUTH and LOYALTY. God allows us to petition Him. He also commands us to obey HIM!

CHRISTIAN ASSOCIATION OF PUBLIC THEOLOGY

Guiding Themes

1. A Christian theology that undergirds and transforms the interactions, functions, and directions of society. To convey sound Christian theological doctrine throughout society by way of teaching, preaching, practice, and service into the public domain,

2. A theology for guiding the humanitarian use of science. To provide the most advanced Christian theological guidance and humanitarian purpose for the peaceful use of scientific technology and scientific technical intelligence.

3. A theology that sets ethical and humanitarian standards for government and bureaucratic operations in society. To provide the Christian theological framework for development of policies and principles for the institutional administration of justice, righteousness, peace, and liberty.

4. A theology that acknowledges the hierarchy of legitimate authority. To establish universally true values and sound principles for community living based on the most noble principles and the highest authority known to humankind.

5. A theology of Christian ethics that determines what is right, true, and just in all human interactions and relations. To provide a theological basis for the scientific method and inquiry that can be used objectively to reflect, evaluate, and validate factual reality, true principles, and valid principles in the areas of science, law, ethics, art, and religion, to avoid

arbitrary decisions, unsound doctrines, and subsequent injurious actions.

6. A theology that supports and advocates major investments (time, money, energy, and resources) in holistic education and Christian ethical training. To provide a Christian theological rationale and concerted leadership to eradicate human ignorance, injustice, and evil through sound contextual education, training, ethics, treatment, and skills for Christian living.

7. A theology that sets character development and ethical training, along with the regular educational curriculum, as a top priority for children and youth. To provide theological initiatives for ongoing character development in children and youth through Christian education, ethical training, treatment, and practice in homes and youth related institutions and organizations.

8. A theology-claiming, proclaiming and advocating the true universality and human inclusiveness of Jesus Christ as the only begotten Son of God and Savior of the world. To provide a theological rationale and a Christian faith-based initiative to enable one to rise above narrow loyalties, conflicting interests, and selfish ambition in order to serve and provide inclusive leadership for the common good of all humanity and God-loving people.

9. A theology that points to and shows the way of righteousness, justice, peace, and salvation for all humanity based on the highest authority in the revealed Word of God, whose name is declared to be above every name. Claim, witness and express a Christian salvation theology that has been validated

in history for over two thousand years and witnessed by over two billion people on the earth.

10. A theology that embraces and witnesses a moral code of ethics, a belief in the truth, a practice of ethical conduct, a cultivation of spiritual values, and a commitment to love and forgive. A theology of person, social, cultural and spiritual transformation.

11. A theology that envisions and proclaims what ought to be as opposed to the status quo or what the present reality is. A theology that points the way, charts the course and sets the conditions on how to get where God wants us to be and do things of God's will.

A theology of public and private service to the poor and needy, spiritual growth, mature stewardship and responsibility, liberation, healing, nurture, restoration, salvation, and wholeness

Rev. Willie James Webb, President
Christian Association of Public Theologians

MENTAL HEALTH IS A
CONTINUING PRIORITY
CAPT, INC.

PRIORITIZING SAFEGUARDS
FOR MENTAL HEALTH

The mental health of Americans is seriously and critically jeopardized. The daily news media is replete with the symptoms of mental disorders and emotional disturbances. Society is bombarded on a daily basis with horrendous reports of brutal crimes against persons, and property and violations against unalienable human rights. There is an epidemic of identity theft, hacking attacks, and drug abuse. The Atlanta Journal-Constitution reported that thirty-three thousand persons died of opioid use-related deaths in 2015. Many of our well-known colleges and universities are experiencing massive student disturbances, violence, and ideological confusion. Social media is saturated with raging ideological warfare, political dissension, sexual crimes, sexual confusion, unbridled greed, and unjustified expressions of hateful words and destructive deeds. Massive numbers of Americans are losing their mental health and spiritual hope and dying silent unceremonious deaths. Mental and spiritual disorders are at the core of America's culture crisis. Basic American institutions are being corrupted by unsound doctrines, irrational ideologies, and social injustice. These imbalances create serious deficits in human potential. These deficits degenerate into mental disorders, toxic relationships, and destructive behavior.

America must make mental health an urgent priority. The mental health of the head determines the health of the whole body. When the head is sick, the health of the whole body is jeopardized. Serious consideration must be given to the mental health status of all heads of organizations, and especially those who head political, military, religious, educational, social and economic organizations. Sick heads make sick groups, sick cities, sick states and sick nations. Sick institutions make sick cultures. Mental and spiritual disorders have contagions that put every individual at risk. Dr. Martin Luther King, Jr. stated that "Injustice anywhere is a threat to justice everywhere." Mental and spiritual illness anywhere is a threat to mental health and life everywhere. Sickness is a prelude to death.

The protection and safeguards for the mind are far behind the protection and safeguards for the body. Much of this is justified because the body houses the mind. The body is the temple of the spirit. Yes, the body must be well cared for. However, in view of the American and world cultural crises, it is urgent that priority be given to mind care and mental health maintenance and enhancement, beginning at birth and continuing throughout life. The criminal and civil statutory laws are voluminous in protecting the physical body and even material property. However, laws designed to protect the mind and individual mental well-being are woefully inadequate and deficient. While there are many lawful and legal remedies to protect the body from threats, abuse, assaults, and violence, those legal protections are not in place for the protection of the mind and mental faculties. There are grossly too few legal protections and remedies to protect and safeguard the mind.

Continuing (Prioritizing Safeguards for Mental Health):

The following priorities, from a theological and cultural perspective, are recommended for restoring and maintaining optimum mental health for the people of God. Adopt legislation that will serve the causes of justice, peace, goodwill, equitable restoration, health, and prosperity in government and society. Heeding the prophecy of Amos would be very helpful, "Let justice run down as water, and righteousness as a mighty stream require Biblical education and literacy in all public education.

Establish impartial government merit systems based on equal education and employment opportunities. Establish fit-for-duty professional standards in all areas of government administration and service. Enforce and ensure public official accountability. Require conflict of interest disclosures for all legal representatives. Require the observance of explicit codes of professional ethics in all government and public service. Establish reasonable time limits for all grievance hearings and judicial litigation.

Legislate and allocate the necessary money, resources, and personnel to provide the needed remedial, preventive, treatment, and growth services for at risk and afflicted persons with mental disorders according to the DSM-V (Diagnostic Statistical Manual of Mental Disorders) by APA (American Psychiatric Association). Include competent theological professionals along with other professionals who make public policy for the care of mentally and spiritually disordered persons.

PLEASE NOTE: THE MENTAL HEALTH CRISIS HAS ALREADY ADVANCED TO AN EMERGENCY IN

AMERICA. IMMEDIATE AND DELIBERATE ACTIONS ARE REQUIRED.

(The Christian Association of Public Theologians, Inc.)
P. O. Box 3148, Atlanta, GA 30302

THE CORE PROBLEMS OF THE AMERICAN SOCIETY
(BASED ON A PUBLIC THEOLOGICAL PERSPECTIVE)

1. The silence(or silenced) Enlightened Prophetic Voices.
2. The Retreat of the Church from the Public Life of Society and from the Raging Ideological Spiritual Warfare.
3. The Growing Compromise of Judeo-Christian Values with Idolatry and Secularism.
4. Spiritual Blindness and Rebellion Against the Revelatory Knowledge and Light of God.
5. The Moral Relativity of Giving Credence to Arbitrary Opinions and Behaviors without Validated Truth or Merit.
6. Ethical Neutrality-The Failure to Give Witness to Truth or to Take a Righteous Stand or to Adhere to a Position of Equity and Justice.
7. The Loss of National Vision, Purpose and Direction along with the Corrosion of Governmental Privatization.
8. Indulgence of Self-Centered Individualism at the Expense of Diluting the Values Essential for the Common Good.
9. Cultural Confusion and Political Instability Influenced by Arbitrary and Capricious Decisions to find Favor with partisan Individuals and Groups of Diverse Ideological Backgrounds and Persuasions.
10. Educational Fragmentation with a Lack of a Unifying Comprehensive Purpose-driven Corporate Focus for the Common Good.

11. Diminishing Merit Systems That Have No Consistency and No Uniformity in Rewarding and Reinforcing Achievement and Success.
12. Lack of Equitable, Sound and Appropriately Elevated Standards as Measures and Incentives for the Growth, Progress and Security for the Common Good.

Most thoughtful men and women would agree with the enumeration of the above Core Problems. Many of the thoughtful and concerned men and women would also agree that there is an urgent need for: A GREAT AWAKENING, A RENAISSANCE, A MASSIVE REFORMATION AND A TRANSCENDENT TRANSFORMATION.

<u>Rev. Willie I. Webb, Author</u>

The Way Our of Darkness: Vital Public Theology Actions to Turn the Lethal Tide

THE DILUTION OF SURVIVAL VALUES

Basic Truths:

All have sinned and come short of the glory of God.
He that is without sin, let him cast the first stone.
Judge not that you be not judged.
Be not deceived, God is not mocked, whatsoever a man soweth that shall he also reap. Spiritual Discernment:
"Beloved, believe not every spirit, but try the spirits, and see if they are of God. (1John 4:1)"

The Congruence of Truth:
True religion, true science, true art and true divine law do not conflict with each other. The pseudo-religion, pseudo-science, pseudo art and pseudo laws conflict with each other.

Basic Foundational Truths:
God's Creationism as taught in the Bible is true.
God's (ID) Intelligent Design in Creation is true.
God's revelation in the Bible is true.
God's Revelation in Biblical Prophecy is True.
God's Revelation in Jesus Christ is True.

Faith in the Revelatory Truth of God:
The faith in these truths became highly concentrated in America between 1600 and 1970. These truths were expressed in abundance by black African Americans.

These concentrated survival values blessed America to become a prosperous, powerful, and blessed country due to its values of truth and faith in God.

The Concentration of Survival Values Corresponds with Racial Segregation:

The Black African Americans developed the most nonviolent and civilized values known. In the midst of slavery and oppression, they built families, churches, schools, communities, and businesses. No other group had ever done so much with so little and against such great odds. Their strides coward civilization, self-help and altruism bear the hallmarks of great people. The richness of cultural, educational, social, civil, and artistic achievements reached its zenith during the segregated and oppressive era in American history.

THE DILUTION OF SURVIVAL VALUES

The integration and globalization beginning in the 1970s began to dilute the survival values of Black African Americans. The most significant achievements of Black Americans were made by those who were reared and socialized in a racially segregated society. The concentration of Black survival values contributed significantly to strengthening America. It is ironic that similar social forces that diluted the survival values of Black Americans are now diluting the survival values of America. America has become a borderless country with a diminishing national identity, no standards, and a loss of identity.

THE DUTY OF THE WATCHMAN

I HAVE MADE THEE A WATCHMAN

Son of man, I have made thee a watchman unto the house of Israel: therefore, hear the word at my mouth, and give them warning from me.

WARN THE WICKED
When I say unto the wicked, thou shall surely die; and thou give him not warning, nor speak, nor speak to warn the wicked from his wicked way, to save his life, the same wicked man shall die in his iniquity; but his blood will I require at thine hand.

Yet if thou warn the wicked, and he turn not from his wickedness, nor from his wicked way, he shall die in his iniquity; but thou have delivered thy soul.

Ezekiel 3:18-19

WARN THE RIGHTEOUS
Again, if a righteous man turns from his righteousness and commits iniquity, and I place a stumbling block in his path, he shall die: because thou hast nor warned him, he shall die in his sin, and his righteousness which he has done shall not be remembered, but his blood will I require at thine hand. However, if thou warmest the righteous man that the righteous sin not, and he does not sin, he will surely live because he has been warned; also, thou hast delivered thy soul. Ezekiel 3:20-21

(The watchman has given warning and delivered his own soul).

THE PUBLIC THEOLOGIAN

The Role of the Church in the 21st Century

1. What is the primary role of the Church in the 21st Century?
2. Why is it so important for the Church to evaluate its role and refocus its priorities for the 21st Century?
3. How does the Church go about educating the people about the Gospel, especially in America where there is growing cultural Diversity in a free-for-all democracy?
4. Isn't there a presumption in American Democracy under the U.S. Constitution that one religion is as good as another and that all religions should have equal status?
5. How does Christianity differ from other religions?
6. Why is it so critical and urgent that public theologians and the church take a proactive role in society in the twenty-first century?
7. Redemptive involvement is mentioned a lot in public theology. What is the meaning of that term?
8. How does the Church propose to deal with the challenges of cultural diversity, technology, and cyberspace?
9. We have witnessed individuals who kill innocent people and sometimes take their own lives in the process, feeling that they have done a righteous thing. What must the Church do about destructive ideological mindsets?

"The Public Theologian" is a publication of the Christian Association of Public Theologians and the Christian Institute of Public Theology.

The book, The Way Out of Darkness: Vital Public Theology, by Willie James Webb, teaches about the practice of public theology.

BIBLICAL KNOWLEDGE IS ESSENTIAL FOR HUMAN SURVIVAL

The Bible is the primary universal book of ethics and the primary authority on the nature of human nature and human behavior.

The Bible reveals the Will of God for human life, its purpose, potential and possibilities.

The Bible reveals WHAT IS and the IDEAL OF WHAT OUGHT TO BE in the here and now and the future hereafter.

The Bible teaches the foundations of creation and the regulations for human interactions and human existence.

THE BIBLE IS HUMANITY'S AUTHORITATIVE LAW BOOK AND RULE BOOK FOR LIFE AND LIVING FOR ALL PEOPLE OF THE EARTH.

The Bible's vital knowledge, wisdom, and understanding of the virtues and eternal values of truth, life, goodness, beauty, love, and GOD are limitless. The Bible is the authoritative first and last word about the sole and absolute jurisdiction and sovereignty of God and God's Will for life and Creation.

THE BIBLE IS THE ULTIMATE LIVING RULE BOOK FOR EVERY PERSON, FAMILY, GENERATION, AND NATION: LIVING, DEAD, AND YET TO BE BORN. THE FOREMOST PRIORITY OF EVERY PERSON, GENERATION AND NATION IS TO LEARN THE RULES AND LAWS FOR LIVING IN THE BIBLICAL WORD OF GOD.

The Christian Institute of Public Theology

CHAPTER 2
CIVILIZATION'S VANGUARD OF TRUTH
AMERICA'S CULTURAL CRISIS DICTATES
TRUTH LEADERSHIP

God's commissioned clergy must be the vanguard of truth to advance the human enterprise of civilization. Truth is the foundation for human survival and triumphant living. Truth is the reality of existence. The truth is the light that illuminates reality.

The truth shows the way to the greatest values known to mankind. Truth shows the way to life, love, goodness, righteousness, justice, knowledge, wisdom, understanding, peace, beauty, freedom, and God. The truth reveals what is, what was, what will be and what ought to be. The truth is created and ordained of God. Truth is the foundation of existence. When the truth is denied, distorted, exaggerated, confused, and misrepresented, problematic crises are precipitated in the culture. Such mishaps threaten the quality and existence of life.

It is critical that the clergy of God assume and assert their leadership role as the vanguard of truth in the twenty-first century. The silence and passivity of God's clergy jeopardize humanity and imperil civilization. The clergy must position itself on the front lines of the ideological battle.

The clergy, individually and collectively, must be the prophetic voice of God and the resurrected witnesses of Jesus Christ. The clergy must become involved in the raging ideological and spiritual warfare that threatens human survival. The clergy must not only take a stand for righteousness and social justice; it must also take a position against evil and injustice. It must also warn the wicked of the destructive consequences of their evil.

You, who believe in God, must proclaim with urgency the gospel truth as never before. You must put the spotlight on wickedness, corruption, and perversions. You must challenge misguidance, misrepresentation, criminality, and immorality.

This clergy vanguard for humanity must rise above partisanship, sectarianism, cultism, egotism, racism, and materialism. It must be biblically based on the Word of God and theologically guided by the wisdom of God.

A UNIVERSAL MISSION OF SPIRITUAL REDEMPTION IS REQUIRED FOR THIS CLERGY VANGUARD. IT MUST HAVE A PLAN OF SOCIAL JUSTICE AND SOCIAL SALVATION. IT MUST HAVE A METHODOLOGY OF HUMAN RESTORATION. IT MUST HAVE A VISION OF PEACE AND PROSPERITY. IT MUST CULTIVATE A NEIGHBORHOOD OF BROTHERHOOD. THIS SKILLED VANGUARD MUST ORDER A WORLD OF CIVILITY AND HUMANITY TO GOD'S GLORIFICATION!

The Christian Association of Public Theologians

HUMAN DISORDERS ARE DERIVED FROM CULTURAL CONDITIONS
Cultural Conditions Can be Changed
-The Public Theologian-

SOME CONDITIONS THAT IMPACT THE CULTURAL CRISIS

1. A lack of biblical education, knowledge, and worship of God the Creator. Subsequently, the infiltration of atheistic ideological influences throughout the American culture.

2. The failure to transmit traditional biblical, ethical, moral, spiritual, and patriotic values to the youth and the general society. We must transmit these values to our children.

3. The lack of youth-oriented ethical, moral, artistic, spiritual, and cultural enrichment training in the home and school. Church and community. Public theology must lead.

4. The failure of the Church and the educational institutions to teach boldly and with authority, the primary purpose of life and the roles of men, women, husbands, wives and children according to traditional biblical standards. Public theology can lead the way.

5. The failure of the Church and ecclesiastical leaders to set the patterns for ethical, moral, patriotic, professional, civilized, and humane standards for the general society.

6. There is an increasing moral relativity (no distinction between right and wrong) and ethical neutrality (no stand for right or wrong) in present-day American society.

7. Dehumanizing and divisive personal and political identities disassociated from the Human Family and the Household of God. We are people of God, First and foremost.

8. There is a growing secularism that seeks to eliminate God, Jesus Christ, and biblical influence and symbols from American society and culture. This must be reversed.

9. Spiritual demoralization is pervading American society with a loss of faith and hope in God. People are surrendering to helplessness, hopelessness, despair, and defeat.

10. There is pervasive sexual misuse, abuse, and gender role confusion. There are diminished traditional family values of child rearing, family cohesion, and public responsibility.

11. There is increasing denial, distortion, and demonization of the reality of validated truth in society and public life. There is even hostility against truth and traditional values.

12. Merit systems are being eliminated. Judicial systems are dysfunctional. The required due process of law under the U.S. Constitution is routinely violated. Can be changed.

"THE PUBLIC THEOLOGIANS MUST LEAD THE WAY IN TRANSFORMING CORRUPT CULTURES"

FOUNDATIONAL TRUTH FOR THEOLOGICAL LEADERSHIP

HUMAN LIFE IS GOD'S GREATEST GIFT TO HUMANITY

Human life is God's most precious, sacred, and valuable gift to mankind. Human life is the creation of God that bears the image of God. God shows favoritism to mankind.

Biblical Reference: "So God created man in his own image, in the image of God created he him; male and female created he them (Genesis 1:27)."

GOD'S INITIAL COMMANDMENTS ARE RELEVANT AND VITAL

The commandments that God gave to the first man and the first woman have continued relevance for each generation on the face of the earth. The violation of these commandments is detrimental to human life.

Biblical Reference: "And God blessed them, and God said unto them, BE FRUITFUL, and MULTIPLY, and REPLENISH the EARTH, and SUBDUE IT: and have DOMINION OVER THE FISH OF THE SEA, and OVER THE FOWL OF THE AIR, and OVER EVERY UVING THING that moves upon the earth (Genesis 1:28)."

THE EARTH BELONGS TO GOD

Mankind inhabits the earth by the grace, generosity, and mercy of God. The earth provides mankind with all of the essentials for human life. God has given mankind the position of stewardship over the resources of the earth. The earth is a perpetual source and resource for the sustenance of human life. Man is a temporary tenant of the earth and not a permanent owner. It is time for man to seriously reassess his sacred responsibility as steward of the earth. Is the management, supervision, administration, accountability, and leadership satisfactory?

Biblical Reference: "The earth is the LORD'S and the fullness thereof, the world and they that dwell therein (Psalm 24:1)."

SOCIAL JUSTICE IS A HUMAN RIGHT

Social (human) justice is the God-given methodology of cultivating, distributing and consuming the resources, values, and services of the earth through the equitable administration of justice according to the righteousness, mercy, and will of God. God has elevated justice as a foremost priority in governing the relationships among human beings. Justice is a balance of the scales of human rights. It is an equitable sharing of what is rightfully due to each individual based on divine law and the righteousness of God.

The Bible is replete with references to justice. Proverbs 11:1 describes justice most succinctly, "A false balance is an abomination to the Lord: but a just weight is his delight." Injustice has negative consequences when the requirement of justice is not met. Injustice creates a deficit in human potential. Injustice is an act of violence. Humanity cannot continue to absorb these deficits without cataclysmic consequences. When humans fail to act justly and fail to be worthy stewards of the earth and its resources, the possibilities for human life are significantly diminished.

(The Christian Institute of Public Theology, Atlanta, Georgia)

HUMAN EFFECTS OF DEMORALIZATION

In the absence of strong, positive, visionary leadership, social organizations become unglued and fall apart. Thus, a permissive culture is created where everyone does what is right in his or her own eyes. (Judges 21:25).

Therefore, an environment is created where the common goal of the whole human enterprise disintegrates into fragmented, misguided, individual conflicting goals, confusion, and chaos. A socially disintegrating society where the moral compass and traditional survival values have been disrupted, many people become demoralized.

Demoralization

Demoralization is the diminished desire of the human spirit to live and succeed. It is the progressive diminution of the will to live. It is the acceptance of defeat by the human spirit. Demoralization represents cooperation with the demoralizing forces by the victims who are being demoralized.

Some Root Causes of Demoralization

Some of the root causes of demoralization are as follows: Injustice, heartbreak, rejection, dehumanization, disappointment, helplessness, hopelessness, adverse discrimination, deprivations, intimidations, subjugation, Involuntary servitude, alienation, isolation, internalized anger, rage, and fears

Some Effects of Demoralization

1. Loss of faith in others and oneself.
2. Loss of feeling
3. Loss of self-esteem.
4. Loss of dreams.
5. Loss of vision for the future.
6. Loss of future hope.
7. Loss of autonomy.
8. Loss of spirit to confront and challenge obstacles.
9. Loss of the spirit to care about life.
10. Loss of the spirit to fight for the values of life.
11. Loss of external and internal interests
12. Loss of the spirit to live.

Some (Unhealthy) Methods Used in Coping with Demoralization

1. Denial of Reality-Self-deception.
2. Social Avoidance-Self-imposed blindness and deafness to reality.
3. Rationalization-Create excuses and alibis to avoid facing reality
4. Distortion-Create comfortable fantasies and delusions to avoid the truth.
5. Projection-Select others or something else to place blame.
6. Psychological ventilation-Curse the darkness and fight the air.
7. Give up-Stop fighting and surrender to defeat.
8. Become irresponsible-Turn self over to other's care.
9. Sedation and tranquilization through alcohol and other drug addiction

10. Become mentally and physically ill-Stop striving.
11. Criminality, theft, fraud, etc. -wreak havoc on society.
12. Homicide, suicide, and other forms of self-destruction.

REVERSING DEMORALIZATION THROUGH REGENERATION, REFORMATION, AND TRANSFORMATION

The corrupted culture, misguided ideologies, and permissive pathological environment can be ameliorated through competent, God-connected, and God-inspired leadership. There are scientific, rational, and spiritual remedies for the list of root causes of our human demoralization. Demoralization is no mystery. The causes are known or knowable. Each root cause of demoralization can be isolated, studied, assessed, and eliminated.

There are remedies and solutions for the debilitating effects of demoralization. There are answers and means to reverse the lethal tide of demoralization. The personnel, resources, methodologies, and expertise exist to begin to get the job done. The individuals and institutions that claim to know the will, the ways, the wisdom and the works of God, must take the initiative to mobilize and utilize the personnel and resources necessary to heal the land and restore the people of God. It is incumbent upon the enlightened clergy of God to develop the plans and strategies and provide theological guidance and leadership.

As long as we continue to evade the escalating crisis of our serious ethical, moral, spiritual, and serious human predicament in America, the implosive, explosive, and destructive demoralization will continue to take its lethal toll.

The Public Theologian
CAPT, Inc.
P. O. Box 3148
Atlanta, Georgia 30302-3148

VITAL SUBJECT FOR A WORLD IN CRISIS
Survival Issues for Urgent Response
The Christian Institute of Public Theology

The following enumerations are vital subjects for consideration, exploration, dissertations, and messages for the people of God to respond to the urgent national and world cultural crises. The gravity of these crises demands the full utilization of the best of science, art, law, and theology. It is an alarming wake-up call for every soul to be subject to the higher power of God. It is high time to get real. It is time to set top priorities. It is time to major in majors. It is time to put on the whole armor of God. It is time to respond to the high calling of God in Christ Jesus. It is time for the prophetic voice. It is time to choose your loyalty and decide your destiny. The implementation of these proclamations is public theology.

(1) Attack on Civilization. (2) Attack on Humanity. (3) The Horror of Evil. (4) Are We Taking Evil Seriously? (5) When Hell is Unleashed in the World. (6) To Rid the World of Evil is Everybody's Business. (7) How can Evil be Overcome with Goodness? (8) How can Evil be Uprooted? (9) The Challenge to Overcome Evil. (10) Do We Have the Courage to Confront Satanic Forces? (11) The Tragedy of Evil to Humanity. (12) The Ugly Face of Evil in Manhattan. (13) The Containment of Evil in a Free Society. (14) A Plan and a Strategy to Combat Evil. (15) How to Fight Spiritual Warfare Effectively. (16) Ungodly and Blinded by Wickedness and Evil. (17) The Fight Against Spiritual Wickedness and Evil in High Places. (18) God's Word Declares that Evil will be Cutoff. (19) The God of Love Speaks Against

Injustice, Unrighteousness and Evil. (20) When American Commercial Airlines Became Bullets, Missiles and Bombs Targeting the Heart of America. (21) Who Is Watching on the Wall Watchtower? (22) When there is No Watchman on the Wall. (23) At Ease and Laxity Invite Destruction. (24) The Enemy is Watching and Waiting for the Nation to Doze. (25) No Time to be At Ease in Zion. (26) Facing the Reality of Terrorism and Technology. (27) Wake Up America. (28) Grow Up America. (29) Get Real America. (30) The Nation of God Must Lead the world in Truth Righteousness and justice. (31) Follow the Mandates of Christ or Reap the Madness of the World. (32) The Danger and Tragedy of Unsound Doctrines. (33) The High Cost of Incompetent Leadership. (34) The High Cost of Ignorance and Arrogance. (35) The Pragmatism of Survival. (36) Restructuring America for Security and Survival. (37) American Priorities for the 21st Century. (38) The Watchman Must Watch and the dog must Bark. (39) Rise and Shine - Your Light is Come. (40) The Triumphant Spirit of Christ. (41) Civilization's Only Hope. (42) Spread the Hope and Share the Love. (43) Embrace the Decency and Order of God. (44) Jesus Came to Make All Things New. (45) pared to be a Witness. (46) Spared to Proclaim the Gospel. (47) Spared to Tell the Story. (48) The Urgent Priorities of the Church. (49) The Courage to Add Works to Faith. (50) The Courage to Declare the Truth. (51) Hold on to the Light of Truth. (52) Begin Living or Die. (53) Living is Giving and Protecting Life. (54) Courage to Unite and Turn the Lethal Tide. (55) God's Message to America.

(Continuation):

56) God's Message to Heads of Nations. (57) How Relevant is the Church in the Arena of International Evil? (58) How Long Will the Church Remain Silent? (59) Courageous Believers in Christ can Make a Difference. (60) God's Message to the World. (61) The Extraction of Evil. (62) Evil is a Reminder that We Left Something Undone. ((63) Evil Reinforces the Seriousness of Life and Living. (64) Evil is a Reminder of the Admonitions of the Gospel. (65) God is Our Ultimate Rescuer from Evil. (66) Evil is a Preview and a Glimpse into Hell. (67) Evil Makes More Urgent the Need to Embrace the Truth of The Gospel. (68) The Will and the Courage to Cut Off and Pluck Out the Offenders to the Body. (69) Wrestling Against the Powers of Darkness. (70) Doing All to Stand. (71) The Danger of Technology without Theology. (72) Biblical Knowledge is Survival Knowledge. (73) The Bible is Humanity's Book of Life. (74) The Bible is God's Vital Message to Man. (75) The Rejection of God's Word and Son is Death. (76) Rejection of God is Mental Insanity and Spiritual Death. (77) To Deprive a Child of Christian Education is Criminal Negligence and Evil. (78) STEM Education without Christian Education is Irresponsible and Dangerous. (79) No Government is Authorized to Prohibit Biblical Knowledge from Public Education. (80) Man's Statutory (manmade) Laws are Subordinate to God's Divine and Natural Laws. (81) A Nation Under God Has a Duty to Lead the World Ethically

and Morally. (82) King Jesus Leads Nations Under God.

(83) The Bible is the Absolute Value Book for Humanity. (84) Governments that Ignore the Bible are in Rebellion Against God. (85) Those Who Reject Jesus Christ Choose Damnation. (86) The Bible is the Book of Light and Life. (87) Jesus Christ is the Ultimate Demonstration of God's Power. (88) The Lethality of Un-Christian Nations Must be Considered (89) The Assimilation of Christian Values for Nations Under God Must Go Forth. (90) The Exercise of Freedoms Outside of the Will of God are Destructive and Lethal Threats to the Civilized Body of Humanity. (91) The Un-Godly are not Authorized to Govern the People of God. (92) The Creator God of the Universe is the God of Intelligent Design, Order, Laws, Justice, Goodness, Mercy, Truth, Knowledge, understanding Wisdom, Beauty, Love, Light, Life, Prophecy, Salvation, Resurrection and Revelation. (93) Man and Woman are Created in the Image and Likeness of God. (94) Humanity was Created for Love and to Love, reverence and Glorify God. (95) God Shares his Nature and Will in Creation, In Christ, the Mind of Christ, The Holy Bible and in the Holy Spirit.

The above subjects, messages, issues, truths, mandates, theological knowledge, and ethical discourses are more than sufficient for the public theologians and the people of God to turn the lethal tide of darkness that is attempting to engulf the earth and humanity. If God allows it, the implementation of these 95 theological issues has the potential to cleanse our nation and the world of evil, wickedness, unrighteousness, sin, and corruption, as well as to bring about a renewal, restoration, healing, and forgiveness to our nations on the earth. TO GOD BE THE GLORY AND PRAISES FOR THE RISEN SAVIOR, JESUS CHRIST, Forever, Amen.

THE RELEVANT ROLE OF MINISTRY IN THE 21ST CENTURY
CAPT, INC

WHAT'S GOING ON IN THE AMERICAN SOCIETY?

In the broad daylight of this 21st century civilization, the local, state, and national governments' policymakers are ignoring the Bible in their administrative, executive, judicial, and legislative practices. The divine laws of God are being ignored. The natural laws of the Creator are being ignored. The statutory laws of the U.S. Constitution are being ignored.

These respective public officials are making their own laws but not according to righteousness, justice, or truth.

God's people are being misled by the dark, arbitrary, and- tyrannical law of worldly secularism. Alien-ideological politicians and atheistic judges are using their judicial discretion to make laws without regard to justice, righteousness, or truth. Justice is denied when it is ignored or delayed. If America has moved into a post-Biblical and post U.S. Constitution era, why have the people not been informed? Laws that are not sanctioned by divine authority, natural law, or U.S. Constitutional law are not validated laws. If such is the case, the American Judicial System is legitimizing injustice through human subjectivity and personal bias.

QUESTIONS FOR CLERGY AND THE CHURCH

Is God calling only political lawyers, peanut farmers, actors, military leaders, or billionaires to lead America, or is God also calling theologians and pastors to lead God's people? Why are ministers and theologians relegated to pastoring churches, teaching at seminaries, officiating at weddings, funerals, and other sacramental services? What responsibilities do ministers have for the general, national, and global welfare? Are theologians and ministers trained by their educational institutions for the general, national, and global welfare?

AN INVITATION FOR CLERGY AND THE CHURCH

Come from under the veils of ignorance, fear, and confusion. Come from under the veil of lies and deceptions. Come from under the veils of foolishness and wickedness. Come from under the veil of darkness and embrace God's knowledge, wisdom, and light of truth, justice, and righteousness. Come from under the bondage of self-imposed inferiority and limitations.

The Christian Association of Public Theologians

CRISIS IN AMERICAN LEADERSHIP

But when he saw the multitudes, he was moved with compassion on them, because they fainted, and were scattered abroad, as sheep having no shepherd. (Matthew 9:36)

Woe be unto the pastors that destroy and scatter the sheep of my pasture! Saith the Lord. (Jeremiah 23:1)

You have scattered my flock, and driven them away, and have not visited them: behold, I will visit upon you the evil of your doings, saith the Lord. (Jeremiah 23:2)

Woe be the shepherds of Israel that do feed themselves! Should not the shepherds feed the flock! (Ezekiel 34:2)

As for my people, children are their oppressors, and women rule over them. O my people, they which lead thee cause thee to err, and destroy the way of thy paths. (Isaiah 3:12)

The diseased have you not strengthened, neither have you healed that which was sick, neither have you bound up that which was broken, neither have you brought again that which was driven away, neither have you sought that which was lost; but with force and with cruelty have you ruled them. (Ezekiel 34:4)

Therefore, said he unto them, the harvest truly is great, but the labourers are few: Pray ye, therefore, the Lord of the harvest, that he would send forth labourers into his harvest. (Luke 10:2) (God's Spiritual Prescriptions by W. J. Webb)

FOUNDATION COMMUNITY CHURCH
Process of Spiritual Alienation
(Cultural Dysfunctions)

1. Discrimination (Selective disfavor and disregard)
2. Separation (Remove from primary proximity and association)
3. Segregation (Systematic assigned designations according to certain social characteristics)

4. Isolation (Withdraw association and resources)
5. Stagnation (Retardation of growth, development and progress)
6. Deprivation (Deny basic needs and vital resources)
7. Domination (Suppress, exploit, misuse, and abuse)
8. Demoralization (Discourage motivation and inspiration, mutilate the aspirations of the spirit)
9. Dehumanization (Degradation of human dignity and assault on human integrity)
10. Concentration (Herded and circumscribed victimization)
11. Starvation (Deprived, robbed and denied of resources for livelihood and living)
12. Annihilation (Utter destruction of life and the values for living)

The process of spiritual alienation is accelerating progressively in American society. It is infiltrating and diluting the ethical, moral, and spiritual values that have traditionally provided an optimum level of social and cultural health. This most insidious alienation process is corrupting the culture, causing confusion, destroying ethical values, and sowing seeds of political and economic instability. Sick cultures breed sick minds, sick souls, sick spirits, and sick societies.

The challenge of public theology is to reverse spiritual alienation trends and eliminate society's destructive cultural dysfunctions.

Willie James Webb, MDiv, MA, MS, CACII, CCS
Pastoral Addiction Counselor

JUSTICE REQUIRES SYSTEMS OF MERIT

GOVERNMENT SYSTEMS WITHOUT MERIT PERPETUATE CORRUPTION & INJUSTICE

In a democratic form of government, the allocation of human resources, goods, and services by the government requires systems, laws, regulations, policies, and procedures of equitable merit. This is to assure that each person receives his or her due according to fairness and justice. Arbitrary systems of non-merit favoritism create confusion, corruption, and chaos.

Personnel administration merit systems have a long history in both the federal government and state governments. Policies and procedures were in place that required the documentation of the respective qualifications as well as the administration of written and oral examinations to be objective in the selection of applicants based on merit. It was common practice in the 1950s, 1960s, and 1970s to go through a merit-based qualification process for government jobs and contracts. During this period of time, the State of Georgia had a merit system that processed applicants for jobs. The State of Georgia also had an office called GOFEP (Georgia Office of Fair Employment Practices). These merit-based systems have been discontinued. What are the motives and rationale for this discontinuation of merit systems?

The advent of the 1964 Civil Rights Act and the creation of the EEOC (Equal Employment Opportunity Commission) engendered some hope for equitable, merit-based fairness and justice in government employment and in the allocation of other government resources and services. Affirmative action programs were also created to bridge the gaps for those who were left behind to pass racial and other forms of discrimination. However, the intended purpose of the 1964 Civil Rights Act and the EEOC have not accomplished the intended goals and objectives. The corruption and dysfunctionality in the EEOC and the judicial system have diluted and nullified equitable fairness, systems of merit, and judicial justice. The unethical and immoral forces of secularism appear to be pushing the ideas, concepts, and notions of merit systems out of the culture. Have thoughtful people considered a society without justice?

Merit systems in government are being replaced with arbitrary, partisan political identities, and ethnocentric favoritism systems. Government personnel systems are becoming openly weaponized with arrogant administrative intimidation, re-constitutional procedures, dictatorial dismissals, punitive and vindictive no-hire lists, or no-rehire black lists; without any DUE PROCESS OF LAW as required by the U.S. Constitution. There are serious consequences when human justice is violated. Human justice requires merit systems in the allocation of God's resources and values. Justice requires government merit systems. Injustice is a threat to democracy. Social injustice violates human rights. Injustice is a threat to America. Injustice is a threat to civilization. THE RESTORATION OF MERIT SYSTEMS AND JUSTICE IN THE AMERICAN GOVERNMENT MUST BE A TOP PRIORITY FOR SURVIVAL AS A NATION!

The Christian Institute of Public Theology

GOVERNMENT'S DUTY PROTECT HUMAN RIGHTS

The government's protection of the inalienable God given human rights fosters the optimum actualization of the God-given human potential to achieve and experience the following blessings of God to:

1. Embrace the reality of truth.
2. Seek knowledge's life-giving and enlightening power.
3. Experience the balance and congruence of justice.
4. Appreciate and extol the virtues of goodness.
5. Follow the ways of righteousness.
6. Embrace and savor the preciousness and value of love.
7. Enjoy and behold the aesthetic beauty of artistic expressions.
8. See and visualize the illumination of light and enlightenment.
9. Wait with patience for the resilience of hope.
10. Hold on and hold out with the perseverance of faith.
11. Realize the gift and understanding of wisdom.
12. Use wisely and gratefully the autonomy of freedom.

THE LOVING GOD OF LOVE HAS ENDOWED MANKIND WITH UNLIMITED AND INEXHAUSTIBLE POTENTIAL FOR THE GOOD LIFE, THE ABUNDANT LIFE AND EVEN ETERNAL LIFE. IT IS WRITTEN AND CONFIRMED IN THE BIBLICAL WORD OF GOD! Governments are instituted to protect these inalienable rights from God!

(The Christian Institute of Public Theology)

AMERICANS' RIGHT FOR COMPETENT REPRESENTATION
Competent Leadership has been Neglected Christian Institute of Public Theology

The right to vote must be balanced by the right to competent leadership and democratic representation. The political advocacy for the right to vote gets substantial news coverage, promotion, and legislation. Voting rights and associated issues such as the alleged suppression of voting, the handling of ballots, proper personal identification, and other prerequisites for voting are prevalent topics in the news media. However, the preoccupation with voting rights and associated concerns has totally neglected and ignored the complementary, essential, and even vital right for competent elected officials, competent leaders and competent democratic representatives. Hardly any credible, valid, relevant, or meritorious requirements are stipulated for the candidates for public office. More concern is expressed about the diversity of candidates for public office than about their merit and fitness for the responsibilities and duties of the respective public office.

The lack of specified basic requirements for public office work goes against the U.S. Constitution, democracy, America, and common sense. The American electoral process and requirements have not kept pace with cultural changes, global connections, and technological advances. The American standards for competent and effective political administration and leadership do not measure up to the new, escalating demanding complexities of the heterogeneous, globalized 21st Century. Incompetent leadership and undemocratic leadership nullify and even defeat the noble purpose and reasons for voting. Voting in a democratic form of government is intended to assure the best representation of the collective will of the citizens based on their guiding constitution and values of justice, freedom, and equality for the common good of society, nation, and humanity.

The social processes of immigration, acculturation, socialization, and assimilation of a variety of populations of people extend far beyond their race, skin color, language, accents, and customs. Human beings also have belief systems, ideologies, and social values, that influence their thinking, values and behaviors. Many of these ideologies, nationalities, and belief systems are incompatible, irreconcilable, and even conflicting. The conglomeration of these social, political, and cultural values must be acknowledged in a heterogeneous society such as America, which has been known as a melting pot. Many values that people adhere to are not easily assimilated. These differences must be acknowledged and reconciled with the established guiding principles, values, and laws of America. There is great space for freedom and differences of ideas and opinions. However, the legally and officially established standards must prevail in the leadership of the American Government. These values and guiding principles of the Nation must be taught and embraced, especially by the American Government's political leadership and political representatives.

It is true that America is a country of immigrants, with people of diverse backgrounds from all around the earth. Traditionally, immigrants came to America and were willing to assimilate, embrace American values, and democracy and become full-fledged Americans. That trend has changed. Many people who migrate to America desire to hold on to the values, political systems, ethnicities, and cultures of their native countries. Many of these different newcomers to

America do not embrace America's democracy, its Constitution, social values, or the Judeo-Christian faith. Some newcomers and those who come to study at universities or for other reasons prefer to influence the American government and society. During this 21st century in America, great emphasis is placed on diversity. Political identities are rampant in America. The emphasis being placed on identities, especially race, gender, LGBT, Democratic, Republican, Independent, Conservative, Liberal, and so forth, is precipitating significant division in America. These differences pervade education from kindergarten through the university. These identities are being used for political influence. Substantial indoctrination is taking place. Political leadership and other institutional leadership are challenged. Therefore, it will require more than just voting or even integrity in voting to cultivate the quality of enlightened leadership that is needed.

The guiding doctrines and principles have served America well. They have brought about great social and political reform in America. They propelled America to become the greatest nation in history in terms of individual liberty, prosperity, and national political power. These values are still sound. They have already withstood the test of time. These values and guiding principles must be taught more thoroughly and deliberately. America must keep its identity as ONE NATION UNDER GOD. INDIVIDUAL FREEDOMS IN THE AMERICAN GOVERNMENT MUST BE SUBJECTED TO AND GUIDED BY THE CONSTITUTION OF THE UNITED STATES. THE DECLARATION OF INDEPENDENCE, AND PLEDGE OF ALLEGIANCE, HOLD ONTO IN GOD WE TRUST, THE TRADITIONAL BIBLICAL VALUES THAT UNDERGIRD AND SUPPORT A DEMOCRATIC FORM OF GOVERNMENT.

To assure the true sound responsible leadership of the Democratic Government from the local, state and federal levels; all candidates for public office must meet designated requirements that assure their mental and physical professional competence, their ideologies and belief systems are compatible with the U. S. Constitution, Declaration and traditional Biblical values and be otherwise fit for duty standards. The American citizens have a right to ethical, competent, and representative public office holders and leaders of justice, righteousness, and liberty. THIS IS AN URGENT AND IMMEDIATE PRIORITY FOR THE US CONGRESS AND THE PRESIDENCY TO ESTABLISH COMPETENT REQUIREMENTS AND STANDARDS FOR CANDIDATES FOR AMERICAN PUBLIC OFFICE FOR THE HEALTH, SAFETY, SECURITY, LIBERTY, PEACE, GOOD-WILL FOR ALL AMERICANS AND THE PEOPLE OF GOD.

WHAT ARE THE CONSEQUENCES
OF A SILENT CHURCH?
Humanity's Vital Need for the Word of God
(The Christian Institute of Public Theology)

A silent Church fails to plant and cultivate the seeds of life. This moral failure and ethical duty allow the evil seeds of destruction and death to grow and multiply. The teaching, preaching, and practicing of the Biblical Word of God are so vital that human life is aborted, withers, deteriorates, and is destroyed without God's Word. God's Word enlightens the mind, nurtures the body and soul. God's Biblical Word gives life, shares life, and protects life. Jesus declares that he came to give life and to give it "more abundantly." John 3:16 proclaims that God so loved the world "that He gave his only begotten Son, that whosoever believe in him should not perish but have eternal life."

The destructive consequences of the deprivation of the Biblical Word of God can be measured, predicted, and correlated with the following human, cultural, and societal degeneration and deterioration:

1. Religious Idolatry. (The worship of idols and false gods.)
2. Mental Confusion. (Mental disorders and insanity.)
3. Human Disorders. (Hatred, personality dysfunctions and social maladjustments.)
4. Spiritual Wickedness. (Orientation and practice of evil behavior against life.)
5. Cultural Dysfunction. (Confusion of social roles, values and traditions.)
6. Government Corruption. (Abuse, misuse & weaponization of government authority.)

7. Political Destabilization. (Divisive political identity, ethnic & ideological confusion.)
8. Social upheavals, crime. (disrespect for law, order, human life & civilization.)
9. Institutional Dysfunctions. (Dysfunctional families, education, religious, business, etc.)
10. Social/economic/political/religious/cultural/chaos. (Devoid of humane survival values)
11. Chaotic, confused, disordered, corrupted government and culture. (Decline of civility.)
12. National catastrophic disruption of civilized living, humane living and quality of life. (Total human ruin; loss of freedom, humanity, civility, government, lives, nationhood)

These twelve destructive consequences of the silent Church are not mysterious. They have been predicated on the predictability of human nature through numerous demonstrations that have been played out on the real stage of history for thousands of years. No nation in history has survived the worship and practice of secularism, materialism, atheism, and the willful rebellion against the Word of God. The words of Hosea (Hosea 4:6) still ring true, "My people are destroyed for lack of knowledge... forgotten the law of God." This knowledge refers to theological knowledge (knowledge about God.). The loving God has given mankind a true, historical, time-tested rule book and blueprint for living. This Rule Book and Blueprint for Living is known as THE HOLY BIBLE. THE TIME IS HERE WHEN CHURCH LEADERS AND BELIEVERS MUST SEND FORTH GOD'S WORD THROUGH EVERY MEDIA POSSIBLE WITH URGENCY THROUGHOUT THE EARTH. GOD'S WORD WILL NOT RETURN VOID (Isaiah 55:11)

CHURCH AND STATE ALLIANCE
Truth and Justice

The truth of religion does not conflict with the administration of justice in government. True religion and a just government are complementary. Biblical knowledge provides the foundation for the administration of justice, law, and public policy for all governments and all nations. God, the Creator, is the source and the authority for all laws and authority in the administration of human justice and government. It is God who endows human beings with human rights. It is the responsibility of the government to administer justice and protect the individual human rights given by God to all human beings. The truth of God and the justice of God do not conflict.

It is the injustice in government and hypocrisy in religion that conflict. It is the travesty of justice and the deception of truth that conflict. The love of God does not conflict with the goodwill of mankind. The truth does not conflict with reality. True science and true religion do not conflict. It is pseudoscience and pseudo religion that conflict. The obedience of man and the righteousness of God does not conflict. The church and state form alliances for truth, righteousness, and justice by adhering to God's divine laws. The integration of truth and justice by the Church and State creates harmony, goodwill, and peace in society.

It is important to emphasize true religion as opposed to the general, inclusive use of the word religion. There are many belief systems and activities that fit the definition of religious or religion, but are not true religion. Worshiping idols is a religious practice. An idol can be anything except God.

The worship of anything less than God is idolatry. There are many religious cults, sectarian, ethnocentric, and ideological groups that do not subscribe to God with the capital G. True religion must be based on and connected to the real Revelatory God of history. The Holy Bible has knowledge of the Revelatory God of history on earth.

True religion, true science, divine laws, natural laws, righteousness, and justice do nor conflict. They are integral parts of the divine creation of the world of reality. It is erroneous to separate these integral parts from each other. True religion, true science, true righteousness, and true justice cannot be separated from each other. The Bible contains the authority, education, knowledge, wisdom, and understanding for decency and order for all governments, societies, and all nations. The Bible is the primary source of human behavior and governance.

The Bible contains vital knowledge about God and Jesus Christ for all people. However, this knowledge does not force anyone to believe it or accept it. Every person has the freedom to choose to accept this knowledge or to reject this knowledge of the Bible. God gives humans the autonomy to choose according to their decisions. God made man free to choose to accept or reject God. This freedom that God gives mankind is very precious.

Jesus Christ is not forced on anyone. It is left to the free will of the individual to accept the Bible or Jesus Christ. God gives individuals freedom of choice and autonomy. It is the duty and responsibility of parents, educational institutions, and society to provide essential education for every child and person to enable them to succeed in life and be a contributor to society. It is very important for each child to get an education to make a living. It is also very important for every child to get an education to make a good life for themselves and others. There is no other book greater than the Bible to enhance the good life. Considering the importance of the Bible, it should be required education for every child born into the world. Every child may not accept the biblical teachings. It should still be the responsibility of parents and society to provide it.

It is tragic that the Establishment Clause of the First Amendment of the U.S. Constitution prohibits prayer and Bible education in public schools and the public domain. This Establishment Clause states that Congress shall make no laws "respecting an establishment of religion or prohibiting the free exercise thereof." This clause, based on a faulty definition and misinterpretation of religion, has deprived millions upon millions of children and other persons in America the greatest literary knowledge known to mankind. This deprivation of knowledge has also deprived the Nation and the world of incalculable blessings and benefits. Only God knows the tragic, unethical, immoral, criminal, inhumane, and evil damages that have been done due to the deprivation of biblical knowledge and education.

Inasmuch as the Bible is not a religion, the First Amendment does not make reference to the Bible. Therefore, the Bible must be exempted from the implied presumption of the Establishment Clause that it is a religion. The Bible is not a religion, and the Bible does not contain any compulsion to force anyone to accept its knowledge, education, or information. The Bible does not force, compel, or require anyone to believe its knowledge or doctrines. There are no biblical requirements in the Bible for anyone to be a Jew, Christian, Muslim, or of any other faith or belief persuasion. Specifically, the Christian faith is not forced on anyone.

It is ironic but true that, according to the First Amendment, the prohibition of teaching the Bible in public schools and public domain is an abridgment of freedom of speech and the press. Laws prohibiting the Bible from being taught in public schools and public domains are in violation of the First Amendment of the Constitution itself. The prohibition and restriction on teaching the Bible in public schools and the public domain, as well as other knowledge domains, is clearly an infringement on free speech and press, as well as some form of discrimination against biblical knowledge. The Bible is clearly a nonpartisan and non-sectarian general historical and universal theological book for all people. It is the greatest work of classical literature.

The misinterpretation and lack of definition of religion, and the unverified presumption that the Bible is a religion or restricted to the nebulous interpretation of a religion, disparage the Bible as a document restricted to a nebulous definition of religion. Because of this grave error, the Bible has been censored and restricted as free speech and freedom of the press in public schools and other public domains.

It is self-evident that the knowledge, history, and truths of the Bible, transcend race, government, religion, nationality, science, art, law, theology, the earth, creation, and time within eternity. It is the most widely known and publicized book in the history of mankind. It is indigenous to humanity and the earth.

The deprivation of this vital knowledge for humanity is reflected in the world's impoverished cultures, conflicts, pandemics, violence, hatred, and confusion of nations on the earth. This cultural crisis is escalating to a civilizational emergency.

It is petitioned and recommended that Bible study and Bible education be required in all public educational institutions and educational institutions that teach education for the public. IT IS REQUESTED THAT THE U.S. CONSTITUTION BE AMENDED TO REQUIRE BIBLE EDUCATION IN ALL PUBLICSCHOOLS. IT IS RECOMMENDED THAT THE ESTABLISHMENT CLAUSE BE NULLIFIED DUE TO THE MISINTERPRETATION OF BIBLE EDUCATION AND UNDEFINED RELIGION.

THE PRIMARY SACRED DUTY OF AMERICA TEACH AND TRANSMIT HUMAN SURVIVAL VALUES

EDUCATE   LEGISTATE   MANDATE   ASSIMILATE

THE FOUNDATIONAL AMERICAN HUMAN SURVIVAL VALUES

1. RECOGNIZE THE SOVEREIGNTY OF THE CREATOR GOD.
2. ACKNOWLEDGE THE SALVATION OF JESUS CHRIST.
3. LEARN THE BIBLICAL WORD OF TRUTH OF SCRIPTURE.
4. ACKNOWLEDGE THE SACREDNESS OF HUMAN LIFE.
5. RESPECT THE HUMAN DIGNITY OF EVERY PERSON.
6. RESPECT GOD GIVEN HUMAN RIGHTS & FREEDOM.
7. OBSERVE EQUAL JUSTICE & EQUITY UNDER THE LAW.
8. RESPECT & OBSERVE INDIVIDUAL RELIGIOUS LIBERTY.
9. PRACTICE JUSTICE & FAIRNESS IN ALL RELATIONSHIPS.
10. LEARN AND ABIDE BY THE REQUIREMENTS OF A DEMOCRATIC FORM OF GOVERNMENT.

VALUES OF TRUTH FOR ALL HUMANITY

EDUCATION PROHIBITED BY RELIGIOUS DEFINITION
The Bible Defies Constitutional Religion Clause
The Christian Institute of Public Theology

The nebulous definitions, meanings, and connotations of religion as used in the First Amendment of the United States Constitution arbitrarily mischaracterize the Bible as a part of the nebulous meaning of religion and subsequently prohibit the unique, inexhaustible, educational, cultural, historical, social, legal, and theological values of the Bible. The Bible is nor ordinary, general, or nebulous in its description. The Bible is not synonymous with religion as presumed in the First Amendment of the United States Constitution's "religion establishment clause."

The Bible is a distinct, unique, and specific historical, legal, ethical, and theological composition of sixty-six specifically named books, combining the Old and New Testament eras of Jewish History. It covers the whole spectrum of life from Genesis to Revelation in the New Testament. The Old Testament contains 39 books: five books of law, twelve books of history, five books of wisdom and poetry, five books of major prophets, and twelve books of minor prophets. The New Testament contains 27 books: four books of Gospels, one book of history, twenty-one letters, and one book of Revelation.

It must be acknowledged that the Bible is not a book of sectarianism, cultism, or any other ism that is less than monotheism. It is not a book of fiction, mythology, or perceptual creations of the imagination. The Bible is a one-of-a-kind historical book that reveals and historically represents one monotheistic God, one humanity, and one Savior. It teaches only the existence of one God who is omnipotent, omnipresent, omniscient, infinite, immortal, and eternal. The Bible teaches further that the worship of any entity or being less than God is idolatry. According to the Bible, there is only one God with a capital G. The polytheistic gods with the small g are idols and are not the monotheistic gods of Abraham, Isaac, and Jacob. This God resurrected Jesus Christ from the dead. The Bible teaches against religious idolatry. The God of the Bible is the God of love and truth.

DEFINITIONS OF RELIGIONS:

The World Book Dictionary (1998, World Book, Inc.) provides four credible definitions of religion as follows: (1) Belief in God or gods. (2) Worship of God or gods. (3) A particular system of religious belief. (4) Anything done or followed with reverence and devotion. These academic and professional definitions of religion from the World Book Dictionary illustrate the expansive, general, and broad definitions of religion. These general and nebulous definitions of religion clearly raise the question of how the specificity of the Bible and its criticisms of idolatry and dishonesty can be considered any part of a false and idolatrous religion. The Bible is not synonymous with God. It is not a book to be worshipped. It is not a being that worships. It is not a being that follows. The Bible is not a devout or revered being. The Bible is not a religion. It is a book of history, knowledge, education, truth, God's love, historical acts, and instructions for the salvation of mankind.

THE NATURE OF RELIGION MERITS SERIOUS STUDY:

Individual decisions and choices from a universe of things, objects, and beings connect and relate the four definitions of religion in the World Book Dictionary to personal and individual beliefs, worship, reverence preferences, and devotions. The core meaning of religion seems to reside in the personal feelings, belief systems, and choices of the respective individuals or groups. Based on the limited information provided, a rational analysis must conclude that the Bible is not a religion. Contrarily, anything can be considered religious. Therefore, the government cannot be isolated from the definition and concept of religion. Based on the nebulous definition of religion, the U.S. Constitution and the American Government, itself, could be considered a religion.

The Bible itself, proclaims that the worship of anything less than God is idolatry. Human beings adore, revere, and worship a variety of things, objects, and beings. Religion appears to originate and reside in the minds, hearts, spirits, souls, and wills of individuals and groups as they focus on objects of devotion, reverence and worship. These objects, things or beings are not necessarily specifically limited or defined. The conglomerate complexities of religion and the associated consequences must not be taken lightly. Serious attention is needed.

REVISITING THE RELIGION ESTABLISHMENT CLAUSE:

The Religion Establishment Clause is based on the First Amendment to the United States Constitution. The

Religion Establishment Clause is used as the legal basis to prohibit the Bible from being taught in the government's public schools in America. This law is used to justify the prohibition of and use of Bibles in government agencies and other places of public accommodations, such as hotels and motels. The words, quotations, and references to the Bible are often censured, discouraged, and disparaged. Some candidates who are being sworn in for American public office refuse to place their hand on the Bible for the administration of the oath of office. The legal restrictions and public prohibitions against the Bible and the use and content of the Bible are being done without sufficient competent legal investigation and study. A serious revisit of this "Religion Establishment Clause" is urgently needed. In addition to reviewing the legality of the "Religion Establishment Clause," a competent social, national, political, economic, cultural, health, educational, and theological impact study would be of great service to America and the world. The heterogeneous and technological complexities of the world have critically, narrowed the margins of error. This error is unaffordable.

THE READING AND LANGUAGE OF THE FIRST AMENDMENT OF THE U.S. CONSTITUTION:

"Congress shall make no law respecting an establishment of religion, or prohibiting the free exercise thereof, or abridging the freedom of speech or of the press; or of the right of the people peaceably to assemble and to petition the government for a redress of grievances."

THE CONSTITUTION OF THE UNITED STATES OF AMERICA RELATIONSHIP OF THE BIBLE TO AMERICAN LAW:

The influence of the Bible predates the 13 American Colonies that began about 1607 AD. Christian ministers and other Christians spread the teachings of the Bible throughout the Thirteen Colonies in America. The spread of the teachings of the Bible and the salvation news of Jesus Christ eventually brought about what is called the "Great Awakening" in the American Colonies. The great spiritual awakening resulted from a massive Christian led movement of evangelistic teachings, revivals, conversions, and dedication to freedom to live, work, and worship without government restrictions and hindrance. It must be noted that Black Africans (Negro slaves) were first brought to the Colony at Jamestown, Virginia, in 1619, and they were not considered as fully equal or equally human as their white counterparts. However, they became part of this vibrant social and political movement in the new world.

The culture of the Colonies became saturated with the ethical teachings, enlightening knowledge, and liberating spirit of the biblical knowledge of the Bible and the soul salvation knowledge of Jesus Christ. The Colonists were inspired and motivated to build communities, churches, and schools and to engage in free enterprise endeavors. This new beginning was inspired and sustained by Christians and Bible believers. The Bible was their primary reading and teaching book. Many could not read or write, but they learned through the oral quotations of Scripture in the Bible. The Bible became a motivator to learn to read, write, and get an education. Many schools were established during this colonial period. Many African American slaves were motivated to read and get an education so that they could read the Bible. The American Negro slaves never considered the Bible a "White man's religion."

It was the influence of the Bible that initiated the Declaration of Independence in 1776 and the Constitution of the United States in 1787. The Bible influenced the ratification of the Bill of Rights in 1791, and the recognition of a democratic form of government described by President Abraham Lincoln in 1863 as "a government of the people, by the people, and for the people," and the issuance of the Emancipation Proclamation in 1863 that freed the Negro American slaves in 1863. In subsequent years, the Bible influenced the Pledge of Allegiance to the U.S. Flag as "One Nation under God" and the American Motto on American currency, "In God We Trust," Show influence of the Bible is deeply imbedded in American culture, education, social, economic, and political institutions. The single most important document that has made the greatest difference for good in America and the world has been and is the Holy Bible. This magnificent, unfathomable, and extraordinary gift to humanity must be respected, re-examined, revisited, reconsidered, reunited, reclaimed, replenished, renewed, and revitalized. Generations, civilizations, and nations have been enlightened, guided, nurtured, and strengthened by the knowledge, understanding, wisdom, spiritual concern, and love contained in and radiating from the Bible.

EXPLORING THE BIBLICAL AND LEGAL PARADOX:

Considering the massive enlightening and constructive influence of the Bible on American culture and its founding documents, as well as Western Civilization as a whole, this paradoxical irony must be emphatically noted and explored. It is an egregious ironical paradox that the Religion Establishment Clause of the First Amendment of the U.S. Constitution is used (paradoxically) to prohibit the Bible from being taught in the public government schools, along with disparaging attempts to build a wall of separation between the Bible and the government; cloaked as "separation of government and religion," and "separation of "Church and State," How is this rational, legitimate and reconcilable when the unique Bible has been influencing cultures, civilization and nations for civility and good for over five thousand years? Biblical knowledge and the foundation and guidance for the governing documents, the Constitution and the democracy of America are based on biblical influence. The Bible is the foundation for America's Constitution, Democracy and civilization's humanizing influence.

The disparagement, marginalization and misrepresentation of the Bible, in reference to the "Religion Establishment Clause" is based on dogmatic ignorance of the Bible's manifested significant truths and pro-life human values for over five thousand years of world history. The expansive disparagement and prohibitions against the Bible are also based on the false premises and presumptions that the Bible is a religion (undefined). The disparagement and subservient relegated status of the Bible in the American Government and general society has and continues to cause tragic human deprivations, cultural damages, political corruption and national calamities beyond description and calculations.

REQUEST, APPEAL, AND RECOMMENDATION: IT IS HEREBY APPEALED, REQUESTED AND HEREBY RECOMMENDED BY THE DULY INCORPORATED

CHRISTIAN INSTITUE OF PUBLIC THEOLOGY OF THE STATE OF GEORGIA, USA

TO: THE PRESIDENT OF THE UNITED STATES; UNITED STATES CONGRESS; THE UNITED STATES SUPREME COURT

IT IS RESPECTFULLY REQUESTED THAT THE APPROPRIATE AGENCIES OF THE AMERICAN GOVERNMENT:

1. DEFINE THE MEANING AND ROLE OF RELIGION IN THE FIRST AMENDMENT OF THE CONSTITUTION OF THE UNITED STATES.
2. CLARIFY THE LEGAL PLACE, PUBLIC ROLE, EDUCATIONAL CLASSIFICATION, THE RELATIONSHIP OF THE GOVERNMENT TO THE BIBLE AS RELATED TO THE FIRST AMENDMENT TO THE CONSTITUTION OF THE UNITED STATES OF AMERICA.

The Christian Institute of Public Theology, Inc.

EDUCATIONAL DEFICIENCY OF CRITICAL RACE THEORY
Readiness & Relevance for Learning are Critical

It is self-evident that a child must have a series of readiness, development, and maturational levels in order to comprehend certain concepts, ideas, and realizations. The educational gradations of kindergarten, early and advanced elementary, middle school, and four years of high school exist to accommodate the child's educational readiness from childhood, adolescence, to young adulthood. These series of developmental stages of the child involve physical, mental, emotional, and social growth of the child.

Human beings, unlike lower forms of life, require years of developmental growth and learning that correspond with their overall maturational and developmental processes and learning readiness. These developmental and growth stages involve the physical, mental, emotional, social, moral, and ethical components of the human individual. Although this process evolves naturally and is very fascinating, it is also very delicate and complex. The failure to recognize this delicacy and complexity in the growth, development, and education of children can be very detrimental to their health, lives, and well-being.

The primary flaw of Critical Race Theory supporters is their failure to recognize the delicate and complex nature of human development. This totally dependent child must learn to crawl on its hands and knees before it can walk or stand on its legs and feet. This totally dependent child must be compassionately cared for and nurtured for a long period of time. During this process, a child must consciously discover and recognize itself and its own self-consciousness. The child must learn its name, identity, and the identities of others in relation to itself and the world around it. A child must learn words and speech before it can communicate ideas in an intelligible language. It usually takes about five years before a child is ready to begin kindergarten. The child must learn to read before it can read to learn. The child must learn the alphabet, how to recognize and spell words, and the art and skills of communicating orally and in writing. This lengthy elementary indulgence in childhood development is a solicitous plea on behalf of children to all who are entrusted to work with them. This plea is especially for educators to be extra compassionate and sensitive to the natural limitations of each child's respective developmental stages. The imposition of tasks and complexities beyond the child's comprehension readiness is detrimental, abusive, and cruel. The imposition of Critical Race Theory on children is a blatantly detrimental example of abuse and cruelty to innocent, and mistreated children. American students from kindergarten through twelfth grade do not have the historical nor the educational developmental foundations to understand the historical, cultural, political, and sociological implications of Critical Race Theory. Most college students are not equipped to fully understand the complexities and multiplicity of variables involved in the analysis of Critical Race Theory. No person born is responsible for his or her race, human characteristics, gender, nationality, or ancestry.

PREREQUISITES FOR OBJECTIVE TEACHING

An objective merit-based and needs-based teaching and learning of Critical Race Theory would require graduate-level competence in Public Education, American History, Black American History, Sociology, Psychology, Cultural Competence, Political Science, Christian Ethics, Constitution of the United States, Declaration of Independence, and the Pledge of One Nation Under God. There is no evidence to suggest that such prerequisites exist with the current administration of Critical Race Theory.

The current administration of Critical Race Theory in American Educational School Systems ignores the readiness and competence of the students to understand the contextuality of such teaching. No known publicized credible educational needs for Critical Race Theory have been established. Critical Race Theory ignores the primary cognitive domain of learning. The cognitive domain of learning takes precedence over the affective and emotional domain of learning. This imbalanced major in the emotional domain aspect of learning jeopardizes the mental, emotional, and social health of all students involved. This also highlights the detriment of SEL (Social Emotional Learning) that is spreading in American Schools and American Educational Institutions. The primary domain of learning, cognitive (intellectual), is being neglected and hijacked by the SEL (social-emotional learning) that is prevalent in many American educational school districts.

This is nor the time in history to minimize and neglect the cognitive domain of learning. The technological, global, and space ages require the utmost objective, scientific, artistic, legalistic and theistic objectivity than ever before in the history of mankind. America and humanity cannot afford the superficial, counterproductive indulgence of misguided miseducation, unsound doctrines, deceptive ideologies, and blind emotionalism for leadership and guidance. Humanity must be guided by validated truth, justice, and righteousness already established by God. The margin of error has become too narrow and the cost too high to gamble with naive and infantile incompetence.

HISTORICAL REALITIES OF RACIAL INJUSTICE

Let it be known that Black Americans lived with, dealt with, and survived the tragic reality of 250 years of racial slavery and another hundred years of racial segregation and discrimination in America. During all of these atrocities. Black Americans significantly contributed to the building of the greatest and most blessed nation on earth as "One Nation Under God." America is an exceptional nation. The Black Americans are significant contributors to this exceptionalism. It is difficult to imagine America becoming a great nation without the presence and contributions of Black Americans. America is the national home of Black Americans. The documented presence of Black people in America dates back to 1619. America is the national home of Black Americans. Subsequent to 1619 Black Americans were born, lived, worked, and died in America. They helped to build the country. They have fought and died in all of America's wars and international conflicts, unlike any other ethnic group.

In spite of enslavement, segregation, discrimination, and degradation, the Black Americans remained more loyal to America than any other American group. Marcus Garvey, a Black Jamaican came to America in 1916 for the purpose of meeting with Booker T. Washington of Tuskegee. However, Booker T. Washington died in 1915, before Garvey's arrival. Garvey started the "Back to Africa Movement" in America in 1916. Garvey had an estimated two million followers among Black Americans. However, the majority of Black Americans considered America as their home. Garvey was released from prison in 1927 and returned to Jamaica. Most Black Americans, as did Booker T. Washington, accepted America their home, and disavowed the invitations and enticements as being Africans or claiming citizenship or a homeland in

Africa. Most indigenous Black Americans, the offspring of slaves, and especially those who believe in the Bible and Jesus Christ, have resisted the alien influences to hate America and White Americans. Psalmist 24 says, "The earth is the Lord's, and the fullness thereof, the world, and they that dwell therein." This makes people aware that no one and no nation have a monopoly on the blessings of God. America was exceptionally blessed because its founding documents were based on Biblical Judeo-Christianity. The prosperous blessings of America were and are not based on geography or the color or race of its inhabitants. It was based on their faith in God and biblical belief systems. Those who are familiar with Black American history know that their faith in God was foundational for their survival, progress, and accomplishment in a hostile environment. America is the official and God ordained national home of Black Americans. Those who would deny the equal rights and privileges of this homeland to Black Americans and/or teach Black Americans to hate America are in violation of all of America's founding documents, governing laws, and the Biblical Mandates of God.

THE SIGNIFICANCE OF BLACK AMERICAN HISTORY

The failure to seriously and broadly teach Black American History is an indictment against American educational, theological, and governmental institutions. Black American History has universal and significant lessons and values for America and the world. It is an integral part of the sacred Judeo-Christian redemptive American history as "One Nation Under God." Biblical Ethics and the Spirit of God are at the center of Black American History. The American

Civil War, the Emancipation Proclamation, and the freedom of the Negro slaves was acts of God in answer to over two hundred fifty years of prayers and supplications. This was an extraordinary epoch played out on the stage of American History.

To highlight this extraordinary history of epic proportion, consider that God sent Moses to Egypt to lead the children of Israel out of captivity and bondage. This intervention on the part of God required the opening of a pathway through the Red Sea. As related in the Bible, Pharoah's army chased them and they drowned in the sea. In America, the Negro slaves had nowhere to go and no weapons to fight with. HOWEVER, GOD PERFORMED A MIRACLE BY FREEING THE NEGRO SLAVES IN THE MIDST OF THEIR CAPTORS. Booker T. Washington describes witnessing this miracle as a child on a slave plantation in Virginia in his book, Up From Slavery.

THE EMANCIPATION PROCLAMATION

Booker T. Washington stated that all the slaves were summoned to the Plantation Big House. He said that a White man rode up on a horse at the gathering of the plantation slaves and read the Emancipation Proclamation to the gathered slaves the Emancipation Proclamation. After the man finished reading, he told the slaves that they were free and that they were free to leave the plantation. They left in jubilation and celebration. After 244 years of slavery, they left the plantation as free men, women, and children. This was a miracle of God. White Americans could no longer reconcile slavery with the truths of the Bible and the Gospel of Christ. This sacred, redemptive Black American History is ennobling and significant, with lessons for America and the world. All

American educational, social, and theological institutions have a duty to teach American Black American History.

THE AVAILABILITY OF BLACK AMERICAN HISTORY

The libraries, museums, colleges, universities, churches, state capitols, the Capitol of Washington D.C. and other historical places are replete with the annals and archives of Black American History. Great lessons and blessings for the Nation and the world are enshrined in Black American History. The bountiful sharing of this vital knowledge has the potential to enlighten, enrich, and elevate America to more noble and celestial civil and moral heights. When this dynamic evolutionary history is judged in its totality, all true Americans will be repentant and humbled, but also grateful and proud to be an American of "ONE NATION UNDER GOD."

A very comprehensive Afro-American History of Selected Bibliography has been put together by Monroe Fordham. This extensive bibliography covers topics ranging from West African origins and the Atlantic Slave Trade to the current era of the Black American Civil Rights Movement. It is recommended that all American public schools, Colleges, and universities utilize this comprehensive and rich bibliography to develop an ongoing Black American History curriculum and courses. The rich content of this scholarly and professionally written authentic Black American history will provide enlightening knowledge, pride, and appreciation. It is recognized that many of the advocates of Critical Race Theory are sincere and have good intentions. It is hoped that they will embrace this more enlightened and constructive means of educating our youth and all Americans about Black

American History and its significance for America and the world. If the CRT Advocates would use their great energy, time, and resources to enhance Character Education and Biblical Knowledge, it would revolutionize Educational Achievement, the Prosperity of the Nation and Blessings for Humanity and Generations for Years to Come!

The Christian Institute of Public Theology

THE BIBLE AND GENDER DIVERSITY

GENDER CREATION

Man and woman, males and females are distinct and separate genders. They are distinctly different. However, they are complementary and interdependent. Their physiological and psychological differences are required to be fruitful, multiply, replenish the earth, perpetuate civilization, and carry out the will of God.

The separate genders, respective functions, and roles are the will of God. Any attempts on the part of man to change these genders, their functions, and roles, go against the natural creation and will of God. Such futile and ill-advised attempts create confusion and detriments to the well-being of humankind, society and civilization.

God expressed his approval of his creation of the man and the woman by saying in Genesis, Chapter 1:31, "And God saw everything that he had made, and behold, it was very good. And the evening and the morning were the sixth day." God affirmed his approval and pleasure in his creation of man and woman.

Is it reasonable to believe or imagine that any man or woman of wisdom, knowledge, or power would consider improving God's handiwork and creation of man and woman? Is it rational, logical, or sensible for any human being to consider changing or modifying God's creation of man and woman? ' Would not such thinking be arrogant and delusional, or some other mental or spiritual disorder?

The creation of man and woman, along with their purpose and duties, have been made very clear from the Book of Genesis through the Book of Revelations. God's will and authority for all human beings have been made known throughout the sixty-six Books of the Bible. It is the solemn duty of every competent person to learn the will of God, especially for one's personal life.

The oppositions, violations, and deviations from the will and the laws of God create confusion, corruption and destruction. God has designed his creation and creatures to operate and function in specified ways. God has created and instituted natural and divine laws to govern and regulate his creation according to the will of God. The Bible contains in abundance God's will, truth, ways, wisdom, commandments, methods, mercy, grace, love, redemption, and Salvation. Biblical illiteracy is an ongoing human tragedy.

GENDER SOCIAL ROLES

The social roles of men and women in the Bible are compatible and congruent with their biological, physiological, psychological, and theological human natures. The man's body, mind, and emotional temperament are more conducive to manual dexterities and activities that require greater physical strength, mental, and emotional capabilities for labor, living, and survival skills, especially in challenging environments. In most cases, man's body and temperament in most cases, are more conducive to the role of manually producing goods and services; providing food, shelter and clothing; and protecting self and family from a myriad of external dangers.

The woman's physiology, psychology, emotionality and spirituality are different from the men. The woman's body is designed with reproductive apparatus to conceive, develop and nurture a fetus and birth and nurture and rear a child. The mother's body is even designed to feed the infant after birth. Needless to say, the conception, birthing and rearing of children is a primary and significant difference between the male and female genders. It goes without saying that males do not have this type of physiology or psychology.

The Creator made this remarkable and unmistakable difference between men and women. It is a difference that ought to be praised and celebrated; not questioned, denied, or belittled. It is only natural that the woman, as the sacred God-ordained laboratory for creating life, deserves more care and protection than her male counterpart. Females are more vulnerable to rape and other assaults by males, who are typically stronger and more aggressive toward women. The female is less capable of self-defense against most males. Women are equipped with many abilities that men do not possess.

Traditionally, more men end up in more leadership positions than women because the man is more predisposed for leadership. Traditionally, women have had more responsibility for child care and household duties. There is an expansive network of interdependence beginning in the home and spreading throughout the community. Men and women work in a cluster of interdependent and complementary social and human services throughout the community.

The mother is the child's first and most significant teacher of the child. This is the period where significant foundational values are instilled. The mother, the father, and the family constitute the most significant institution that shapes the destiny of a child, a people, and a nation. This gift of God endowing children to be conceived, birthed, and nurtured by mothers ought to be esteemed to the high heavens. Women can and do play many other significant roles beyond child-rearing and the home. However, there is no other role more significant than training up a child in the way he should go (Proverbs 22:6)

THE NOBILITY OF MEN AND WOMEN

(The following artistic pronouncements are biblically-based in the Word of God and theologically guided by the Will of God)

Men and women were not made for opposition to each other, but rather, For submission to each other.

They were not meant to be foes against each other.
They were meant to be friends for each other.

Men and women were not meant to be competitors, They were meant to be partners.

Men and women were not meant to be alienated adversaries against each other.
They were meant to be united missionaries for each other.

They were not made for negative detractions;
They were made for positive attractions.

Men and women were not made to be suppressive and possessive;
They were made to be blessed, progressive and successful.

Men and women were not made for animosity and negativity;
They were made for generosity and civility.

Men and women were not made for envy and enmity;

They were made for gentility and intimacy.

Men and women were not meant to be debaters and haters;
They were meant to be innovators, creators, and liberators.

Men and women were not made for slothfulness and sin.
They were made to be constructive and industrial in order to win.

Men and women were not created to be violated and intimidated.
They were made for conciliation, restoration, and glorification.

Men and women were not meant to be shamed and blamed;
They were meant to be lifted up to reign with good names and fame.

GOD'S STANDARDS FOR GENDER ROLES

Gender roles and gender purposes are set by God in the Universal Holy Bible. The predominant expressions of patriarchy in the Bible are consistent with God's Will for creation, salvation, and redemption for mankind. The predominant expressions of patriarchy in the Bible do not subordinate nor minimize the significance of matriarchy in the Bible. The complementary roles of men and women are interdependent and inextricable.

There are natural reasons why the role of men in the Bible is more pronounced than the role of women. That is neither a denial of the roles of women nor the significance of the role of women. The significance of giving birth to all children cannot be overstated. The role of the matriarchy is omnipresent in civilization. The Biblical roles of men (to name a few) have been priests, prophets, kings, disciples, apostles, missionaries, etc. The Savior, Jesus Christ, is of the male gender. God is referred to as "Our Father, Father, The Father." However, all of these men, leaders, and patriarchs were brought into the world by women. God saw fit to have his "Only Begotten Son, Jesus Christ, be born of a woman.

Based on this brief Biblical gender information, it can be concluded justifiably that the Biblical Matriarchy in the Bible and in the world is real, foundational, significant, and in accordance with the Will of God. The matriarchal and patriarchal gender roles are the earthly arrangements made by God according to Scripture. According to Jesus, those that rise from the dead (Mark 12:25) "but are as angels, which are in heaven." In the body of Christ on this earth, "there is neither male nor female: for ye are all one in Christ Jesus." (Galatians 3:28)

God declared that his creation is good. The creation of man and woman are the crown of God's creation. God created the man and the woman, male and female, in the image of God. Ir is incumbent upon these special God's Image bearing creatures, man and woman, to be reverent, obedient, humble and ETERNALLY GRATEFUL FOREVER MORE!!!

The Christian Institute of Public Theology, INC
Atlanta, Georgia

BENEFITS AND REWARDS OF BIBLE STUDY

The Bible Study Fellowship Group has numerous benefits and rewards. It helps members find faith, hope and love in God. It helps members grow faith, hope, and love for God. It helps members to share faith, hope, and love in God.

The Bible Study Fellowship helps members apply faith, hope and love in God and the world. It enlightens the mind and enhances spiritual growth. It is a place to unload burdens and be refreshed with the love and spirit of God. It is a place to discover the greatest revelations known to mankind.

The study of the Bible is an available lifelong privilege and honor essential for sustaining spiritual and human growth. It is an invaluable and indispensable resource for the prosperous and abundant life. The knowledge, resources, and revelations of the Bible are an inexhaustible blessing for all who will avail themselves of its unsearchable riches. Biblical knowledge is that knowledge that provides the key to making sense and purpose out of all other knowledge and life experiences. It is truth, light, and the pathway to God and eternal life.

There are many keys to understanding the Bible. One key is to recognize the Bible as progressive revelation. That means that this revelation had a beginning. This beginning can be considered a birth. The Bible can be considered a living organism. As in the case of all living things and beings, they are born and grow from infancy, childhood, adolescence, young adulthood, and adulthood. The progressive revelation of the Bible had such a historical development. This helps explain the perceived contradictions in the Bible. For example, "an eye for an eye, and a tooth for a tooth" cannot be reconciled with the Gospel of love and forgiveness taught by Jesus. Jesus makes it clear that he did not come to condemn the world but to save it. He also said that he did not come to destroy the laws or the prophets, but to fulfill them. Therefore, the Bible cannot be accurately judged by its early beginnings and developments. It must be judged by what it came to be or grew to be in its adult fulfillment in Jesus Christ.

The Bible contains the greatest classical literature and history known to mankind. This history has relevance for all of history. The literature of the Bible has produced more universal artistic expressions and the highest aspirations of the human spirit than any other volume in the annals of human history. Get to know the characters in the Bible. Get to know the first man and the first woman, Adam and Eve. Get to know the patriarchs, Abraham, Isaac, and Jacob. Get to know Joseph, the dreamer. Get to know Moses, the leader and lawgiver. Get to know Samson and the Judges. Get to know Hannah's son, Samuel. Get to know King David, the other Kings of Israel. Get to know the Hebrew prophets and priests. Absorb yourself in the Psalms of David and the Proverbs of Solomon, and the suffering of Job. Concentrate on the Gospels and the New Testament. Learn about the great events of the Bible. Examine the creation, the Tower of Babel, the Flood, the Red Sea crossing, the birth of Christ, his miracles, his gospel, his crucifixion, resurrection, the great commission, the ascension, Pentecost, and the church's growth.

The Bible Study Fellowship transforms our spirits and renews our minds. This Bible study offers a transcendent message from above and beyond the culture that we live in. It is the most exciting, fulfilling, and rewarding journey that anyone can embark upon. It has therapeutic healing, spiritual guidance, and growth. It teaches healthy personal and social interaction. Members who are qualified and interested in group leadership and social interaction coaching are trained. It offers an opportunity to learn listening and communication skills in a group setting. It is an accepting and caring forum to feel safe in sharing one's feelings, ideas, and thoughts. It is a forum that offers the opportunity to learn how to relate to other members of the group in positive and helpful ways. It is an opportunity to learn, in a clinical setting, how to facilitate focused, goal-oriented and problem-solving discussions. The Bible Study Fellowship Group is a training opportunity to develop group leaders and proficient Bible study teachers. In addition to the verse-by-verse study of the Bible, it is essential to use reputable Bible commentaries, concordances, other literary sources, and relevant current events to maximize the benefits of the Bible study.

INFORMATION TECHNOLOGY AND BIBLE STUDY

It is vitally important that the Church and believers in Christ and the Word of God utilize and encourage others to use the IT (Information Technology) of smartphones, iPads, and other information technology containing the Bible and Scriptural information. It is the duty of the Church and believers to make known that smartphones and other technological instruments contain the Bible. Making people aware that they have a Bible in their smartphone or iPad is a powerful and useful realization. We must hold on to the Book that contains the Bible and also enhance the technology that contains the Bible as well. The very fact of having this convenient and readily available access to the Bible may be a motivating factor and an incentive to increase Bible reading and Bible study. Special efforts must be initiated to capitalize on this technological opportunity to promote increased Bible study. Special outreach efforts to youth must be made to teach them Bible use and study via smart information technology. It is suggested that those who are skilled in this area of information technology be encouraged to create a curriculum and begin offering a smartphone or iPad Bible study class. This ought to be a priority project in every Church to help overcome our Biblical illiteracy deficits and dangers.

The Christian Institute of Public Theology, Inc.

CHAPTER 3
AMERICA'S VITAL GUIDING PRINCIPLES
PREREQUISITES FOR EFFECTIVE LEADERSHIP
The Christian Institute of Public Theology

The guiding and leadership principles of America are established by specific laws, certain truths, traditions, and documents. The U.S. Constitution contains the specific laws. The Declaration of Independence contains certain specific truths. The United States Pledge of Allegiance as One Nation under God and its motto, "In God we Trust," contain the mandates, values, and traditions. The Holy Bible is the universal foundational document for all of America's governing laws, ethical values, and guiding principles.

The American guiding and leadership principles incorporate a long list of specific ideas and values (along with their enumerated antitheses, which must be defeated). These following specific universal ideas and values are not random, arbitrary, or frivolous. The enumerated ideas and values are congruent with God's revelation of truth contained in the Holy Bible and in the life and Gospel of Jesus Christ. Jesus is at the center of history, which creates a point in time that designates the backward count before Jesus Christ came and the forward count after he came into the world and history. B. C. is the backward count to the past. It means Before Christ. A. D. is the abbreviation for the Latin word, Anno domini, which means "In the Year of Our Lord." It is the forward count from the birth of Christ. The Book of Matthew (Matthews 1:1-17) contains a genealogy of Jesus Christ that counts backward from Christ's birth to David and Abraham. The Book of Luke records the genealogy of Jesus Christ from

Christ back to David, Abraham, Adam, and God (Luke 3:23-38). The current date of this writing is 10/28/2021 AD, in the year of our Lord. Christ was born on the earth two thousand Twenty-One years ago. Every time a date is made or referenced in world history, it is an acknowledgment of JESUS CHRIST'S BIRTH AND COMING.

Inasmuch as Jesus is proclaimed as Lord of Lords, King of Kings, and Prince of Peace, why not learn about the noble governing and guiding principles of Jesus Christ? Why try to deny history's most well-known, celebrated, and exalted figure? Why ignore the best-known and most universally validated book of history? It is the ultimate book of law, history, truth, and the guiding principles of government and human life. The world's deaf ears, deceptive minds, hateful hearts, and evil spirits do not qualify for any position of leadership or public policy-making in the American government. Only those with the competence, compassion, and commitment to be guided by established laws, Biblical principles, and survival values should be considered for positions of human leadership in the American government or any other human leadership position of GOD'S PEOPLE.

JESUS CHRIST IS THE ULTIMATE PROLIFE, ABUNDANT LIFE, ETERNAL LIFE, ALL TIME LEADER. HIS LIFE AND MINISTRY INCORPORATE ALL THE PRINCIPLES AND VALUES FOR LEADERSHIP. GOD HAS PROVIDED SPECIFIC IDEAS, LAWS, PRINCIPLES AND VALUES CONGRUENT WITH THE VALIDATED TRUTH OF SCIENCE, ART, LAW, THEOLOGY AND CHRIST, TO DEFEAT EVIL AND SPIRITUAL WICKEDNESS IN THE RAGING WARFARE AGAINST HUMAN SURVIVAL VALUES.

THE SPIRITUAL AND CULTURAL BATTLEFIELD
The Warfare Against Survival Values

SURVIVAL VALUES			DESTRUCTIVE VALUES
1.	Goodness	VS	Evil
2.	Truth	VS	Lies
3.	Love	VS	Hatred
4.	Justice	VS	Injustice
5.	Knowledge	VS	Ignorance
6.	Wisdom	VS	Foolishness
7.	Understanding	VS	Confusion
8.	Hope	VS	Despair
9.	Faith	VS	Doubt
10.	Godliness	VS	Idolatry
11.	Reason	VS	Irrationality
12.	Mercy	VS	Cruelty
13.	Order	VS	Chaos
14.	Peace	VS	War
15.	Sacred	VS	Secular
16.	Enlightenment	VS	Cognitive Deficiency
17.	Righteousness	VS	Wrongful
18.	Wholeness	VS	Divisive
19.	Civility	VS	Barbarianism
20.	Purity	VS	Corruption
21.	Beauty	VS	Offensive
22.	Charitable	VS	Self-Centered
23.	Innocent	VS	Guilty
24.	Positive	VS	Negativity
25.	Humility	VS	Arrogance
26.	Secure	VS	Endangered

SURVIVAL VALUES			DESTRUCTIVE VALUES
27.	Progressive	VS	Regressive
28.	Goodwill	VS	Envious
29.	Refinement	VS	Crude
30.	Joyful	VS	Miserable
31.	Inspiration	VS	Demoralization
32.	Generosity	VS	Greed
33.	Sacrificial Service	VS	Fraudulent Exploitation
34.	Benevolence	VS	Malevolence
35.	Altruistic	VS	Jealousy
36.	Restoration	VS	Destruction
37.	Elevate	VS	Denigrate
38.	Freedom	VS	Bondage
39.	Salvation	VS	Damnation
40.	Life	VS	Death

The above enumerations of SURVIVAL VALUES and their opposite, DESTRUCTIVE CHOICES can be clearly separated and distinguished. The human attitudes, values, and behaviors associated with these survival values and destructive choices can be determined through a variety of human actions and expressions. These clear choices make possible wise and intelligent decisions. The loving God created man and woman in his image with the autonomous ability to make decisions based on God's knowledge, truth, and wisdom. God created a dichotomy of opposites to avoid confusion. He created men and women. God created light and darkness, day, and night. He created sweet and bitter, up and down, north, and south, east, and west. God enables man (woman, too) to make choices between survival values and disobedient, destructive choices. God provides the blueprint for human survival in the Holy Bible. He sent messengers prophets, kings, and angels. The Bible is a comprehensive law book containing priests, laws, commandments, principles, ethics, and values to govern and guide mankind and the nations in all walks of life. Last of all, God sent Jesus Christ as the unmistakable embodiment of all survival values. Jesus Christ is the GREAT ULTIMATE AM OF ALL MANKIND'S SURVIVAL AND SALVATION VALUES. HISTORY HAS VALIDATED THE UNIQUE TRUTH OF JESUS CHRIST

THE SPIRITUAL AND CULTURAL WARFARE IN AMERICA AND THE WORLD IN THIS 21 CENTURY, AD, REQUIRES AND DEMANDS THE STEADFAST ADOPTION OF THE SURVIVAL VALUES AS PROVIDED BY THE LOVING GOD AND SACRIFICIAL SON, JESUS CHRIST

The Christian Institute of Public Theology

BIBLICAL AND US CONSTITUTIONAL GUIDES
Sound Doctrine Public Policy Preferences For
A Just, Free, Healthy, Peaceful, and Prosperous America

1. Pro-Human Life as Sacred from God the Creator.
2. Patriotism for America as a Nation under God.
3. Acknowledge America and all Nations as Nations under God.
4. Acknowledge the Truth of the Holy Bible as Validated by History.
5. Accept Jesus Christ as the God-sent Savior's historical truths.
6. Uphold the Truths of the Bible and the Laws of the U.S. Constitution.
7. Support Judicial Equal Justice under Just Laws, God, and the U.S. Constitution.
8. Support Individual and religious Liberty under God and U.S. Constitution.
9. Acknowledge and Respect the Sacredness of Christmas, the Cross and other Validated Religious Celebrations and Historical Monumental Symbols.
10. Establish and Utilize Just Merit-Based Administrative and Judicial Systems for Fairness, Justice and Equality.
11. Respect, Support, Teach and Encourage the True, Sound, Ethical and Moral Traditional Social Values Based on Historical Precedents, Scientific Knowledge and Biblical Truth.
12. Provide the Utmost Support for Public Education as Standard Education Designed for the Public Good as Paid for by Public Funds. Accommodate Charter Schools and other Private Bono-fide Educational Institutions with Private Funding.

13. As Mandated by Law in Georgia, Teach Comprehensive Character Education from Kindergarten through Twelfth Grade. THE SERIOUS LETHAL MORAL VIOLENT CRISIS IN AMERICA DEMANDS MAJORING IN CHARACTER EDUCATION UNDER-GIRDED BY CHRISTIAN EDUCATION

14. As Mandated by Georgia Law, TEACH THE OLD TESTAMENT AND NEW TESTAMENT AS HISTORY, LITERATURE AND BIBLICAL KNOWLEDGE. THE DESTRUCTION OF THESE CHILDREN FOR LACK OF BIBLICAL (THEOLOGICAL) KNOWLEDGE IS DESTROYING AMERICA AND THE BLESSINGS OF GOD UPON AMERICA.

15. Support Israel and Its Democracy and All God-Fearing Nations. AMERICA HAS BEEN BLESSED TO BE A BLESSING TO THE WORLD. CHRISTIANITY WAS BORN OUT OF ISRAEL Judaism). AMERICA HAS BEEN KNOWN AS A CHRISTIAN NATION. USA IS IN THE MIDDLE OF JERUSA)LEM. THE UNITED STATES OF AMERICA HAS A CONNECTION WITH ISRAEL AND JERUSALEM. AMERICA MUST NOT FORFEIT THE BLESSINGS OF GOD!

16. Establish Appropriate Educational, Ethical, Moral, Patriot, Professional, and Otherwise Competent and Fit for duty, Responsibility and Accountability

Standards for All Elective and Public Officials Who Represent the People.

AMERICAN DEMOCRACY AND PUBLIC THEOLOGY
By
Willie James Webb

The 1ˢᵗ Amendment of the U.S. Constitution prohibits a theocratic form of government in the name of religion. America has a democratic form of government that was created by a philosophy of Judeo-Christian doctrines. The American Democracy proposes to be a representative form of government for the people, by the people, and of the people. It is the longest-lasting constitution of any other known government.

It is significant to note that Christian believers developed the American democratic form of government and constitution on September 17, 1787, at a time when there was no significant heterogeneity in America besides the native Americans and the Negro slaves. It is significant that these Christian believers developed a universal constitutional form of government that was inclusive of all people. However, at this point in American history, the practice of democracy excluded black African American slaves. Religions do not have a monopoly on the universal moral and ethical principles essential for the equitable administration, allocation, distribution, and accountability for the goods, resources, and services existing in a society. Therefore, the laws of the U.S. Constitution were not "religious" laws, but they were laws in congruence with truth, justice, and righteousness.

God created and required specific laws and commandments to govern the conduct of all people regardless of their form of government or type of religion. God requires all leaders and all people to live according to the truth, justice, righteousness, goodness, mercy, love, and the will of God. God's laws and principles are not arbitrary and do not depend on individual opinions for their validity. God's laws and principles are true, just, righteous, and based in reality. God's laws are not relative, neutral or fictional. They are real with real consequences. No person, nation or religion is exempt from God's laws and judgement.

God is the creator of the universe with absolute jurisdiction over everything and every being (Genesis). The earth and everything therein belong to God (Psalm 24). God demands that every soul be subject to God (Romans 13:1). Contrary to the expressions of many judges and legal scholars, religion is not synonymous with God, the Bible, or Jesus Christ. Religions are created and born in history. They also died in history. However, God, the Bible, and Jesus Christ are above history and human culture. The autonomous nature of man made by God, has free will to choose. Man can choose to ignore God, Jesus, and the Bible. However, man's independent negative choice does not negate God, Jesus, or the Bible. Man's independent choice does not excuse man's duty to obey God and God's commandments. Man's autonomous free will does not excuse man's rebellious spirit against God. God's jurisdiction is inescapable. His commandments cannot be suspended. Personal responsibility and accountability to God cannot be delegated or evaded. God's divine laws and natural laws are absolutely supreme. MANMADE LAWS ARE ONLY VALID WHEN THEY ARE CONGRUENT WITH GOD'S LAWS & WILL.

Christian Institute of Public Theology

GUIDING PRINCIPLES FOR DEMOCRACY
U.S. GUIDING PRINCIPLES OFFER UNITY FOR AMERICA

America has the most noble human uniting governing principles known to humanity. America is a republic of 50 united states, embracing the Declaration of Independence, which proclaims that God created equality of all people. The Declaration of Independence proclaims the inherent endowment by the Creator of certain unalienable rights for all men (all people; among these rights are life, liberty, and the pursuit of happiness. The sound doctrine of the Declaration of Independence is a guiding principle for the unity of the United States and for all the citizens and people of America.

The founders and architects of the creeds to govern the United States formulated a noble idea for governing the United States. A democratic form of government was this noble idea. A democratic form of government insures a government by the people, for the people, and of the people. This noble idea of democracy evolved and resulted in the written document of the United States of America's Constitution, as well as a Bill of Rights. The Constitution of the United States of America and the Bill of Rights confirm that America is covenanted to be governed by the Law and not by men.

The governing and guiding principles of the Declaration of Independence and the Constitution of the United States of America were founded upon Biblical, Judeo-Christian principles. It is historically documented that the men who wrote the Declaration of Independence and the U.S Constitution were Christian Believers. Additionally, a large number of these men were theologically trained. Christianity is inclusive of all humanity. It does not force itself upon anyone. It is consistent with God's gift of autonomy to each individual to choose. No one is forced or can be forced to be a Christian or to accept Jesus Christ as Lord and Savior. It is the individual's autonomous choice.

It is well documented in American Church history, along with names, places, and dates, that Christianity was spread throughout the thirteen colonies, beginning in 1607. American Church history records The Great Awakening in America in 1726. This Great Awakening consisted of massive proclamations, exhortations, teaching, preaching, revivals, conversion, and spreading the Gospel of Jesus Christ. This Great Awakening accelerated the American culture with biblical study, Christian beliefs, and doctrines.

This seeding of Christianity in American culture in the sixteenth and seventeenth centuries was precursory and foundational for the Declaration of Independence in 1776 and the signing of the Constitution on September 17, 1787. This is suggestive that the founders of America's guiding democratic documents were based on available ethical, just, legal, and theological, sound moral doctrines and principles.

These governing documents were derived from a rich, knowledgeable, ethical, social, and spiritual American culture.

These true, time-tested universal principles, equitable laws, ethical values, and God-inspired human spirits transformed America into the most prosperous, powerful, and blessed nation on earth. America is considered an exceptional nation because it acknowledges itself as "One nation under God, with liberty and justice for all," and the "evidentiary truths that all men are created equal and are endowed by their Creator with certain "unalienable rights-among these-life, liberty, and the pursuit of happiness."

Serious problems have been detected regarding the maintenance and continuation of America as an exceptional nation under God. Can America neglect or stray from its guiding principles and remain an exceptional nation under God? Many American problems could be analyzed to explore answers to this question. The last two decades have produced problems in the general political election process. The voting process in recent years has caused massive confusion, litigation, bitterness, and debate.

There are two faulty presumptions in the American political election process. The first presumption encourages optimum utilization of voting to have a successful democratic government. However, voting alone does nor assure a successful democracy. Incompetent and unfit candidates can, and often are, voted into office. Candidates who do nor believe in democracy can be overwhelmingly elected to public office. The emphasis and priority placed on encouraging people to vote are not sufficient to maintain and sustain American democracy. The second faulty presumption in the political election process is that the majority makes the best choice for the people and the nation. However, majority decisions and choices are not always the most ethical or best for the people or the nation. It is clear and logically concluded that a majority can be against the guiding principles of a democratic government.

This brief discourse on Guiding Principles for Democracy makes it clear that a true and effective democratic form of government requires specified true knowledge, comprehensive education, professional competence, sound philosophical ideologies, ethical and moral standards congruent with sound biblical doctrines, and the benevolent spiritual compassion of Jesus Christ.

In order to maintain and sustain the indispensable and vitally needed democratic form of government, America must begin now to revolutionize its public educational systems with the required Biblical Education as History and Literature, Character Education, Ethical and Moral Education, Health Education, Legal Education, Artistic Education, Marriage and Family Education, Vocational Education, Patriotic Education, Theological Education, Liberal Arts Education, Technological Education, Science Education, Engineering Education, Sanctity of Life Education, Religions Liberty, Human Individual Freedom Education for Civilized Living.

The above educational curriculum, truths, knowledge, standards, and values have been rested and validated guiding principles for democracy is tantamount to disavowing civilization cursing mankind, and declaring open rebellion against the Creator God.

What has happened to American Democracy in the 21ˢᵗ Century? Why is there so much confusion, so much conflict, and divisiveness in the United States? In my book, The Way Out of Darkness, some foundations for the American Culture Crisis are addressed. Here, a very brief synopsis is provided. In the early years of American history from the 17ᵗʰ to the early 20ᵗʰ centuries, millions of immigrants came to America with multiple nationalities, races, ethnicities, religions, and cultural backgrounds. However, these immigrants with their multiple cultural backgrounds assimilated into the American Culture and became identified as Americans. Most of them assimilated, accepted, or were influenced by the predominant Judeo-Christian faith and values of the American Democracy.

The doctrines, of the Judeo-Christian faith, make possible a human assimilation and acculturation of differences into a great and glorious harmonious heterogeneous oneness. It allows human beings to maintain their unique God-given ethnicities and differences, and still be civil, benevolent brothers and sisters. The Biblical Word says," There is neither Jew nor Greek, there is neither bond nor free, there is neither male nor female: for you are all one in Christ Jesus (Galatians 3:28).

Those guiding Biblical, Declaration of Independence, and one Nation under God principles sown into the American Culture, brought America through the Civil War and reunited the North and South. These guiding principles led to the emancipation of Negro-American slaves. These biblically based democratic principles, through the leadership of Dr. Martin Luther King, Jr., brought about the greatest nonviolent social revolution in world history in America.

America is blessed with God-inspired and -directed democratic guiding principles that welcome all people of goodwill. These standards of governance for mankind are set and authorized by God. The time rested and validated guiding principles for The United States of America are THE BIBLE, THE DECLARATION OF INDEPENDENCE, THE CONSTITUTION OF THE UNITED STATES OF AMERICA, THE PLEDGE OF ALLEGIANCE TO THE FLAG AND THE REPUBLIC FOR WHICH IT STANDS, AS ONE NATION UNDER GOD, INDIVISIBLE, WITH LIBERTY AND JUSTICE FOR ALL, and THE MOTTO: IN GOD WE TRUST (NOT MAN). These are the GOD INSPIRED INFALLIBLE PRINCIPLES TO LEAD AND GUIDE AMERICA AND ALL GOD's PEOPLE ACCORDING TO THE DEMOCRATIC FORM OF GOVERNMENT!

AMERICAN CITIZENS FOR DEMOCRACY
AMERICAN COALITION

A DOCUMENT FOR HUMAN EQUITY AND JUSTICE GENTRIFICATION MUST CONFORM TO HUMAN RIGHTS & U.S. CONSTITUTION

The Administrators of gentrification are not licensed to violate human rights. Civil rights, property rights, the Bill of Rights, and the U.S. Constitution. The justification for intrusive building constructions that disrupt neighborhoods, and residential private property must be based on a critical community need and the community's overall good. The Atlanta Beltline has not identified or established that it provides community needs and basic benefits for the community. Unfortunately, the Atlanta Beltline Impact Study by ARC (Atlanta Regional Commission) has not been shared publicly with the Southwest Atlanta Community. The justification and the merits of the Atlanta Beltline, based on a cost/benefits analysis, have not been publicly shared with the Southwest Atlanta Communities.

The Atlanta Beltline's impact on Atlanta residents and the state of Georgia is becoming increasingly unsustainable. As this clandestine, uncertain adventure unfolds, it becomes clearer that it is an unwise, superfluous, extravagant, and hazardous enterprise. There are many more worthy and urgently needed infrastructural projects in Atlanta than the Beltline. It would be wise to redirect the vast resources allocated for the Beltline to relieve traffic congestion, water supply systems, protective disaster shelters, and environmental hazards of falling trees, floods, dangerous storm shelters, building codes for more secure structures, shelters, and resources for the homeless and mentally disordered. THE POSITIVE REAL NEED LIST GOES ON AND ON.

The Beltline is initiating and transforming peaceful, stable, and safe communities into ones characterized by confusion, conflicts, chaos, and catastrophic disasters. The naive bicycle, scooter, and nature trail planners, engineers, and collaborators do not comprehend the human heterogeneous complexities of social chemistry, political physics, legal math, and theological ethics well enough to embark on such an unpredictable project with such wide-ranging ramifications. These serious knowledge deficiencies in government leadership unleash destructive social consequences upon us all. We "PERISH FOR LACK OF KNOWLEDGE." RECONSIDERATION IS A VIABLE OPTION.

THE TRAVESTY OF GENTRIFICATION

The taking away of residential private property through Eminent Domain or through the arbitrary raising of property value beyond the affordability of the homeowner is a serious and damaging personal deprivation and an unjust human rights and property rights violation. According to the 5th Amendment of the U.S. Constitution, the violated property owner is entitled to "JUST COMPENSATION." Currently, the gentrification trend, in conjunction with unscrupulous investors and home buyers, is to pressure the homeowner to sell the home at the lowest price before the impending home values escalate. Therefore, the homeowner gets cheated by yielding to a quick sale. Therefore, the buyer gets the benefit of the increased value of the property. The homeowner who has lived in the home for multiple years and accrued significant equity, investment, improvements, and other benefits and amenities sustains a significant net loss through the gentrification process. However, the 5th Amendment requires "Just Compensation."

It is unjust and a violation of human, civil, and property rights to arbitrarily increase the value of private property beyond the invested residential property owners' affordability. The 5th Amendment provides a legal and equitable remedy for this property right violation. Simply stated, the 5th Amendment requires "Just Compensation." This just compensation legal remedy must be brought to the forefront as an equitable remedy for the gentrification-related human and property rights violations of the citizens of Atlanta.

THE COST OF JUST COMPENSATION

Just compensation is the equitable payment to the victimized residential property owner by the administrators of the specific party or parties affecting the deprivation and confiscation of property through the unlawful processes of gentrification. Just compensation must consider the total cost of the residential property along with the commensurate losses and damages associated with the violation of property rights and human rights. The loss of a residential property after multiple years of occupancy extends beyond the mere physical structure and geographical location. A HOME IS MUCH MORE THAN A HOUSE. A home is a special place of personal attachment, retreat, reprieve, comfort, security haven, intimacy, and privacy, a private and confidential depository, and sharing. It is the basis for family planning, childbirth, growth, and development. It is the primary place where values of life and survival are taught and instilled in the family. The home and the family are the primary social units where values for the nation and civilization are transmitted.

Homes and families form communities and develop institutions such as schools, churches, businesses, industries, governments, commerce, and global social connections and interactions. It is the ideal social unit to which every person should belong. It is a Primary value.

The "Just Compensation" must consider more than merely the deprivation or confiscation of residential physical property. Just compensation under the 5th Amendment must include damages to family values, emotional and sentimental attachments, investments, personal safety, liberty rights, peace of mind, and the pursuit of happiness. Just compensation must cover the loss of reputation and character, as well as the incapacitating and destabilizing pain and suffering.

According to the 5th, 14th, and 1964 Civil Rights Acts, A US COURT OF COMPETENT JURISDICTION MUST CONSIDER THE PLAINTIFFS CHARGE OF HUMAN RIGHTS, CIVIL RIGHTS, AND PROPERTY RIGHTS VIOLATIONS AND THE REMEDY OF "JUST COMPENSATION."

(US Citizens, Stakeholders, Social Justice Advocates, and Public Theologians in Atlanta)

A RESOLUTION FOR LEGISLATION ENACTMENT
BASIC REQUIREMENTS FOR GOVERNMENT PUBLIC OFFICE REPRESENTATIVES

Whereas the health, prosperity, and survival of the United States of America require all of its constituted public officials and leaders to have ideological and philosophical belief systems compatible with the truth of the Bible, the Declaration of Independence, the Constitution of the United States, The Pledge of Trust in God as a Nation Under God, and A Democratic Republic Government Of the People, For the People, and By the People.

It is also resolved that American government representatives, leaders, and candidates for public office must subscribe to a validated professionally recognized body of knowledge, sound truth doctrines as validated by true science, authentic art, just laws, and validated theological codes of ethics.

It is further resolved that the American individual freedoms, values of life, and inalienable human rights endowed by God the Creator; must not be subject to arbitrary, chaotic, irresponsible, and unprotective laws. God-given life and liberties must be diligently protected by just laws and purpose-driven by the good of society, American citizens, and humanity. The Candidates for public office, elected and appointed representatives, must be professionally validated as competent, duly qualified, and fit for the respective office or position.

Pursuant to these ends, laws must be enacted that require the professionally validated health of mind and body, pertinent educational achievements, pertinent work experience, patriotic commitment, and ideological, philosophical, and professional ethical values compatible with the founding and guiding principles and doctrines of the United States of America. All public officials, leaders, and candidates for public office must be validated as competent, duly qualified and fix for their respective government duties, responsibilities and obligations to American citizens and the Democratic Republic of the United States of America.

The Christian Institute of Public Theology

THE GOLDEN RULES OF SUCCESSFUL LIVING

Sociologically speaking, human beings live interdependent group lives. Psychologically, human beings need to have a conscious awareness of themselves, others, and the world around them. Economically, human beings are in need of a livelihood support system. Politically, they need equitable rules and laws to govern their interactions and protect each other as individuals with certain natural and God-given rights and entitlements. Theologically, human beings need validated instructions from the Creator of their being and the world regarding the purpose of their lives and authoritative knowledge as to how to govern their lives in community and fellowship with each other.

Human beings on the planet Earth are blessed beyond measure and comprehension that they have been provided with an inexhaustible book from their Creator about the universe, creation, mankind, and the Creator Himself. That book is known as the Bible. It is the book of unrivaled golden rules for living. It is a book of revelation from God that tells about God's involvement and engagement with mankind. It is the book that defines what exists and what should exist. It is the book that reveals the will of God for mankind. It is a book that can be understood by science, art, law, and theology.

It is said by scholars that every civilization has some form of the Golden Rule in their respective languages. The Bible is the ultimate rule book. It is foundational to all laws on earth. The first five books of the Bible are law books. It is the book with the greatest knowledge, wisdom, and understanding about the universe, about mankind, and about life and existence itself. The Bible is the most widespread and universally known book on earth. It has the greatest classical literature known to mankind. It is shameful, disgraceful, pathological, and sacrilegious that such a book, such a precious and invaluable gift, could be so neglected and marginalized. The Bible is the book that documents the birth, life, teachings, love, crucifixion, resurrection, and ascension of the Savior of the world, Jesus Christ with invincible evidence and infallible proof. This is the individual who was born, lived, was crucified, arose from the dead, and ascended in history. Jesus Christ is the historical event that splits history into B.C. and A.D.

AMERICA'S AUTHORITATIVE GOVERNING VALIDATED DOCUMENTS

1. The Holy Bible
2. The Declaration of Independence
3. The Constitution of the United States
4. The Pledge of Allegiance to:
   One Nation Under God with Liberty and Justice For All
5. The American National Motto: "In God We Trust" (Not Man)

These documents of law create a democratic form of government. A democratic form of government is a government "BY THE PEOPLE, OF THE PEOPLE AND FOR THE PEOPLE." This Democratic Republic form of government has created an Exceptional Nation on earth. America has afforded more individual freedom to more people than any other nation. This AMERICAN EXCEPTIONALISM has been created by the God-inspired Documents that govern America. Thanks be to God!

THE MAINTENANCE OF HISTORICAL INTEGRITY (KEEP THE RECORD STRAIGHT) CAPT, INC

BCE (Before Common Era) and CE (Common Era) are dishonest, misleading historical deceptions. BCE and CE are contrived to avoid and eliminate B. C. (Before Christ) and A. D. (Anno Domini, In the Year of Our Lord) from the two-thousand-year factual historical tradition on earth. These deceptions are designed to get Jesus Christ, the center of history, out of history. To avoid the names Jesus Christ and Lord, elementary school students have already begun to use BCE and CE instead of BC and AD. The phrases "before common era" and "common era" have no specific or substantive meaning. They are deceptions and attempts to distort history.

Who gave writers, authors, publishers, and teachers the authority to eliminate BC and AD and adopt BCE and CE? Were the clergy, theologians, and faith-based representatives a part of the decisions to make these changes? It may be helpful to learn how these deceptions were conceived and initiated.

The believers and guardians of truth and sound doctrine must challenge, oppose, and eliminate this false, unethical, and deceptive usage of BCE and CE. How can the professed believers of Christ and those who are knowledgeable of the documented historical facts and records of history allow this open deception to proceed without serious challenge and opposition? Can the keepers of sacred history remain silent in the face of this serious assault on two thousand years of documented world history?

Every person who believes in truth, righteousness, justice, and civilization has a duty to oppose these audacious deceptions in the 21st Century A.D. There must be written and verbal protests. Books and publications with the dates BCE and CE must not be purchased. The theological seminaries, Bible colleges, colleges, and universities, as well as the public school systems, must stop buying these books with these deceptive references. We must not buy into lies that are substituted for the truth. We must take a stand for our children and the oncoming generations. Legislation must be initiated to safeguard the accuracy and integrity of documented history. It is illogical and irrational for anyone to attempt to deny the reality and the historical centrality of the most widely known person who ever walked the earth with a 2000-year documented history. Jesus Christ is the timeline of history. No historical date is credible without the acknowledgement of Jesus Christ. What other person in history would be more deserving or appropriate?

The Christian Association of Public Theologians

USING PERSONAL GIFTS TO REDEEM HUMANITY

What are your special gifts? What are your special talents? How can you use your special gifts and talents to uplift and redeem humanity?

1. How can your gifts and talents be used to highlight the eternal values of truth, goodness, and beauty in this world?
2. What can you do or what can you invent to make God's word a more convincing reality in this world?
3. What can you do or what can you invent to demonstrate more love, compassion, sensitivity, and caring for human life in society?
4. What can you do, improve, or invent that will reduce disappointments, heartaches, pain, and stress?
5. What can you do with your special gifts and talents to enhance the sacredness of life and the divine purpose of life ordained by God?
6. What can you do or what can you invent to contribute to a more just, civil, and humane society?
7. What message can you give to captivate the imagination of humankind for good?
8. What art can you create and demonstrate to lift the moral values of mankind and glorify God?
9. How can you use art, law, theology, and science to eliminate destructive wickedness and the rough edges of human nature and mold it into a more refined creature of God.

The Christian Institute of Public Theology

CHAPTER 4
COURAGEOUS STANDARDS FOR AMERICAN LEADERSHIP
STANDARDS MUST BE
TRUE, JUST, AND RIGHTEOUS

America must prioritize competence and qualifications for public and political office consistent with democratic values, the United States Constitution, the Declaration of Independence, and the biblical foundational creeds as a Nation under God. The National self-interest and the security of America require adherence to the Nation's ethical, Constitutional values, moral, social, and civil humanitarian standards.

CORE STANDARDS FOR LEAERSHIP

1. Biblical and historical confirmation of God's righteousness
2. Biblical validated Truth of the Unique Holy Bible.
3. Validated competent just leadership representation.
4. Representation for the common good of humanity.
5. Human justice, righteousness, and truth leadership.
6. Adherence to Sound doctrines and validated ethical values.
7. Professional competence in science, art, law, and theology.
8. Pro-human life reverence in all human representative services.

9. Guided by excellence in all qualitative products and services.
10. Respect for autonomous human freedom and rights endowed by God.
11. Observance of the equitable acquisition and allocation of God's gifts.
12. Faithful stewardship of God's gift of life and infinite resources.

AMERICA MUST BEGIN NOW TO ESTABLISH, REQUIRE AND ASSIMILATE THESE CORE SURVIVAL VALUES AND STANDARDS FOR ALL PEOPLE WITHIN THE JURIS-DICTION OF AMERICA. THESE VALUES CAN BE SUSTAINED THROUGH THE FOLLOWING EDUCATION: Biblical Education, Declaration of Independence, Theological Education, Patriotic Education, Constitution of the United States, Christian Education, Moral & Ethical Education, Liberal Arts Education, Character Education, Democratic Government Education, American History Including Black American History, World History, Vocational Education, Free Enterprise System, Science, Art, Law and Theology. THIS EDUCATIONAL CURRICULUM ENCOMPASSES THE MOST NOBLE AND ADVANCED KNOWLEDGE KNOWN TO MANKIND.

-KNOWLEDGE TO KEEP HUMANITY FROM PERISHING-

AMERICANS' RIGHT FOR COMPETENT REPRESENTATION
Competent Leadership has been Neglected Christian Institute of Public Theology

The right to vote must be balanced by the right to competent leadership and democratic representation. The political advocacy for the right to vote gets substantial news, promotion, and legislation. Voting rights and associated issues such as alleged suppression of voting, the handling of ballots, proper personal identification and other prerequisites for voting are prevalent topics in the news media. However, the preoccupation with voting rights and associated concerns have totally neglected and ignored the complementary essential and even vital right for competent elected officials, competent leaders, and competent democratic representatives Hardly any credible, valid, relevant, or meritorious requirements are stipulated for the candidates for public office. There is more concern about the diversity of the candidates for public office than there is about merit and fitness for the responsibilities and duties of the respective public office.

The lack of specified basic requirements for public office work against the U.S. Constitution, democracy, America, and common sense. The American electoral process and requirements have not kept pace with cultural changes, global connections, and technological advances. The American standards for competent and effective political administration and leadership Do not measure up to the new escalating demanding complexities of the heterogeneous globalized Twenty First Century. Incompetent leadership and undemocratic leadership nullify and even defeat the noble purpose and reasons for voting. Voting in a democratic form of government is intended to assure the best representation of the collective will of the citizens based on their guiding constitution and values of justice, freedom, and equality for the common good of the society, nation, and humanity.

The social processes of immigration, acculturation, socialization, and assimilation of a variety of populations of people extend far beyond their race, skin color, language, accents, and Customs. Human beings also have belief systems, ideologies and social values that influence their thinking, values, and behaviors. Many of these ideologies, nationalities and belief systems are incompatible, irreconcilable, and even conflicting. The conglomeration of these social, political, and cultural values must be acknowledged in a heterogeneous society such as America which has been known as a melting pot. Many values that people adhere to are not easily assimilated. These differences must be acknowledged and reconciled with the established guiding principles, values, and laws of America. There is great space for freedom and differences of ideas and opinions. However, the legally and officially established standards must prevail in the leadership of the American Government. These values and guiding principles of the Nation must be taught and embraced, especially by the American Government's political leadership and political representatives.

It is true that America is a country of immigrants with people of diverse backgrounds from all around the earth. Traditionally, Immigrants came to America and were willing to assimilate, embrace American values, democracy and become full-fledged Americans. That trend has changed. Many people who migrate to America desire to hold on to the values, political systems, ethnicities, and cultures of their native countries. Many of these different newcomers to America do not embrace America's democracy, its Constitution, social values nor the Judeo-Christian faith. Some of the newcomers and those who come to study in the universities and for other reasons prefer making changes in the American Government and the American society as well.

During this Twenty First Century in America, great emphasis is placed on diversity. Political identities are rampant in America. The emphasis being placed on identities, especially, race, gender, LGBT, democrat, republican, independent, conservative, liberal and so forth, are precipitating significant division in America. These differences are pervading education from kindergarten through the universities. These identities are being used for political influence. Substantial indoctrination is taking place. Political leadership and other institutional leadership are challenged. Therefore, it will require more than voting or even integrity in voting to cultivate the quality of enlightened leadership that is needed.

The guiding doctrines and principles have served America well. They have brought about great social and political reform in America. They have propelled America to be the greatest nation known to history in providing individual liberty, prosperity, and national political power. These values are still sound. They have already withstood the test of time. These values and guiding principles must be taught more thoroughly and deliberately. America must keep its identity as ONE NATION UNDER GOD. INDIVIDUAL FREEDOMS IN THE AMERICAN GOVERNMENT MUST BE SUBJECTED TO AND GUIDED BY THE CONSTITUTION OF THE UNITED STATES. THE DECLARATION OF INDEPENDENCE, PLEDGE OF ALLEGIANCE, HOLD ONTO IN GOD WE TRUST, THE TRADITIONAL BIBLICAL VALUES THAT UNDERGIRD AND SUPPORT A DEMOCRATIC FORM OF GOVERNMENT.

To assure the true sound responsible leadership of the Democratic Government from the local, state, and federal levels, all candidates for public office must meet designated requirements that assure their mental and physical professional competence, their ideologies and belief systems are compatible with the U.S. Constitution, Declaration and traditional Biblical values and be otherwise fit for duty standards. The American citizens have a right to ethical, competent, and representative public office holders and leaders of justice, righteousness and liberty. THIS IS AN URGENT AND IMMEDIATE PRIORITY FOR THE US CONGRESS AND THE PRESIDENCY TO ESTABLISH COMPETENT REQUIREMENTS AND STANDARDS FOR CANDIDATES FOR THE AMERICAN PUBLIC OFFICE FOR THE HEALTH, SAFETY, SECURITY, LIBERTY, PEACE, GOOD WILL FOR ALL AMERICANS AND THE PEOPLE OF GOD.

GOD'S WORD AND GOD'S AUTHORITY
Lessons for Judging and Disparaging Others

Let every soul be subject unto the higher powers. For there is no power but of God: the powers that be are ordained of God. (Romans 13:1)

Judge not that you be not judged. For with what judgment you judge, you shall be judged; and with what measure you mete, it shall be measured to you again. Why beholdest thou the mote that is in thy brother's eye, but consider not the beam that is in thine own eye? Or how will thou say to thy brother, Let me pull out the mote out of thine eye; and, behold, a beam is in thine own eye? Thou hypocrite, first, cast out the beam out of thine own eye; and then shall thou see clearly to cast out the mote out of thy brother's eye. (Matthew 7:1-5)

There is a way which seemeth right unto a man, but the end thereof are the ways of death (Proverbs 14:12). The way of a fool is right in his own eyes: but he that hearkeneth to counsel is wise (Proverbs 12:15). He that speaketh truth sheweth forth righteousness: but a false witness deceit (Proverbs 12:17). Deceit is in the heart of them that imagine evil: but to the counsellors of peace is joy (Proverbs 12:20). Lying lips are abomination to the Lord; but they that deal truly are his delight (Proverbs 12:22).

Woe unto them that call evil good, and good evil; that put darkness for light, and light for darkness; that put bitter for sweet, and sweet for bitter! Woe unto them that are wise in their own eyes, and prudent in their own sight! (Isaiah 5:20-21).

Therefore, thou art inexcusable, O man, whosoever thou art that judgest: for wherein thou judgest another, thou condemnest thyself: for thou that judgest doest the same things (Romans 2:1). For they being ignorant of God's righteousness, and going about to establish their own righteousness, have not submitted themselves unto the righteousness of God(Romans 10:3). As it is written, There is none righteousness, no not one (Romans 3:10). FOR ALL HAVE SINNED AND COME SHORT OF THE GLORY OF GOD. (Romans 3:23)

TO ALL AMERICANS AND ALL EDUCATIONAL INSTITUTIONS THE CULTURE CRISIS MANDATES EDUCATION FOR THE WHOLE PERSON: THE HEAD, HEART, HANDS & HEALTH (HUMAN HATRED AND TECHNOLOGY HAVE MADE THIS AN URGENT NECESSITY)

CARE	EDUCATION
C haracter	Education
A rtistic	Education
R eligious	Education
E thical	Education

MUST UNDERGRID AND GUIDE

S T E M	Education
S cience	Education
T echnology	Education
E ngineering	Education
M ath	Education

The Christian Institute of Public Theology

QUESTIONS FOR CANDIDATES SEEKING PUBLIC OFFICE

1. Identity theft is a serious and growing problem. What will you do to reduce and eliminate identity theft?
2. How will you guarantee that the municipal water supply is clean, sanitary and safe for drinking, consumption, and other use for all persons with constant sustainable monitoring?
3. What will you do to prevent the malfunctioning of water meter reading that frequently results in excessive charges?
4. What will you do to regulate the prices of legal drugs and medications within reasonable and just humane limits?
5. Many court cases linger and languish for years without adjudications and dispositions, what Initiatives will you take to establish reasonable time limits for hearing and adjudicating judicial and administrative cases?
6. What will you do to maximize the relevance and usefulness of the K-12 public school Curriculum for learning marketable skills for students to make a living and achieve a successful life beginning after completing high school?
7. What will you do in your public service capacity to prevent poverty and help those who Are afflicted with poverty, homelessness, drug addiction, crime, and other detrimental Victimization?
8. What will you do to protect vulnerable children and youth from insufficient, improper Guardianship, exploitation, neglect, and abuse?

9. What plans do you have to protect and promote the health, wealth, safety, and dignity of the elderly in their homes, assisted living and community in general?
10. What policies, procedures and regulations can you initiate to assure the utmost safety and care in hospitals and other healthcare facilities?
11. What will you do to reform building codes to assure safe construction of homes and other structures in the event of severe weather and catastrophic events?
12. What will you do to protect consumer interests from utility and other companies?

EFFECTIVE BIBLE STUDY GUIDE

INTRODUCTION AND PURPOSE

True biblical knowledge is declining in America at a time when it is most needed. Biblical illiteracy in any society is very dangerous. Biblical foundational truths are indispensable for ethical guidance in the way of truth, righteousness, and justice. These truths are essential and needed for civilized living, peace, hope, love, prosperity, and human and spiritual salvation. Biblical knowledge from God is mankind's only hoped to be saved from the destruction of ideological and spiritual wickedness and misguided technological warfare. Biblical knowledge is God's blueprint for human survival. The Bible is the unique historical record of God's demonstrated and illustrated communications and revelations to mankind. It is the Book with the authoritative message and commandments from God. It is The Book with the un-equivocal and undeviating Will of God to reach mankind. It is the authority on life, human nature and how to live. The Bible teaches that God is the Creator of the universe with all power and all knowledge. The Bible is The Book of Absolute Good News. The Bible is The Book of Salvation that reveals in human history God's Love and God's Word that became flesh and dwelt among us in JESUS CHRIST. The primary purpose of this Bible study guide is to make the Word of God known to as many persons as possible with the most optimum effect.

BIBLE STUDY DEVOTION AND ACKNOWLEDGEMENTS

A thirty-minute devotional and acknowledgement period immediately before the actual Bible study begins can be very helpful and therapeutic for the members of the Bible Study Group. This facilitates the Bible Study Group evolving into a fellowship group. It is appropriate to use five, ten or fifteen minutes for an opening musical selection, followed by prayer, Scripture and a second musical selection. This may vary with the specific circumstances. After this brief devotional period, the Bible Study Teacher/ Coordinator will greet the Bible study members and allow each member, voluntarily, to register their presence and express whatever relevant concern they may have on their minds and hearts. At the conclusion of the devotion and acknowledgement period the Bible Class Coordinator or Teacher will begin the Bible class at the designated beginning time.

EFFECTIVE BIBLE STUDY GUIDES

The purpose of the Bible Study Fellowship Class is to learn the Word of God and the teachings of the Old Testament and the New Testament through scheduled systematic study procedures by an experienced and qualified credentialed professed believer in Jesus Christ. It is recommended that the Bible Study Class be scheduled for one hour or one- and one-half hour a minimum of once each week at a place conducive for serious and sacred Bible study.

A standard and effective method of studying the Bible is to select one of the 39 books in the Old Testament or one of the 27 books in the New Testament in Chronological order.

It is preferable to study one chapter from the chosen book rather than covering it all during each meeting session. The key is to study in a thorough way, each sentence and verse of the chosen chapter. Listen exactly to what the sentence and verse say and discuss the meaning objectively. To encourage inclusive participation of the class members, the teacher may ask for a volunteer or request a designated class member to read a segment of the chapter being studied. More interest and participation can be generated by allowing class members to express their ideas and opinions about the passage of Scriptures studied. it is ideal to complete the assigned chapter at each meeting session. However, additional sessions may be required to complete one chapter due to varying interests and discussion time.

To get the most from the Bible study, it is important to be prayerful, faithful, and sincere in searching of the truth of God's revelation in Scripture. Along with God's revelation in God's creation, it is important to understand that the whole Bible is Good News. This does not mean that everything stated in the Bible is good, because the Bible talks about good and evil, Justice and injustice. The Good News is that the Bible is a book of truth about the world of reality it deals with the real and the Ideal. It deals with what is, and what ought to be. Much of the Bible is prophetic, the fulfillment of consequences of rebellion and disobedience on the part of men and nations.

It is essential to understand the connection and the relationship of Jesus Christ to the Old Testaments. The study of the Bible and the spiritual journey through the Bible become even more fascinating and exciting when "the root and the offspring of David," is made along with "And the Word was made flesh and dwelt among us." There are references to Jesus Christ in all the books of the Bible. Jesus is the only person known to history that it can be said that everything he said and did was in good news. Additionally, everything others said about him and the things they did to him, is good news. Even the sacrificial crucifixion was and is good news. Jesus is God's sacrificial gift to the world.

There is no other book that can be substituted for the Bible. There is no other book or collection of books with a coherent account of creation and man's genesis and purpose as the sixty-six books of the Bible proclaim. There is no other book with a validated salvation plan and a Savior for mankind. There is no other book that remains relevant and vital for all times, ages and for all persons and nations. The Bible speaks to every person, every age, and every civilization. Its message is always enlightening and redemptive for mankind.

The Bible is the primary and foremost authority for mankind. No man or secular authority is authorized to take away or add to the canonized books of the Bible. The Bible knows mankind better than all the laws, arts, science, and religions of mankind. It is the account of man's search for God and God's revelation to mankind. The Bible is the historical account of God's communication to and with mankind on the planet Earth. The Bible is the account of God's visitation in his Only Begotten Son, Jesus Christ. The Bible has a personal message from God to each person. It is a message of love, redemption, and salvation.

BENEFITS AND REWARDS OF BIBLE STUDY

The Bible Study Fellowship Group has numerous benefits and rewards. It helps members to find faith, hope, and love in God. It helps members grow faith, hope, and love in God. It helps members share faith, hope, and love in God. The Bible Study Fellowship helps members to apply faith, hope, and love to God and the world. It enlightens the mind and enhances spiritual growth. It is a place to unload burdens and be refreshed with the love and spirit of God. It is a place to discover the greatest revelations known to mankind.

The study of the Bible is an available lifelong privilege and honor essential for sustaining spiritual and human growth. It is an invaluable and indispensable resource for a prosperous and abundant life. The knowledge, resources, and revelations of the Bible are an inexhaustible blessing for all who will avail themselves of its unsearchable riches. Biblical knowledge is that knowledge that provides the key to making sense and purpose our of all other knowledge and life experiences. It is truth, light, and the pathway to God and eternal life.

There are many keys to understanding the Bible. One key is to recognize the Bible as progressive revelation. That means that this revelation had a beginning. This beginning can be considered a birth. The Bible can be considered a living organism. As in the case of all living things and beings, they are born and grow from infancy through childhood, adolescence, young adulthood, and adulthood. The progressive revelation of the Bible had such a historical development. This helps explain the perceived contradictions in the Bible. For example, "an eye for an eye, and a tooth for a tooth" cannot be reconciled with the Gospel of love and forgiveness taught by Jesus. Jesus makes it clear that he did not come to condemn the world, but to save it. He also said that he did not come to destroy the laws or the prophets, but to fulfill them. Therefore, the Bible cannot be accurately judged by its early beginnings and developments. It must be judged by what it came to be or grew to be in its adult fulfillment in Jesus Christ.

The Bible contains the greatest classical literature and history known to mankind. This history has relevance for all history. The literature of the Bible has produced more universal artistic expressions and the highest aspirations of the human spirit than any other volume in the annals of human history. Get to know the characters in the Bible. Get to know the first man and the first woman, Adam, and Eve. Get to know the patriarchs, Abraham, Isaac, and Jacob. Get to know Joseph, the dreamer. Get to know Moses, the leader and lawgiver. Get to know Samson and the Judges. Get to know Hannah's son, Samuel. Get to know King David and the other Kings of Israel. Get to know the Hebrew prophets and priests. Absorb yourself in the Psalms of David and the Proverbs of Solomon and the suffering of Job. Concentrate on the Gospels and the New Testament. Learn about the great events of the Bible. Study the creation, the Tower of Babel, the Flood, the crossing of the Red Sea, the birth of Christ, His miracles, His Gospel, His Crucifixion, Resurrection, Great Commission, Ascension, Pentecost, and the growth of the Church.

The Bible Study Fellowship transforms our spirits and renews our minds. This Bible study offers a transcendent message from above and beyond the culture that we live in. It is the most exciting, fulfilling and rewarding journey that anyone can embark upon. It has therapeutic healing, spiritual guidance, and growth. It teaches healthy personal and social interaction, members who are apt and interested learn about the art of group leadership and social interaction guidance. It offers an opportunity to learn listening and communication skills in a group setting. It is an accepting and caring forum to feel safe in sharing one's feelings, ideas, and thoughts. It is a forum that offers the opportunity to learn in a clinical setting, how to facilitate focused, goal oriented and problem-resolution discussions. The Bible Study Fellowship Group is a training opportunity to develop group leaders and proficient Bible study teachers.

In addition to the verse-by-verse study of the Bible, it is essential to use reputable Bible commentaries, concordances, other literary sources, and relevant current events to maximize the benefits of the Bible study.

INFORMATION TECHNOLOGY AND BIBLE STUDY

It is vitally important that the Church and believers in Christ and the Word of God to utilize and encourage others to use the IT (Information Technology) of smart phones, iPad and other information technology containing the Bible and Scriptural information. It is the duty of the Church and believers to make known that smart phones and other technological instruments contain the Bible. It is powerful and useful realization to make people aware that they have a Bible in their smart cell phone and iPad. We must hold on to the Book that contains the Bible and enhance the technology that contains the Bible as well. The very fact of knowing this convenient and readily access to the Bible may be a motivating factor fact of knowing this convenient and readily access to the Bible may be motivating factor and an incentive to increase Bible reading and Bible study. Special effort must be initiated to capitalize on this technological opportunity to promote increased Bible study. Special outreach efforts to youth must be made to teach them Bible use and study via the smart information technology. It is recommended that person who are proficient in this specific information technology, be encouraged to develop a curriculum and begin providing a Smart Phone/iPad Bible Study Class. This ought to be priority in every Church to help overcome our Biblical illiteracy deficits and dangers.

The Christian Institute of Public Theology, Inc.
Atlanta Georgia

BIBLICAL SYSTEMATIC THEOLOGY
(Evaluation components of true religion)

The Bible represents the whole gospel for the whole person and the whole world. Based on the Bible, the structural content of a comprehensive systematic theology can be developed. Systematic theology consists of the following doctrines enumerated with the Bible as their source. Does the doctrine conform to rational, theological, historical, or externally documented reality? (Verifiable beyond fantasy and imagination):

1.	Bibliology	What is the doctrine of SCRIPTURE?
2.	Theology	What is the doctrine of GOD?
3.	Christology	What is the doctrine of CHRIST?
4.	Pneumatology	What is the doctrine of the HOLY SPIRIT
5.	Anthropology	What is the doctrine of MAN?
6.	Soteriology	What is the doctrine of SALVATION?
7.	Ecclesiology	What is the doctrine of CHURCH?
8.	Eschatology	What is the doctrine of LAST THING?

THE UNIQUE SCRIPTURES OF THE BIBLE

The Bible is God's displayed and illustrated living human and divine expressions and revelations of real human life as it unfolds on the stage of human history. The Bible and the Gospel of Jesus Christ are uniquely interwoven with human nature and human history. They are expressions and revelations of truth about the essence of the human existence and the predicament of mankind. The Bible and Jesus Christ have been perused, analyzed, and synthesized by massive minds for over two thousand years, and they still stand with unscathed solidarity.

The purpose of this structural outline of systematic theology is to help believers to examine the validity and soundness of their faith and belief systems during the raging warfare of ideas, ideology, cultism, sectarianism, alien spirits, and false doctrine; fueled by cultural diversity, perversity, false religions, and secularistic technology.

The Christian Institute of Public Theology, Inc.

THE TEST FOR EVALUATING TRUE RELIGION
THE PUBLIC THEOLOGIAN
MAGAZINE

I. God is:

1.	Omnipotent	All-Powerful
2.	Omniscient	Knows Everything
3.	Omnipresent	Present Everywhere
4.	Infinite	Unlimited, Unbounded
5.	Eternal	Without Beginning or End, Everlasting
6.	Immortal	Eternal Existence, Not Subject to Death
7.	Creator	Originates Existence

II. Are the Religious Doctrines Congruent with the Following Universal Values and Principles?

1.	Life	Autonomous Animated Self Conscious Will
2.	Truth	Identifiable existential Reality
3.	Justice	Balanced Equitable Fairness
4.	Goodness	Genuine Virtue, Moral Soundness and Purity
5,	Righteousness	Just Actions with Positive Regard
6.	Love	Compassionate Caring and Affection
7.	Light	Illumination that makes sight possible
8.	Beauty	Expression of Elevated Pleasant Sensations
9.	Faith	Hopeful Belief for Desired Fulfillment
10.	Hope	Intuitive Faithful Optimistic Expectation

III. Are the dichotomies (Opposites) of the Universal Values, Clear, and Distinguishable in the Respective Religion or Doctrine?

IV. Does the Religion Conform to Theological, Historical, Existential Documented Reality? (Verifiable reality beyond fantasy and imaginary fictions.)?

V. Is the Religion, Doctrines or Principles, Inherently, Universally Inclusive of the lives and humanity of all Human Beings?

VI. Does the Religion Allow for the Autonomy of the Individual's Free Will and Conscience as Opposed to Coercive Intimidations that mitigate against Individual Conscience?

VII. Has the Religion Outgrown and Transformed Itself from Limited Ideological Isms to the Inclusive Universal Household of God?

VIII. Does the Religion Contain Redemptive Revelations from God, and Specifically manifested in History, with Invincible Evidence and Infallible Proofs?

IX. Enumerate Who or What is the Competently Validated, Timeless and Universal Authority of the Religion or Doctrine and When was the Authority Established?

X. What is the Competently Validated, Ultimate Divine Goal(s) or Benefit(s) of the Religion?

NOTE: Religions, Prophets, Doctrines, and Principles can be False, although sincerely believed!

Christian Association of Public Theologians, Inc.

THE STRUCTURAL CONTENT OF SYSTEMATIC THEOLOGY
The Bible is the only Authoritative Book for Constructing Systematic Theology)

Outline for systematic theology		General Content
1.	Doctrine of Scripture	The Revelation of God and God's
2.	Doctrine of God	Word God as Absolute Creator & Sustainer
3.	Doctrine of Christ	Incarnate Son and Savior of the World
4.	Doctrine of Holy Spirit	Communal Omnipotence
5.	Doctrine of Creator	Originality of Reality & Existence
6.	Doctrine of Earth	Habitation of Human Life in God's Image
7.	Doctrine of Time	Limited & Limitless Infinity & Eternity
8.	Doctrine of Mankind	Beings with Souls & God's Image
9.	Doctrine of Love	Ultimate Caring for God, Self & Others
10.	Doctrine of Evil	Wicked Forces Against God's Will
11.	Doctrine of Justice	Equitable Balance of Human Values
12.	Doctrine of Freedom	God-given Autonomous Will to Choose
13.	Doctrine of Faith	Ultimate Belief in Unseen Power Source

14.	Doctrine of Righteousness	A Virtuous, True, Just, & Godly Way
15.	Doctrine of Salvation	Abundance & Eternal Life in Jesus Christ
16.	Doctrine of Goodness	Moral & Ethical Virtues Without Flaws
17.	Doctrine of Beauty	The Elevated Ideas of God-Inspired Art
18.	Doctrine of Sin	Rebellion & Disobedience to God's Will
19.	Doctrine of Last Thing	Absolute Fulfillment of God's Will
20.	Doctrine of Trinity	Father, Son, and the Holy Ghost

The above doctrines can be built on the Old and New Testaments of the Bible. These doctrines (and others) evolved through the revelatory history of Israel. These doctrines are found in the living, illustrated, and demonstrated experiences of God's intervention and revelation in the history of Israel on the planet earth. They contain the message and the will of God for all mankind. No other book contains these authoritative, sound doctrines for constructing a holistic, systematic theology. The Bible is the unique revelation of God to all mankind. No other book offers the sound doctrines necessary to construct systematic theology.

The Bible is a record of real historical people, geographical locations, and events that took place on the planet Earth. It is inspired by God. It is real. It is ideal. It tells the story of humanity in relationship to God. It explores the human nature of mankind. It is the authority on human nature. It illustrates and demonstrates the high and noble capabilities of humanity's potential. It illustrates and demonstrates man's fall to low moral depths. It illustrates and demonstrates the high and noble capabilities of the potential of mankind. God has shown man what is good, just, righteous, true, and loving. The Bible is the book that tells mankind what the will of God is. It tells man that he (mankind) is made in the image of God. The Bible illustrates and demonstrates, on the stage of history, the Savior of the world, Jesus Christ. The Bible is the greatest story and the greatest message ever shared in history. The failure to share the message of the Bible and the failure to receive this message is among the greatest tragedies of history.

The Christian Institute of Public Theology, Atlanta, GA 3031

THE CHRISTINAN INSTITUTE OF PUBLIC THEOLOGY

GUIDES FOR CHOOSING SCRIPTURE AND SERMON/MESSAGE SUBJECTS

The messenger or preacher must have a deep desire and burden to share a relevant, redemptive, Biblically based message of ultimate enlightenment, truth, hope, love, and fulfillment with the listeners and hearers of the Word. The process begins with meditating on the most current, relative, present, and pressing spiritual needs of the people assembled to be nourished and have the Word proclaimed. This meditative process includes petitioning God to reveal the problems that need solving, the brokenness and diseases that need healing, the damages and losses that need restoring, the courage, confidence, faith, hope, truth, and love needed to live and overcome according to the will of God.

A PRAYERFUL ASSESSMENT OF NEEDS

Some of the common problems and common needs among the people are:

1. Ignorance about the knowledge, truth, understanding, wisdom and salvation of the Bible, God, Jesus Christ; the will, ways, love, and power of God. People are perishing for the lack of theological knowledge (knowledge of God).
2. Many people are struggling with selfishness, pride, disobedience; rebellion against man and God; jealousy, envy, vainglory, greed, indifference, self-righteousness, hatred, addiction problems,

materialism, worldliness, slothfulness, no goals, no purpose, no mission, no hope, no faith, lostness, lonely, heartbroken, disappointed, hopeless, and defeated.

3. People are oppressed, downtrodden, beaten down and victimized by injustice and evil of the world. Some are deprived, neglected, abused, exploited, deceived, mislead; robbed of freedom, education and survival resources and values. Some people work under stressful conditions of intimidation, discrimination, demoralization and threats of incarceration and annihilation.

SELECTION OF BIBLICAL TEXTS AND SUBJECTS

Select Biblical texts and subjects that most appropriately encompass the message and spirit that will best express and address the answers and solutions to the specified targeted needs and specific problems described above. The Scripture and subject must provide the inspired Prescription and answers according to the Word of God. It must be a Scripture and a subject that are internalized emotionally (passion and feelings), conceptualized intellectually for clear and orderly presentation, (with love, conviction, and compassion); empowered by the Holy Spirit. These guidelines help to bring together the spiritual needs and problems with the answers and solutions according to the Will of God. Whatever that spiritual or human need may be, the answer and solution are found in the Word of God in the Holy Bible through the communion of the Holy Spirit and the grace of Jesus Christ.

THE RATIONALE FOR RESOLUTIONS
Proposals for Solving Problems and
Elevating Humanity
-The Public Theologian-

The initiatives of salvation resolutions for cultural transformation are based on the words of Jesus, "And I say unto you, ask, and it shall be given you; seek, and ye shall find; knock, and it shall be opened unto you (Luke 11:9)." It is essential to make real the appeals to the appropriate persons, representatives, and authorities. There is a need to be explicit in your request and what you want. The heart of your resolution appeal must be based on truth, righteousness, justice, and the validated word of God for the public good.

The resolutions are written proposals and appeals for responsive action. To get things done, some form of action is required. Faith without works is dead. Cursing the darkness is not productive. Negative moaning, groaning, and complaining rarely accomplish anything of significance. Hatred and ill will against perceived enemies are not redemptive for cultural transformation. The resolution proposal and appeal not only make a formal request, but it makes known the just, righteous, and humanitarian beneficial resolution to the issue or problem at hand. It is empowered by the grace and the congruence of God's Will.

The well planned and written resolution explains the existing problematic concerns and the means and methods of resolving the problematic concerns. Inasmuch as the resolution has enumerated the problem and provided the written recommendations, proposals and solutions, the receiving authority only need to receive, accept, adopt, and implement the submitted resolution. The public theologian assures that the sound doctrine of Scripture is incorporated into the resolution.

SOME NEEDED RESOLUTIONS FOR CULTURAL TRANSFORMATION

1. Resolution for Character Education from K-12 in all Public Schools.
2. Resolution for Biblical Education from K-12 in all Public Schools.
3. Resolution for Black American History Education in all U.S. Educational Institutions.
4. Resolution for Black American Music Art in all Public Educational Institutions.
5. Resolution for Black American Restoration for Racial Enslavement & Discrimination.
6. Resolution for Government Administrative Equity & Merit Systems for all citizens.
7. Resolution for Required Bible Courses for All American Law Schools & Judges.
8. Resolution for Validated Educational, Ethical, Mental & Moral Fitness for Public Office.
9. Resolution for Establishment of Validated Professional Competent Code of Ethics.
10. Resolution for Vocational Education and Artistic Education in all Public Schools.
11. Resolution for Protective Holistic Child Care, Nurture, Education, Health & Training.
12. Resolution for Reaffirmation of Strict Observance of U.S. Constitutional Law Equitably.

THE PUBLIC THEOLOGIANS WHO ACCEPT THE WHOLE GOSPEL FOR THE WHLOE PERSON FOR THE WHLOE WORLD MUST BE RESOLUTE IN THE PURSUIT OF TRUTH, JUSTICE & SALVATION.

BOOKS OF THE BIBLE

OLD TESTAMENT – 39 BOOKS	NEW TESTAMENT – 27 BOOKS
LAW – 5 POETRY MAJOR PROPHET – 5	GOSPEL – 4 PAULS LETTER TO FRIENDS - 4

GENESIS	JOB
ISAIAH	MATTHEW
1TIMOTHY	EXODUS
PSALMS	JEREMIAH
MARK	2 TIMOTHY
LEVITICUS	PROVERBS
LAMENTATIONS	LUKE
TITUS	NUMBERS
ECCLESIASTES	EZEKIEL
JOHN	PHILEMON

HISTORY – 12	MINOR PROPHET - 12	HISTORY – ACTS
JOSHUA	HOSEA	
JUDGES	JOEL	
RUTH	AMOS	
1 SAMUEL	OBADIAH	
2 SAMUEL	JONAH	
1 KINGS	MICAH	
1 KINGS	NAHUM	

1 CHRONICLES	HABAKKUK	
2 CHRONICLES	ZEPHANIAH	
EZRA	HAGGAI	
NEHEMIAH	ZECHARIAH	
ESTHER	MALACHI	

PAULS LETTER TO CHURCHES – 9	GENERAL LETTER – 9
ROMANS	HEBREW
1 CORINTHIANS	JAMES
2 CORINTHIANS	1 PETER
GALATIANS	2 PETER
EPHESIANS	1 JOHN
PHILIPPIANS	2 JOHN
COLOSSIANS	3 JOHN
1 THESSALONIANS	JUDE
2 THESSALONIANS	REVELATIONS

WHAT IS A PROBATION OFFICER?
by ... Willie James Webb

A probation officer is an officer of the court and a peace officer of the community. His or her role is not prosecution, defense, judicial decision-making or rendering verdicts of guilty or innocent. The probation officer is an investigator who seeks to present the relevant facts and contextual truths concerning the litigation and disposition of the client to make possible a more equitable administration of justice by the court. The image of the client portrayed by the probation officer to the court is a very significant image. It is an image created by the investigation and observation of the probation officer. The probation officer uses his or her skills to make a composite report based on what he or she has seen, heard, witnessed and observed. The probation officer weeds out and screens out irrelevancies from a universe of social facts and circumstances to present a picture of the client that will assist the court in rendering a decision that will be in the best interest of the client and society. The wide and varied vantage point of the probation officer is one of the unique characteristics of his or her job. The probation officer sees the client from many points of view based on many frames of reference. The probation officer deals with the legal, economic, social, cultural, religious, scientific, and artistic aspects of the client's life. The probation officer is entrusted with authority and influence over the most important and sacred values of the client. These include freedom, economics, education and various other kinds of opportunities and responsibilities and rights and privileges. The probation officer seeks to harmonize and reconcile the individual interest of the client with the common interest of society.

As the probation officer takes his or her investigative journey through the social and cultural environment of the client, he or she examines it for those rough spots, deprivations, excesses, negations, abuses, negligence, antagonistic relationships and for those significant others who may have eaten "sour grapes and set their children teeth on edge." The probation officer often sees the inheritance of generational blessings and misfortunes.

Unlike the theoreticians, statisticians and accountants who deal with theories, numbers and machines, the probation officer deals with facts, persons, things, and events. He or she relates to specific persons, places, things, and circumstances. He or she visits homes, schools, businesses, job sites and other places in the community. The probation officer must deal with real people, real problems in the real world. The probation officer attempts to work with the whole person from various perspectives to arrive at a more complete picture of his or her client. This more complete picture is based on firsthand personal knowledge, personal acquaintance and a synthesis based on many perspectives.

WHAT IS A PROBATION OFFICER?

The probation officer is a case manager and a mentor. He or she is an advocate for the client assigned by the court. The Probation officer cuts "red tape" and links the client to essential developmental, remedial, sustenance and growth services. He or she cultivates community support systems and builds alliances for opportunities and advancement. The probation officer offers more than lip service, lectures, and platitudes. He or she provides focus, direction, motivation, and inspiration for self-actualization and personal achievement. The probation officer is often involved in passionate confrontations, difficult decisions, and courageous actions of creative casework and bold advocacy. He or she is a teacher of personal achievement and social progress. He or she teaches respect for the rights, property and person of others, respect for law and patriotism for America. The probation officer is a counselor for moral and ethical values and the integrity and dignity of human life. The probation officer teaches delinquents to be delivered, failures to be successful and losers to be winners.

What is a probation officer? He or she is a specialized generalist in the areas of human behavior, human relations, and human resources. He or she is a correctional practitioner and a rehabilitation counselor. He or she is a skilled evaluator and a social diagnostician. The probation officer is one who has respect for the law, a generous fund of useful knowledge, life skills resourcefulness, spiritual insight, reverence for the Creator and compassion for humanity. The probation officer is one who is engaged to assist a law violator to carry out the court's order by raking the advantage of another chance to prove worthy as a law-abiding citizen. The probation officer is a change agent in the life of his or her clients. The probation officer is a model and an example of what a citizen and a person ought to be like. He leads by what he knows, what he does and where he goes. She is a humanitarian, a reformer, and a transformer. The probation officer is a man or woman with a special calling to do noble work for humanity and to practice a high art for civilization. He and she are extolled and unsung heroes.

Willie James Webb
Former: Probation Officer Supervisor &
Project Director Correction Specialist
Fulton County Juvenile Court Atlanta, Georgia

THE SEVENTH ANNUAL CONFERENCE OF THE CHRISTIAN ASSOCIATION OF PUBLIC THEOLOGIANS
OCTOBER 19, 2012

The Keynote Address:
"Instituting Sacred Knowledge for Leadership in a Secular Society"
Rev. Willie James Webb

Greetings in the name of our Lord and Savior, Jesus Christ, to the Public Theologians and all persons in attendance at this, our Seventh Annual CAPT Conference. Thanks to our President, Rev. Melvin Ware and all persons who have worked on committees to make this Conference a reality.

The growing secularism in American society has become a great threat to our institutions, our quality of life and the survival values that have brought us as a people and as a Nation thus far in the Twenty-First Century. This destructive process of secularization is escalating at a rapid rate, it is fueled by advanced technology, social media, and attacks on religion in the public square.

A secular society is antagonistic and is at war with God and true religion. A secular society attempts to ignore God and influence others to do the same. Secularistic people have developed policies and laws to get religion and anything that represents God out of public life. They want God and religion out of society. They believe that they can get along without God and religious values. The people who embrace secularism have objected to mention God in the Pledge of Allegiance. They have objected to crosses on the graves of soldiers in National cemeteries. They have objected to the

Ten Commandments being in courthouses. They have outlawed prayers in the public schools. They have objected and filed lawsuits to prohibit the Nativity Scene of Jesus' birth on public property and in public places. They have objected to the name of Jesus in public prayers. Efforts are being made to get the inscription, "In God We Trust," off the American currency. The trend continues.

The frightening thing about this trend of secularism is that it has a growing measurable impact. According to a religious research organization, known as PEW Research, there are more people in America for the first time in its history who do not claim any affiliation with religious organizations as the largest singular category. Protestantism has historically been the largest singular religious affiliation category in America. The no religious category is the highest single category now. Parenthetically speaking, Black Americans have been the largest ethnic minority for over 300 years. That has changed in the 21st Century. Hispanics have surpassed the Black Americans as the largest American minority group in America.

The Americans and the American Christians as well as the other American religions were not culturally, spiritually, or educationally prepared to receive over fifty million immigrants to America in the past fifty years. This large influx of other nationalities, religions, cultures, and ideologies have contributed to the culture crisis in America. This blessed, powerful, but juvenile Country, was not prepared and was not taught how to receive, educate, accommodate, and appropriately assimilate with the newcomers to America. The necessary adjustments to the large number of immigrants in America contributed to the inability of America and the Christians to deal effectively with the growing secularism. The American culture has been saturated with other diluting influences. This is not suggest that the recent immigrants have brought bad things to America. Many have brought positive influences to America. My point is - that the Americans and the Christian Americans were not prepared to assert the needed education, training, transformation, and leadership for the newcomers to America.

The growing secularism in America is dangerous. It is a form of Godliness that is permeating and infiltrating the whole culture. It is infiltrating the government, laws, leader, institutions, families, schools, healthcare, sports, and entertainment. It is infiltrating social media and cyber space. It is dumbing down the populous and indoctrinating the youth. It has begun a campaign to rewrite history. It has no respect for truth, facts, science, religion, law, or arts. It is a Pandora Box of evil loosed in the world. You need to get involved with the educational systems. You need to know that they are teaching your children. You need to know who is teaching your children. You must get intimately involved in the political process. You need to know the identification and the competence of the people who are representing you from the local and state level to Washington, D.C. You must keep diligent watch over your Executive, Legislative and Judicial branches of government from local to federal.

Secularism is bringing about another more omnibus danger to America.

That danger is since secularism is eroding the sacred Judeo-Christian foundation upon which America rests. The U.S. Constitution, The Bill of Rights, the Declaration of Independence, the Motto, "In God We Trust," the Pledge of Allegiance and democracy itself is based upon the doctrines of Judeo-Christian. This foundation has made America the most powerful and most blessed of all Nations. Despite slavery and a civil war, it is crystal clear that God blessed America. God blessed America with the Emancipation and the outlawing of involuntary servitude. God blessed America with the passage of the 1964 and 1965 Civil Rights Acts.

However, a series questions arises through the erosion of Judeo-Christian values. Can America survive if it is shifted from its Judeo-Christian Foundation? Blind efforts are being made to shift America from its sacred Christian foundations to an antichrist and secular foundation. That is why this Nation is in confusion, division, gloom, and doom because its fractured foundation. That is why this Nation is in confusion, division, gloom, and doom because its foundations are being shaken. However, Jesus says, "upon this rock I will build my Church and the gates of the hell shall not prevail against it." The hope of humanity is in Jesus Christ.

The present-day leadership is leading society away from the pathways and the values that brought us out of ignorance, bondage and darkness. The blind cannot lead the Many of our elected officials do not have the competence of the qualifications to be an effective representative. Therefore, we must raise the bar. We must raise the standards and spell out the qualifications that we desire in our public representatives. We must also provide them with a job description and duties for what needs to be done. We must not continue to go about business as usual. We must identify the problems and respond to the crisis with specific, positive recommendations. I have already taken the liberty and exercised my duty as a responsible citizen to write a Job Description for the Superintendent of the Atlanta Public Schools. I have also written guidelines and recommendations for School Principals to help them be effective in their jobs.

I am encouraging each of you to tell your story. Do not wait around for someone else to tell your story. If left to others, they may distort your story. You also need to learn to tell the story of your people. And while you are learning to tell the authentic stories of yourself and your people, you must also learn to tell the story of God, as He has shared it with us in the Holy Scriptures. There is salvation and redemptive enlightenment in the story of the African American slaves and their Black-American offspring in America. The story is rich with sacred knowledge and survival values.

Black American history is a significant part of American history. The slaves and their offspring helped make America the most powerful and free country in the world. The biased news media often plays down the significant contributions of Black Americans. That is why it is important to tell individual stories and share them. I am so pleased that we have the story of Booker T. Washington, George Washington Carver, The Tuskegee Airmen, Dr. Martin Luther King, Jr., Rosa Parks and many, many others. I will give you an example of the recent history of news media bias. You recall on 911, terrorists hijacked four American Airlines planes. They had plans to decapitate the head of the American Government by suicide missions of crashing one plane into the Pentagon in Washington, crashing two planes into the two World Trade Center Towers in New York City, and the fourth plane into the Whitehouse Capitol in Washington, D.C. Three of the planes found their targets. However, the fourth plane did not hit its target at the Capitol in Washington. That plane crashed in Pennsylvania. The reason it crashed in Pennsylvania was because a young Black American Pilot refused to give up the controls to the terrorists. The heroic story of a courageous Black American Pilot never came out in the mainstream news media. We must keep the faith. We may be denied and rejected by man. God knows and he will accept us and reward us at the proper time. Just keep the faith.

Lastly, God has set the standards. Creationism is a present reality before our very eyes and ears. The heavens declare his glory. We can see it and behold it. And yet, the secular courts Rejected Biblical Creationism and decided that the schools must teach Charles Darwin's evolutionary theory and not the facts and the truth of God's Creation that is invincibly visible before our very eyes. The courts would rather accept the secular theories and reject the sacred truth. God has provided mankind a universal Book that sets the standards for all mankind. It is the Holy Bible consisting of the Old Testaments and the New Testament. It is a Book that records the progressive revelation of God in history on the planet earth. It gives the beginning and the end. It contains God's love for man and his search for man in his blindness. When the blind keep insisting that the blind lead, the blind will bring about chaos and destruction in the Nation. Their lies, false doctrines, misrepresentations, ignorance, and evil is bringing the Nation closer and closer to the brink of disaster. When we talk about secularism (the exclusion of God and religious values in society) we are referring to an evil that will bring damnation, curses and destruction to the people and the Nation.

When we advocate the institution of sacred values in the leadership of the Church, the people, and the Nation, we are advocating for life and for survival. The sacred must lead the secular. The secular is on a horizontal plane, disconnected from God and disconnected from the redemptive knowledge that comes from God. This disconnection from God precipitates a meltdown of survival values. A meltdown of survival values is taking place as I speak.

During this meltdown, the prophetic voices are being silenced. Where are the prophetic voices? When was the last time you heard a national prophetic voice? When was the last time you heard a serious concern from the NAACP, SCLC, CBC, CORE, SNICK, ACLU American Civil Liberties Union? During this meltdown, when was the last time you heard the voice of a college or university president? When was the last time you heard from the voices of academic scholars? When was the last time you heard a national voice from the Church?

When was the last time you heard from the prophetic voice of a church leader? We have many historical and mega churches. We have many outstanding well known religious organizations. During the meltdown, where are their prophetic voices? Where are the watchmen? Where are the barking dogs to warn the people of the dangers that are lurking ahead?

When was the last time you heard of any significant legislation or contribution made by your political representatives on the local, state, or national level? It is so unfortunate that we usually do not hear from our public officials until they want our vote and support. It is unfortunate that most, if not all, of our public officials are not representing us. They are representing themselves and their interests, not us and our interests. Because they are not representing us, they have made us a voiceless people. We cry out, but our voices are not heard.

It is unfortunate, but too often when we vote elected officials into office, we give them a free, paid vacation with no supervision from us and no accountability to us. When was the last time your political representative asked you for your opinion about the pressing problems and issues that we face in our society and government? When it comes to our elected public officials, we must insist on legislation that will force them to be accountable to us and their constituency. It is shameful that they get a paid vacation without any accountability. Let us initiate legislation immediately to require all public officials to provide quarterly written accountability reports and quarterly opportunities to meet with them to get our input. We must stop being misrepresented and misused.

Sacrificial gift of his only begotten Son, Jesus Christ, for those who believe and receive the Salvation Gift.

Public theology is Biblically based on the Word of God and Theologically guided by the Love, the Light and the Spirit of God.

THEOLOGICAL GUIDES FOR HEALING HATRED ADDICTION

1. Make a commitment to love God, yourself and your neighbor through benevolent associations and human services according to the word of God.
2. Adopt a successful personal identity, a significant life purpose, noble goals, and spiritual empowerment to the glory of God.
3. Internalize in the heart, the mind, the soul and spirit, the eternal values of love, truth, goodness, and beauty to the glory of God.
4. Focus time, energy and resources on creative and positive endeavors that serve Humankind and glorify God.
5. Make it a continuing priority to discover, realize, develop, and actualize your God given gifts, talents and potentials for human services and blessings to the glory of God.
6. Become a vessel of true knowledge, hope, motivation and inspiration for human reformation and transformation according to the word of God.
7. Study the Bible to become the moral compass and theological guide for the knowledge of truth, the ways of justice, righteousness, and peace according to the word of God.
8. Build on a solid foundation to support, protect, develop, sustain, and share the precious values of life and glorify God.
9. Envision, dream, and create virtuous ways and means to enrich, refine and sustain the gift and quality of human life through God inspired art, music and human services to the glory of God.

10. Be a goodwill ambassador: sow seeds of truth, kindness, encouragement, affirmation, and love as you meet, greet and associate with others to the glory of God.

11. Create future oriented ideas and projects to develop and utilize your gifts, talents and potentials as a productive humanitarian contributor and servant to humanity to the glory of God.

12. Attend spiritual growth fellowship groups to find faith, grow faith, share faith, and apply faith to edify sisters and brothers and to glorify God.

CHAPTER 5
ESTABLISHMENT OF PROTECTIVE STANDARDS
FOR ADVOCACY, POLICIES AND ACTIONS

1. Publicly displayed sexual activity is harmful to the common good of society and especially to children and youth. Standards must be established to prevent the public display of explicit sexual activity. The news media must establish responsible policies in this area of programming

2. Same-sex marriage, homosexual activity, and sexually linked same-sex domestic partnerships are deviations from the established standards of the natural order. The promotion of these practices is harmful, confusing, and destructive to the institution of marriage, families, and especially the protection of children. Same-sex relationships are based on invalid principles and unsound doctrines that cannot be universalized. Same-sex marriage and homosexual activity work against the common good of society. This is not meant to be a condemnation of people who identify as same-sex. It is for the encouragement of healthy lifestyles and for the public good. God loves all his children. He has set standards for all his children. God has set standards for all of creation. Divine laws and natural laws are created and authorized by the Creator, God. The fluctuating and sometimes arbitrary statutory laws made by man cannot legitimately and authoritatively usurp the laws made by God. The divine and natural laws of God may be denied, opposed, and ignored. Nevertheless, they are

unmistakably and inherently there or here as abiding realities beyond the power and authority of humankind. We must be careful not to esteem, celebrate, or worship sex beyond the purpose and responsibilities of marriage.

3. The public display of licking, kissing, and other oral contact between dogs (as well as other animals) and humans is an unnatural expression of affection and is harmful to the common good of society. Standards must be set to prohibit the elevation of a dog or other animal to the level of cohabitation with human beings. This unnatural oral behavior of licking and kissing dogs and humans must be prohibited by television and other public media shows.

4. It is grossly irresponsible and outrageous that dangerous dogs continue to attack and kill people. Strict standards, strict laws, and strict enforcement must be established to protect individuals in all communities from the exposure and attacks of dangerous dogs. The responsible government agencies must be diligent and vigorous in solving this lethal problem and public nuisance.

5. There is a gross lack of protection for the public in the food service industry. The laws, standards, and enforcement are woefully inadequate in restaurants and other public eating establishments. Strangers with unknown health histories and unverified backgrounds can get a job in food services at most food service establishments. This is especially true in Georgia. We are insisting that adequate food service laws and standards be established and enforced that require, as a minimum:

    a. A health certificate based on a physical examination by a licensed Board-certified physician;

    b. Sanitary training for food service workers;

      c. Appropriate hygiene and sanitized uniforms by food service workers, and

      d. Regular random inspections of all areas of food storage. preparation, utensils, equipment, and service areas.

6. Customers of barber, beauty, and other body care salons must be assured, with appropriate notices and publications, that the facilities have acceptable standards of cleanliness, sanitation, safety, and certified training, and professionalism. The certifying and licensing agencies must ensure that customers are protected. The burden of protection must not be placed on the customers.

7. Healthcare facilities at every level must develop safety standards that will provide the highest level of protection possible to protect their patients from safety and health hazards while in the care of their healthcare providers. Negligence, health hazards, and medical mistakes are at exceptionally high and unacceptable levels. It is recommended that the appropriate corrections be made and the appropriate inspections, monitoring, and accountability be instituted.

8. Greed, malpractice, fraud, theft, deceptions, and unprofessionalism are rampant in too many businesses. It is strongly recommended that business ethics education and training be required for all persons who work in the business public sector. Adequate and acceptable ethical practices in all businesses serving the public are recommended.

9. How can consumers of the automobile repair industry be protected from deceptive and fraudulent practices? Policies and procedures must be developed to protect customers from fraudulent and unscrupulous practices in the automobile repair industry.

10. It is recommended that the selection of music played in restaurants and other recreational areas be conducive to relaxation, conversation, reflection, peace, and tranquility. Loud, rhythmic, noisy, and emotionally stimulating music works against enjoyment, dialogue, peace, and reflection. It is recommended that the selection of music in public restaurants and similar facilities consider the customer's need for peace, quietness, relaxation, conversation, refinement, and family values, as well as cultural and spiritual values. Loud rhythmic noises contribute to abuse and violence.

11. It is recommended that the legislation be passed requires with specificity, appropriate and sufficient road signals that provide clear and timely directions for motorists to make driving decisions without confusion and jeopardy to highway and road safety.

12. There is a significant problem in seeing and locating addresses from streets in most of our municipalities. It can be frustrating, stressful, time consuming, and a road safety hazard. It is recommended that a legislation will be passed to require the readable visibility of street numbers of all addresses on all buildings from the street. Unclear addresses are distracting to drivers and pose traffic hazards.

13. The disciplinary problems in our Public-School Systems are very detrimental to the educational process and it contribute significantly to our social ills. The school disciplinary problem is fixable. CAPT is appealing to the school superintendents, the Boards, and principals to institute immediately the necessary policies, remedies and procedures to fix the disciplinary problems in the Public-School Systems. Representatives of CAPT are available to make recommendations toward that end.

14. There is a lack of uniformity and seriousness in the presentations of programs in the school during Black History

Month in February. CAPT is appealing to the educational systems to develop a more meaningful, relevant, redeeming, and universally applicable Black History curriculum to be presented in all the public schools in the month of February. Black History in America has invaluable messages for the world and for all people. CAPT representatives are available to aid in this regard.

15. The state of Georgia, during its 2006 legislative session, passed legislation that allows for the literary and historical teaching of the Bible in the Public-School Systems of Georgia. The legislation is said to be permissive and not mandatory. However, CAPT is recommending that each educational entity of the applicable schools in Georgia adopt the curriculum or otherwise make the elective Bible course available to every student who chooses to take the Bible course. Inasmuch as the State has approved the Bible course, it is now the right of every student in Georgia Public Schools to have the Bible course made available to them.

16. A well-planned assembly program in the school system can be very helpful in instilling values, building character, fostering positive self-esteem and identity, motivating for achievement, and promoting excellence, scholarship, leadership, and service. CAPT is recommending to the respective school Boards, superintendents, and principals of Georgia Public Schools, K-12, to institute a well-designed weekly assembly program for all students. A weekly school assembly program has significant potential for building a strong, positive school spirit and school pride. An inspirational singing of the school song once a week would reinforce it.

17. Computerized online technology is effectively eliminating millions of Americans from participating in accessing in the process of getting goods and services to which they are

entitled. The elimination of the traditional means and ways of accessing entitled goods and services is happening unchecked at a rapid rate. This technological deprivation and/or inaccessibility are causing serious civil rights violations.

The necessity and requirement of computerized technology to access the means of goods and services effectively discriminate against a large and growing class of American citizens. This technological discrimination deprives those who do not have computers or access to computer technology of an equal opportunity to access and utilize the availability of goods and services.

Laws must be instituted and enforced to protect and ensure that the entitlement to access and utilize available public services for those citizens who do not have access to computer technology. Computer technology is imposing an unnatural disadvantage on citizens and other persons who do not have the respective technological capabilities. It is an imposed deprivation that is not necessarily due to the fault of the technologically deprived. Laws have been instituted to accommodate the physically and mentally challenged. Therefore, it is only logical, fair, and reasonable to institute technological accommodation laws to ensure equality of opportunity for the technologically disadvantaged.

To avoid complete dependence on computer technology, it is also recommended that adequate traditional means of accessing and utilizing public services be maintained. Computer technology is not absolute. It depends on electrical power, which goes out from time to time.

18. The reformation of the Criminal Justice System has great potential for education, training, rehabilitation, reducing crime, building character, and creating more responsible and productive citizens. This can be done by educating and

training this captive population. It can be done by providing mental health, alcohol, and drug treatment services in all detention and correctional institutions. It can be done through Bible study and worship. CAPT is recommending that funding and professional education, treatment, and pastoral staff be established in the criminal justice detention and correctional facilities. It is recommended that the churches provide ongoing pastoral ministry for the Criminal Justice System.

19. Judges and lawyers arbitrate, litigate, and make decisions regarding the most precious values and sacred rights of human beings. This includes life, liberty, property, the quality of living, and the allocation of resources. Judges and lawyers are trained primarily in statutory law. Most judicial decisions are based on statutory law. Natural law and Divine law provided by God are routinely excluded from judicial decision-making in the American judicial system.

For lawyers, judges, and others who arbitrate the rights of individuals to be more accurate and comprehensive in their deliberations, mediations, and decisions, it is recommended that appropriate theological courses be added to the legal law curriculum. Law schools and theological seminaries must become allies in the training of lawyers and judges. How can a judge legitimately decide the case involving "Creationism us. Evolutionary Theory" without valid theological knowledge?

20. In view of the hazards of crime, fires, floods, and other natural disasters, building codes must be reviewed and modified to build safe and substantial homes and other structures to protect human life and property. The building industry must be monitored by the appropriate authority to ensure that life, property, and human rights and health are protected from hazardous, defective, and otherwise faulty materials,

structures, and environments. Building codes must be written and enforced to provide the optimum protection and security for human life, property, rights of individuals, and the common good.

21. Churches must take the lead in advocating and providing for love, protection, care, and the Christian education and training of children. Churches must get involved in parenting education and the early mentoring of children and youth. Parents must be taught to take greater responsibility for building character and instilling healthy values in their children, and more involvement with the respective schools and the parent or teacher association is a necessity.

22. The elderly population is increasing at a rapid rate. Increasingly, the quality of life declines for the elderly due to the need for more healthcare and services as they get older. Many of these seniors end up in nursing homes with strangers and, in some cases, uncaring workers in deplorable living conditions. The church must lead the way in providing the optimum level of care and compassion for our senior citizens. This will require commitment, training, and resources. We must not be cheap or negligent with those who paved the way for us.

23. Public theology is encouraging technology to use its creativity and innovation to design equipment, instruments, materials, electronics, and devices to enhance the efficiency and independence of the elderly and disabled.

24. The Christian Association of Public Theologians ("CAPT") is appealing to all colleges and universities to include courses in public theology. It is unintelligent and irrational to ignore and exclude the Biblical knowledge of God and Jesus Christ from a liberal and free educational system. The hope of human survival and salvation are found in Biblical Christian theology. It is the duty and responsibility of higher education to make

available the knowledge that has influenced Western civilization and the world more than any other knowledge. This knowledge is contained in the Holy Bible. We must recognize and add ethics to the other three domains of learning.

Secular public education is primarily limited to the following domains of learning:

(A) Cognitive, (B) Affective, and (C) Psycho-motor.

The cognitive includes the intellect and mind. The Affective includes emotions and feelings. The Psycho-motor relates to bodily activity and behavior. The excluded learning domain is the spiritual domain.

The spiritual domain is about the soul, ethics, morality, and religion. It is about the human relationship to the Creator that is contained in the Holy Bible and other expressions. CAPT advocates for the incorporation of spiritual and theological domains into public school systems.

25. Noah did not wait for the flood to come before he prepared to save a remnant of humanity. Noah built the ark out of gopher wood and crude instruments he made himself. Despite the wickedness and corruption of the people of the earth, Noah found grace in the eyes of God. Moreover, God gave Noah instructions on how to survive the Great Flood.

Global warming, tsunamis, earthquakes, and other natural disasters are threats to humanity on the earth. God's grace and mercy are available. He promises his people, who are called by His name that He will heal the land if they "humble themselves, pray, seek His face and turn from their wicked ways." (2 Chronicles 7:14). God has blessed mankind with the knowledge, technology, and resources to live on the water, under the water, and the capability to fly above it.

God has warned humanity of the looming dangers to the people on earth. Why can't the people of the world and the nations of the earth recognize the common threat to all humanity; stop the waste and the squandering of resources, turn to God and be preparing for a survival strategy for humanity? We must do more than talk about dangers and go on with business as usual. God has shown us the dangers. It is now time to respond with the highest ethical, spiritual, and theological guidance and the full arsenal of scientific and technological resources. Human life was the ultimate concern of Jesus Christ. It must be our concern as well!

26. It is urgent that public theologians get involved in the spiritual and ideological raging warfare. It is these evil ideological spirits that is the driving force behind greed, injustice, jealousy, arrogance, crime, violence, and wars. Military might is not sufficient to destroy the various expressions and disguises of spiritual wickedness and spiritual darkness. The theologians must prepare, and devise strategies and methods to get involved in the ideological warfare. God has shown us and demonstrated in nature and in history and in His Word that which is good, true, righteous, just, merciful, compassionate, holy, and loving. The Bible is overflowing with the inexhaustible riches of God and His Christ. The message must get out of "the Book", outside the church walls, and into the public square and marketplaces of the world.

27. Re-evaluate privatization laws and policies. A few questions must be asked about privatization, which includes the following:

    a. Was the establishment of privatization done legally and constitutionally?
    b. Is privatization based on a sound doctrine and established democratic principles?

c. Were the citizens, voters, and general public provided an opportunity to be informed, discuss, approve, and cast votes for privatization?

d. What are the criteria and guidelines for determining what can and cannot be privatized and the qualifications and requirements for privatization contracts?

e. Who and what office in the State of Georgia administers privatization and where is the location or locations of the operation(s)?

f. Who and what office(s) monitor the privatization contractors? What office keeps the list of privatized services and contractors?

Is the list of privatized contractors made available to the public?

g. Please provide the information necessary for the citizens and the public to communicate with the Office of Privatization. This is a request for the name of the director, the address of the privatization office, telephone, e-mail, and website.

28. Effective legislation and policies are requested to protect citizens and the public from identity theft. This legislation must include appropriate safeguard requirements for institutions and agencies that require the provision of personal information, such as birth date, Social Security Number and Drivers' License as a prerequisite to their service. The legislation must require personal and technological safeguards against the transmission, access, and disposal of public personal information that can be used for identity theft. It is noted that the picture identification, along with the accompanying information on drivers® licenses in the State of Georgia, can be retrieved and

reproduced by State Patrol personnel. What policies and procedures are there to safeguard against the retrieval of this personal information by the Georgia State Patrol for unauthorized purposes?

29. The leaders of the international governments and the international leaders representing the one true God of the universe must convene and establish acceptable civilized standards of conduct for all human beings. Those standards must include:

    a. The respect, reverence, and sacredness of all human life.

    b. The inherent right to be free of human bondage and involuntary servitude.

    c. The right to be free from the malice, harm, and violation of other human beings, physically, mentally, spiritually, and socially.

Those uncivilized behaviors must be condemned and eliminated because they harm human life and violate human rights. The international community must condemn the taking of human life and the violation of human rights. The international community must condemn and eliminate the violations, the violence, and the taking of innocent human lives, as well as the social and cultural breeding grounds for such ungodly violations.

30. The government and the church must take the lead in establishing equitable merit systems for equality of opportunities and services. Arbitrary, capricious, and discriminatory assignments of goods and services create unjust and harmful social and political systems in a society. Social justice is a prerequisite for society's higher values. Ethical merit systems are vital for social balance.

31. The bureaucratic automated electronic answering systems are very damaging, as well as costly and inefficient for consumers. It is not unusual to wait for 30 minutes or more to contact a human being for simple services. In many instances, the consumer gives up after a series of redundant, automated, and repetitive referrals. In most cases, these automated services are inefficient, time-consuming, and stressful. This automated system must be evaluated and changed for the benefit and welfare of consumers and citizens.

UNITED STATES OF AMERICA DEMOCRACY REQUIREMENTS FOR PUBLIC OFFICIALS AND ELECTED REPRESENTATIVES

1. Legislated Public Official/Elected Representatives RESPONSIBILITY and ACCOUNTA-BILITY to their respective Constituents.
2. Legislated EDUCATIONAL and ETHICAL Fit for Duty Requirements and Standards for Public Officials and Representatives.
3. Legislated PROFESSIONAL CODE OF ETHICS that embraces sound universal Principles, Loyalties, Ideologies, Doctrines and Personal Character for Public Officials and Elected Representatives.
4. Legislated PERSONAL LIABILITIES FOR ETHICAL, PROFESSIONAL, HUMAN AND CIVIL RIGHTS VIOLATIONS by Public Officials.
5. Legislated Requirement for BIBLICAL LITERACY, THEOLOGICAL AND CULTURAL COMPETENCE as Prerequisites for Serving in Public and Elective Office.
6. Legislated ESTABLISHMENT OF IMPARTIAL MERIT SYSTEMS WITH EXPLICIT FAIR EMPLOYMENT POLICIES, PROCEDURES AND PRACTICES for Government Agencies and Public Businesses.
7. Legislated EMPLOYMENT GRIEVANCE PROCEDURE WITH CLEAR, FAIR POLICIES AND PROCEDURES THAT COMPLY WITH THE DUE PROCESS OF LAW Contained in the 14th Amendment of the U. S. Constitution.
8. Enact Legislation that Requires LIABILITIES AND PENALTIES FOR LEGAL AND PUBLIC REPRESENTATIVES WHO FAIL TO DISCLOSE KNOWN CONFLICTS OF INTERESTS IN THEIR CONTRACTUAL

AGREEMENTS AND PUBLIC DUTIES AND RESPONSIBILITIES.

9. Institute Legislation that Prohibits any government or Private Person or Agency from PLACING ANY CITIZENS. (EMPLOYEE, FORMER EMPLOYEE OR PROSPECTIVE EMPLOYEE) NAME ON A DESIGNATED "NOHIRE LIST® or (Blacklist, Stipulate Penalties and Damages for Such Violations in the Legislation.

10. Institute Legislation That Will Provide Access and Availability to Entitled Services and Resources For Citizens Who are technologically challenged by the restrictions of Online Access and Availability of Entitled Services and Resources.

ISSUES REQUIRING ETHICAL DECISIONS
THE CHRISTIAN INSTITUTE OF PUBLIC
THEOLOGY

1. An outstanding Black U. S. Military General was asked his opinion about having a Person belonging to the Islamic faith as the president of the United States. The General replied, "I would not have a problem with it. What difference does it Make?" What is your ethical opinion?
2. A previous U. S. President made the remark, "We need more women bosses. It Is time to have a woman president of the United States." What is your opinion?
3. An LGBT woman, a racist white man and an atheistic Black man are candidates for president of the United States. What is your ethical choice?
4. An executive decision was made to ban openly gay people from serving in the U.S. Military. What is your ethical opinion?
5. AU.S. Military Commander stated that he would observe gender equality in the Military. Therefore, when it comes to deployment to the battlefield, women are deployed along with the men. What is your ethical decision?
6. The City of Atlanta has a Black female Mayor, a Black female president of the Atlanta City Council, and a White female Chief of Police. What is your ethical opinion Regarding the municipal leadership roles of these women? (During Bottom's Tenure)
7. Two women came to the pastor of the church and requested that he perform a Wedding ceremony for them. They reminded the Pastor that the U.S. Supreme Court legalized same sex marriage in the United States in 2015 and that they were Prepared to pursue their rights

in court if the pastor refused to perform the Wedding ceremony. As a pastor, what would you do?

8. Two same-sex married women are requesting the adoption of a boy and a girl of kindergarten and elementary age. What is your ethical recommendation?

9. Two men who say they are married to each other and are requesting the adoption of a six-year-old girl and an eight-year-old boy. What is your ethical recommendation?

10. Two White men who are married and claim to have adequate economic means to provide a good home and education for a ten-year-old Black boy. What is your ethical opinion about this requested adoption?

11. A 9th-grade male student stated that he is transgender and is requesting that he be permitted to use the "Girls Restroom." What is your ethical opinion?

12. There is an LGBT movement insisting that the public school systems begin teaching a curriculum that includes LGBT and the history of LGBT to all students in the public school systems. What should be the ethical position of the Church and Christian Believers regarding the LGBT Curriculum in public schools?

13. How do you explain the gender equality between men and women? In the world of Work, it is said that men's salaries are higher than women's. Does this suggest that Women are sexually discriminated against in the world of work?

14. There are two candidates, a man, and a woman, running for the Presidency of the United States. Which would be your preference and why?

15. Mayor candidate, Ceasar Mitchell in May 2017, along with over 20,000 other persons Signed a petition asking the City of Atlanta to permanently install a crosswalk in

the gay Colors in the Midtown at 10th and Piedmont. What is your ethical opinion of this decision?

16. A Day Camp at the San Francisco Bay Area with children ages 4-12 practice (gender Fluidity. These children are referred to whichever sex they are comfortable with. Reference (AJC, p. A6,8-8-17). What is your ethical opinion of teaching gender fluidity to the described children?

17. Many Confederate Monuments (including Stone Mountain) are being targeted for Demolition or removal from public property. What are your ethical recommendations?

18. A few cases have gone to courts of law alleging that the monumental crosses in public places (and even crosses on graves in national cemeteries) are in violation of the "religion establishment* clause in the U.S. Constitution. A recent case against crosses on cemetery gravesites alleges that the cross should not be used because many of the buried soldiers were not Christians, but subscribed to other religions. What are your ethical opinions regarding the above cases?

19. Recently, a pastor advised his congregation that the church music would be changing in order to attract more young people to the church. He said the music would Include some Hip, Hop and Gospel Rock. He advised the choirs to prepare to allow This contemporary worldly music into the church to win young people for the church. What is your ethical decision about the pastor's recommendation?

20. Georgia has a law that allows the Old Testament and the New Testament to be Taught as elective courses as History and Literature from ninth through the twelfth Grade. A person made the remark that if the Bible can be

taught in the public Schools, then, other religions, such as Islam should also allowed to be taught in the public schools. What is your ethical opinion about including other religious literature because the Bible can be legally taught in the public Schools in Georgia?

21. Many Black Americans express the idea that Christianity is a White man's religion. Jesus is portrayed as a White man and White Christians had Black folks in slavery. They further allege that the Bible and Christianity have been tampered with. What is your ethical response to this kind of thinking?

22. What are your ethical recommendations to the Democrats, Republicans, President, Department of Justice, and the Supreme Court to heal the great American Divide in this Twenty-First Century?

23. What is your ethical and prophetic message to Christian Americans?

24. What is your ethical and prophetic message to the World?

LEGISLATIVE PRIORITIES FOR A HEALTHY SOCIETY
(Long ignored and long overdue)

1. American Judicial reformation is urgently needed. Judges and lawyers must be taught a sense of justice and righteousness based on truth and sound rational judgement with acknowledgement of natural and divine laws. Judicial decisions are often arbitrary, political, ideological and biased with no justice or relationship to reality.

2. Legislation is needed that requires public officials to be accountable to their political constituency and tax paying citizens. When public officials fail to represent their constituency or when they misrepresent them it is tantamount to political and economic fraud against the American citizens.

3. Legislative Institutional Restoration is urgently needed for the historically deprived and disadvantaged Black American families, educational institutions, religious institutions, businesses, and other Black community enterprises. Historical and continuing racial discrimination continue to take a great toll on these long suffering, sacrificial and loyal Americans. They need legislated restorative help from their own Nation. This is not Just a Black American need. This is a hundred percent American restoration need.

4. Urgent legislation, monitoring and strict enforcement is needed for efficient, reasonable, and just time limits for judicial and administrative investigations, litigations and dispositions in the courts and administrative hearings where Civil and Human Rights are at issue and concerned. It is not unusual for hearings and litigations of Civil and

Human Rights cases to languish in the judicial systems and courts for over 6 years. Justice delayed is not only justice denied but also additional compounded injustice by the Justice System, itself.

5. Legislation is urgently needed to ensure fairness, justice and equality in government employment and personnel administration through a democratic merit system based on an objective quantifiable comprehensive monitored merit system. American citizens must not be subjected to biased, prejudicial, personal favoritism systems and administration by intimidation. Such a non-merit system contradicts democracy and negates the U.S. Constitution and makes a mockery of justice.

6. A government of justice and equality of law for its citizens requires explicit legislation prohibiting the use of arbitrarily placing citizens' names on "No Hire Lists" or "Blacklists" without due process of law mandated by the U.S. Constitution. The arbitrary, subjective, and prejudicial use of "No Hire Lists" is an abominable crime and violation of human and Civil Rights. It makes a mockery of justice and the U.S. Constitution. The vicious and clandestine use of unlawful "No Hire Lists" are destroying professional careers, defaming characters and destroying the lives of good and productive citizens. This should not be allowed in any civilized society, especially in government administration.

Legislative Priorities for a Healthy Society – Continued

7. Legislation is needed to "ban the box," designating references to past employment and job terminations on applications for employment. Such references are often used arbitrarily to deny employment in a prejudicial way

without knowing any information about a past termination on a previous job. Many previous job terminations were not justified or fair at all. There is an extensive movement to "ban the box" for criminal records on job applications. There is also a movement to expunge criminal records so that they will not hinder employment opportunities. Legislate "ban the box" for past job terminations.

8. Legislation is needed to enforce the teaching of Comprehensive Character Education in all public schools throughout Georgia from (K-12) kindergarten through twelfth grade. Ongoing character education is critical for students' well-being as well as the good and safety of society. (Refer to House Bill 605, Ga. 1999).

9. Educational legislation is urgently needed for the establishment of Accelerated Compensatory Education for the historically deprived Black American students with records of low academic achievement, poor attendance, a high dropout rate, and other barriers to educational achievement. Compensatory accelerated education is urgently needed to catch these children up with their peers, or they will forever remain behind. Helping these historically deprived children catch up educationally not only helps them, but it also helps the community and the Nation.

10. Legislation is needed to require for the provision of professional mental health and substance abuse personnel to provide remedial, educational, preventive, and promotional services as needed for all students from (K-12) in the public schools in the State of Georgia. There is a vast and growing need for mental health, drug abuse and addiction services in the public school systems in Georgia and throughout the Nation.

11. Legislation is needed to require the public-school systems to publish the educational Curriculum, along with the books, authors and other educational material used in the classrooms and in the education of children from K-12. This legislation must also require that parents and the community be involved in the development of the curriculum that is taught to their children. Most parents, residents and citizens do not know the content, rationale, values, and significance of what knowledge is being taught to their children.

12. Legislation is needed to require all high schools and boards of education in Georgia to adopt Georgia Law (20-2-148). Elective course in History and Literature of the Old and New Testaments Eras. Presently, this law left the option of this elective course to the local board of education to decide. Although this is an elective course, the Atlanta Board of Education has refused to adopt it in the curriculum of Atlanta Public Schools.

THEOLOGICAL RECOMMENDATION

The following legislative and administrative recommendations will serve the cause of justice, peace, goodwill, health and prosperity in our government and society. It will enhance trust and confidence in the government and create an atmosphere of respect and hope for the future.

Recommendations:

1. PUBLIC OFFICIAL ACCOUNTABILITY - Adopt legislation requiring all public officials, local, state, and federal, to provide quarterly constituent meetings and quarterly written political updates to be made available to constituent communities.
2. FIT FOR DUTY STANDARDS - Adopt legislation requiring a minimum standard of educational, ethical, citizenship and patriotic competence for all public officials, compatible with the laws of the U.S. Constitution.
3. BIBLICAL LITERACY AND THEOLOGICAL COMPETENCE - Adopt legislation requiring Biblical literacy and theological competence courses in the curriculum of all law schools. Statutory laws cannot ignore divine laws and natural laws of God and be valid in the administration of human and social justice.
4. BIBLICAL JUDEO-CHRISTIAN EDUCATION - Adopt legislation requiring courses of the Old Testament and the New Testament to be taught as history and literature in all public schools. Based on theological studies (which are scientific and objective), the Judeo-Christian Bible has been

validated by history to be inclusive (but not coercive) of all people. It has been validated by rigorous scholarship to be progressively revelatory. historical, redemptive, comprehensive, holistic, universal and foundational for democratic, ethical, moral, and spiritual values that are compatible with the disciplines of human nature, law, art, science, and religion.

5. THEOLOGICAL REPRESENTATION IN PUBLIC POLICY - The Church and the faith community must insist on credible theological representation at the local, state and federal levels in regard to the formulation and implementation of public policy for the American people. It is dangerous for the Nation to make decisions for the people without being theologically informed.

6. ESTABLISH IMPARTIAL GOVERNMENT MERIT SYSTEMS - Establish through legislation impartial merit systems with explicit fair employment policies, practices, and procedures. The government must set an example for fairness and justice in its employment practices and contractual agreements and transactions involving the rights of citizens and the equitable allocation of taxpayer money. The subversion of fairness undermines trust in government. True merit systems reinforce trust in government and democracy and contribute to peace and goodwill

7. PERSONAL LIABILITIES FOR RIGHTS VIOLATIONS - Institute legislation for personal liability for any government employee or government agent in the course of their employment, who violates the Civil Rights of a subordinate or another employee

during their employment with the respective agency. This prohibits the violating employee from claiming administrative immunity from prosecution.

8. EMPLOYMENT GRIEVANCE PROCEDURE -- Institute legislation requiring a fair, clear, and understandable grievance policy and procedure that complies with the due process of law contained in the 14th Amendment with reasonable time limits for resolution no to exceed 180 days.

9. PROHIBIT NO HIRE LISTS - Institute legislation that prohibits any government or private agency from placing the name of an employee, former employee, or prospective employee on a designated no-hire list without the due process of law. In the event a person's name is placed on a no-hire list after a due process hearing has been granted, specify the full nature of the no-hire list, including its jurisdiction, effects, duration, removal, and appeal procedure.

10. CONFLICT OF INTEREST DISCLOSURE - Institute legislation that requires legal penalties for an attorney or other legal representative to agree to represent a client for consideration and fail to disclose a known conflict of interest when entering into the contractual agreement with the client of failing to make disclosure after the agreement.

11. CIVIL RIGHTS SEMINARS --- It is recommended that human rights and Civil Rights seminars be held in each government agency monthly at a convenient time and place to keep employees and citizens informed of the laws and the education about the Civil Rights of U.S. Citizens. Such meetings are also recommended for the Church and other faith organizations.

12. PROFESSIONAL CODE OF ETHICS - It is recommended that each government employee be required to subscribe to a designated code of professional ethics with explicit required conduct and behavior. Each employee is entitled to know with specificity what conduct, mannerisms and expectations are required of them. It is recommended that professional codes of ethics be instituted in all agencies where people are served, including the clergy and faith-based organizations.

A SIGNIFICANT LAW FOR
A CULTURE IN CRISIS
Inclusive Character Education

The State of Georgia is able to make a most significant contribution to the Nation, humanity and the World through its ingenuous Character Education Law, House Bill 605, signed into Georgia Law April 1999 by Governor Roy Barnes. This Law mandates the teaching of character education in all public schools throughout the State of Georgia from kindergarten through grade twelve.

This Character Education Law provides for the teaching of twenty-seven non-controversial character traits that are universally acceptable for human development, educational achievement, and cultural enrichment for a humanitarian civilization. These positive character education traits are vitally needed for all the arenas of civilized and productive living for all people. The accelerating American cultural diversity, divisive political identities, ideological conflicts, and increase of crime and violence, warrant serious attention to character education throughout American society.

In his book, New Possibilities for Juvenile Justice, Reverend W. J. Webb enumerates the 27-character traits along with a brief definition of each trait. This information is provided to heighten the awareness of this significant law and to help to disseminate this vital knowledge which is not well known nor publicized. These generic traits for teaching character education are very relevant and vital for the welfare of America and its people.

These universal character education traits are not just needed in the K through 12 classrooms in Georgia, they are needed in all educational, domestic, social, civic, political, religious, business, healthcare, and governmental institutions. It is tragic that this Character Education Law has been in effect for 22 years and so few people are aware of its existence. Although this Law is mandated throughout the public educational districts of Georgia, many of the teachers, principals, and school board members are not aware of this significant vital character education law.

The severity of America's culture crisis necessitates and mandates that all responsible Americans engage in the teaching and spreading of this law!

The Christian Institute of Public Theology

FUNDAMENTAL TRAITS FOR CHARACTER EDUCATION
(Georgia Law, House Bill 605)

The consistent teaching and practice of the enumerated traits of character education below found in Georgia Law have the potential to significantly transform the American culture for good. These character traits are not exhaustive. However, they provide the content for the judgement that Dr. Martin Luther King, Jr. referred to in his classical statement, "Judge others not by the color of their skin, but by the content of their character." These character traits or the noble contents of character, are enumerated and defined so that they can be systematically and intentionally taught and practiced for the ethical, moral, and spiritual transformation of the American culture.

These contents of character can also be seen as golden rules for living. These noble traits and golden rules involve the inner sentiments and aspirations of the mind, heart, and spirit of human beings. The culture of a people and nation reflects the contents of the human beings of the inhabitants of the respective culture and nation. The elevated transformation of societies, cultures and nations must begin and be sustained by the internal values of the minds, sentiments, and spirit of the inhabitants. IT IS CRITICAL THAT CHARACTER EDUCATION BE-COMES A MAJOR PRIORITY IN THE CURRICULUM AND POLICIES OF ALL AMERICAN EDUCATIONAL AGENCIES AND INSTITUTIONS. Additionally, the following 27-character traits are highly and urgently recommended for teaching and practice in all educational, religious, political, business, government, and social institutions. They develop and enhance individual, family, community cultural and national human health and safety.

Fundamental Traits and Definitions for Character Education:

1. Cheerfulness	Be pleasant and encouraging.
2. Citizenship	Be a responsible member of society.
3. Compassion	Develop a caring and positive concern for others.
4. Cleanliness	Practice personal & environmental cleanliness.
5. Cooperation	Learn and practice teamwork with others.
6. Courtesy	Extend friendliness & hospitality to others.
7. Courage	Be brave. Take a stand for the right thing.
8. Creativity	Use your intelligence to think/innovate new things.
9. Diligence	Do not give up. Hold on. Endure to the end.
10. Fairness	Treat all with respect. Give everyone their dues.
11. Generosity	Adhere to a spirit of giving and sharing.
12. Honesty	Be real, authentic, sincere, true.

13. Kindness	Be pleasant, affirming, helpful and positive.
14. Loyalty	Be reliable, dependable, committed, dedicated.
15. Patriotism	Express care, concern, loyalty for your nation.
16. Patience and Virtue	Wait with hope, faith, and endurance.
17. Perseverance	Work, struggle until success is achieved.
18. Punctuality	Be on time or ahead of time for appointments.
19. Respect for Creator	Reverence for God the Creator.
20. Respect for Others	Acknowledge sacredness of human life.
21. Respect for Environment	Keep clean, healthy, productive, and safe.
22. Self-Respect	Value your human dignity, integrity, sacred ness as one who bears God's image
23. Self-Control	Be guided by knowledge, wisdom, respect.
24. Sportsmanship	Play fairly. Lose gracefully. Be a winner.
25. School Pride	Help your school achieve its corporate goals.
26. Temperance	Balance mind, emotions, actions w/reality.

27. Tolerance	Be understanding and considerate of those who do not meet your expectations.

The above twenty-seven-character traits and definitions abstracted from Georgia Law 20-2-145 are universal principles that can be used in a variety of educational settings, growth, fellowship and discussion groups in schools, churches, homes and other agencies and institutions where people gather. These character traits can also be offered for educational and certification credits to participants who wish to teach the Character Education Course on a regular or part-time basis. This information and other related transformational education can be found in the book authored by Willie James Webb, entitled NEW POSSIBILITIES FOR JUVENILE JUSTICE-DIRECTIONS FOR YOUTH TRANSFORMATION.

The Christian Institute of Public Theology promotes and provides information for character education and other culturally transforming knowledge. CIPT, Inc provides certification courses for churches, schools and other institutions and individuals to spread this helpful transforming knowledge for children and all diverse groups with an interest in making a positive difference in these difficult times in America and the world.

CIPT (Christian Institute of Public Theology)

A RESOLUTION FOR THE ENACTMENT OF FEDERAL LEGISLATION KNOWN AS THE AMERICAN ATONEMENT AND BLACK AFRICAN AMERICAN RESTORATION ACT

Preface

This Resolution and proposed legislation are the culmination of the Black African American cry for human and civil justice for 400 years in America. This Resolution and proposed legislation are offered in the spirit of reconciliation, unity, democracy, and patriotism for the United States of America. It is based on the foundations, traditions, Constitution and Declaration of Independence of America. It is biblically based in the will of God. It is based on sound doctrine and theologically guided by the ultimate authority of God. It is socially, morally, ethically, and politically inclusive by the jurisdiction of God, the Creator. The Atonement and Restoration Act is for America to acknowledge, repent and make equitable reparation to Black Americans (Descendants of African American slaves) for the damage of 246 years of slavery and 150 years of subsequent discriminatory damage after the Emancipation Proclamation in 1865 to this present time of 2015 A.D. This Act of Atonement and Restoration is not a time to cast blame and shame on any specific entity or individual. It is a time for national repentance, internal reconciliation, renewal, strengthen and unifying the Nation. This healing, restoration and redemptive process is not solely for Black Americans. It is in the best interest of America to maximize its potential as an exceptional Nation under God.

The American Atonement and Black African American
Restoration Act

Whereas the Black African Americans, the offsprings of Black African American slaves, have endured 246 years of enslavement, from 1619 to 1865 in America, and another 100 years from 1865 to 1965 (1964 Civil Rights Act) of deprivations and subordination through racial segregation and discrimination, and even to this present time of 2015 A.D., fifty years after the 1964 Civil Rights Act. The scales of human and civil justice have never been balanced for the Black African American in America.

Whereas the ongoing accumulative human damages, deficits, suffering and untimely deaths of the Black Americans due to the historical precedents and continuing social injustice, an inhumane toll is taken on the lives of Black Americans as well as the Nation itself. Therefore, it is in the best interest of America and all Americans to enact this legislation for American Atonement and Black American Restoration.

Whereas the corporate and institutional wrongs of 396 years committed against Black African Americans have not been properly acknowledged and corrected by the American Nation, a Nation under God. It is in just, humane, and righteous order for the Nation to set aside a day, a week, a month, or a year to atone for four centuries of wrongs against Black African Americans.

This set-aside time would be healing, renewing and restorative for America. This is a time to focus on the blessings and mission of America according to its moral, ethical, and spiritual foundation. It is a time to refocus on the significance of the foundational documents of the Declaration of Independence, U.S. Constitution, and the

Divine Biblical laws of God. The restorative acts of compensation will bring about prosperity, unity, and strength to the United States of America. The deficits and damages to Black African Americans have also been deficits and damages to America. The enactment of the American Atonement and Black African American Restoration Act will help America purify its spirit and reach a fuller potential as a Nation.

Whereas the Black African Americans have demonstrated for four hundred years unprecedented loyalty to America, the country of their bondage, through sacrificial labor, support, and protection for America, at home and abroad, by giving their blood, sweat, tears, sacrificial service and lives in all of America's wars. It was these Black Americans who chose the civilized pathway of nonviolence that brought about the most successful social revolution in American history and perhaps in the world. The Black cry for social justice, atonement and restoration is the American voice, crying out for healing forgiveness and wholeness.

The American Atonement and Black African American Restoration Act provides for a Federal Commission with appropriate respective state representatives, patriotic Americans, the clergy and Civil Rights organizations appointed by the President of the United States to work out the plans for atonement activities and equitable restoration resources and services to compensate for the damages and deficits to the Black African American citizens (off springs of slaves) of the United States with a twelve month time limit for convening and implementation. The enact of this legislation, the convening of the Federal Atonement and Restoration Commission must complete its work and begin implementation of the ACT before entering into the 500-year century without Black African American restoration.

American Atonement and Black African American Restoration Act

This is a proposal for the above Act of American Atonement and Black African American Restoration along with recommendations for descriptive plans that focus on restoration policies, procedures, activities, and practices developed through the Committees of the Concerned Black Clergy of Metropolitan Atlanta to provide the compensatory restoration for the historically disadvantaged Black African Americans.

Purpose of American Atonement and Restoration Act

The United States of America must begin restoring itself in its most vital, deficient, and neglected areas. The most neglected and deficient segment of America is the Black African American citizens. The Black African Americans have, historically, sustained more human deficits and more social injustice from 1619 to 1865 and even to this present time of 2015 than any other group in America. This includes 246 years of enslavement and another hundred years of racial segregation and racial discrimination. The 1964 Civil Rights Act and the 1965 Voting Rights Act helped, but the problem was not fixed. Fifty years after the death of Dr. Martin Luther King, Jr., systemic racial injustice against Black African Americans persists. A point in time has been reached in America where America, as a Nation, must respond to the four-hundred-year Black cry for justice and prove to the Black Americans and the world that Black American lives matter. There are overwhelming negative disparities indicating that they do not matter as much as White lives. This disparity must be erased for the welfare of the Nation. Black American lives matter because they are human beings and bona fide Indigenous American citizens with U.S. Constitutional Civil and Human Rights. The American Atonement and Black Restoration Act is the most reasonable, just and conciliatory proposal for the critical restoration of America.

Solicitation of Concerned Black Clergy Committee Recommendations

It is recommended that the Concerned Black Clergy Committees, with the approval of the President of Concerned Black Clergy and CBC Board, develop respective written compensatory plans in the most urgent and vital areas for Black African American security, development, and sustained restoration as U. S. citizens with equal rights, opportunities and protection by the U.S. Constitution and the American Government. Compensatory means to elevate, remediate and accelerate to overcome barriers of disparities.

(CBC) Committees, Chairpersons and Restoration Tasks:

Clergy Training Committee   Rev. Willie J. Webb, Chairperson

Devise a plan of educational and theological training for clergy for healthy personal, social, economic, political, spiritual, ethical, and moral development and empowerment of families, educational, religious and community institutions. Teach religious leadership for healthy spiritual growth and the responsible use of science and technology to enhance life for peace, humanity, and civility.

(CBC) Committees, Chairpersons and Restoration Tasks:

Economic Development   Mrs. Alice White Bussey,
Committee   Chairperson

Devise an economic development plan for Black African Americans within the context of compensatory services to elevate and accelerate the advancement of Black American economic development to a restorative level and status compatible with other groups in the American Society.

What kind of support services and resources do the Black Americans need to advance to comparable levels with other groups in America? Identify the barriers that prevent Black Americans from achieving optimum economic development. Describe how these barriers can be removed.

Education Committee   Dr. Carolyn Jackson,
                                                Chairperson

What are the needed sources, resources, personnel, and support to bring about compensatory accelerated learning and educational achievement for Black African American students? Devise a plan to accomplish these objectives and goals for the Black American students. Devise a plan and rationale to justify designating the HBCUS (Historical Black Colleges and Universities) as National Historic Sites to be supported and sustained by the Federal Government due to their significant contributions to America and the world. Devise a plan to designate the approximate 5000 Rosenwald Schools throughout 15 southern states as National Historic Sites and to be utilized for educational and cultural enrichment purposes.

Health Committee	Dr. Reginald Figures, Chairperson

Specify the medical, psychiatric, health and health related educational needs, inclusive of remedial, prevention and promotional of Black African Americans to overcome the gross pathological health disparities of Black Americans. Explore the feasibility of erecting a memorial medical center at Tuskegee in memory of the victims of the Tuskegee Syphilis Study. Tuskegee has had the hospitals. Presently, it has none. Restoration is our context.

Juvenile Justice Committee	Mr. Tony Graves, Chairperson

Specify how juvenile clients can be treated, educated, and reformed while they are in custody and under the supervision of the Court. Create an educational curriculum, a rehabilitative Treatment plan and character development plan for each child who comes into the jurisdiction of the Court. Specify how juveniles can be diverted from the juvenile justice and criminal justice systems. Develop a training, culturally enriching and socially and spiritually transforming program that makes law abiding and law-abiding productive citizens

Political Issues Committee	Councilman Joe Cam, Chairperson

Establish a legal and political network to write, support and advocate for the enactment of the American Atonement and Black African American Restoration Act. Research and share legal and political information to assist Black Americans toward a progressive and sustainable Independent and free citizenship. Institute community schools for political freedom and economic independence in the context of Black restoration. Encourage law schools to require courses in theology, art, and science.

Public Safety Committee	Chief Winston Minor, Chairperson

Evaluate and institute building codes to insure the construction of housing and other buildings in the Black community for safety in structure, materials, and locations, especially in view of natural disasters, such as weather storms, falling trees, fires, floods, erosions, and earthquakes. Keep the Black community educated and informed regarding EPA (Environmental Protection Agency), OSHA (Office of Safety and Health Administration), FDA (Food and Drug Administration) and ARC (Atlanta Regional Commission), Law Enforcement, Fire Department, etc. There is a whole unexploited economic industry in maintaining a safe environment. Many jobs can be created by maintaining a safe environment by the removal of unsafe trees and preventing destructive forest fires.

Religious Affairs Committee	Rev. Timothy McDonald, III, Chairperson

How can the many religious affairs, events, special occasions, different religions, denominations, Black churches, White churches, and others get focused on the religious duty of supporting and making contributions and creating a spiritual environment to restore the historically victimized Black Americans to their rightful place as equals in the sight of God, Democracy, and the United States Constitution in America? How can the Churches, Synagogues, Mosques, Temples, and different religions use their resources of education, art, science and economic resources to support the restoration of the Black Americans in the United States?

Veterans Affairs Committee	Dr. Richard Cobble, Chairperson

Develop a plan, methodology and strategy to insure the appropriate healthcare, and human services for healing, health, and wholeness on a sustainable basis for all veterans and especially the Black veterans who are subject to racial discrimination. Considering that 21 veterans commit suicide daily, nor to mention the neglect in the Veterans Administrations and the many bureaucratic administrative barriers to entitled services, it is urgent that this Restoration Law be enacted.

Voter Registration Committee	Rev. Albert E. Love, Chairperson

Devise a plan, policy, procedure and practice and advocacy to educate and ensure the realization of the optimum voting potential of the Black community within the context of Black restoration through optimum Black voting and Black political participation and empowerment. Write a plan for ongoing sustainable Black voter registration education and community and political involvement.

The above committee reports will serve as guides for the Legislative Commission to decide on what issues to consider for the Black African American Restoration. It is true that Congressman John Conyers of Michigan has submitted Reparation Legislation annually for several decades. However, the concept of Restoration is broader than the concept of Reparation.

Restoration aims at restoring Black Institutions, Townships, Communities, Churches, Schools, legacies, heritage, patents, property, culture, and social standing, etc. The aim of restoration goes beyond just monetary reparation. Restoration is asking for a safe environment for Black people to live without being discriminated against and victimized because of color or any other ethnic, racial, or religious characteristic on a sustainable basis.

Presented to Concern Black Clergy as a report from Clergy Training Committee and submitted to: President Rev. Frank C. Brown, Concerned Black Clergy of Metropolitan Atlanta, Ga.

Clergy Training Committee Report, Chair, Rev. Willie J. Webb, CIPT, Inc.
Atlanta, Ga. August 17, 2015

SALVATION RESOLUTIONS FOR THE PUBLIC GOOD
Resolutions for Cultural Transformation
-The Public Theologian-

1. Resolution for Character Education	
2. Resolution for Ethical Education	
3. Resolution for Biblical Education	
4. Resolution for Artistic Education	
5. Resolution for Vocational Education	
6. Resolution for Theological Education	
7. Resolution for Administrative Merit Systems	
8. Resolution for U.S. Constitution Education	
9. Resolution for Declaration of Independence Education	
10. Resolution for Pledge of Allegiance to U.S. Flag	
11. Resolution for Gender Education and Roles	
12. Resolution for Religious Pluralism Education	

13. Resolution for Cultural Diversity Education & Competence	
14. Resolution for Church and State Synchronization	
15. Resolution for Human heterogeneous Cooperation	
16. Resolution for Nations Under God	
17. Resolution for Democratic Government	
18. Resolution for Child Care and Child Rearing	
19. Resolution for Courtship and Marriage	
20. Resolution for Transmission of Moral Values	
21. Resolution for Assimilation of Christian Values	
22. Resolution for Public Office Qualifications	
23. Resolution for Maintaining Quality Public Schools	

It is recommended that a thorough one-page resolution be written of each of the resolutions above to be presented, submitted, and transmitted to appropriate representatives, pastors, ministers, churches, educational and governmental institutions. These resolutions are written to become public policy, ordinances, legislation, and laws. These resolutions are to be studied, discussed in various groups, classes and incorporated in educational curricula in all educational institutions from the public schools through the university systems of higher learning. The basic universal truths contained in these resolutions must be incorporated in the established American institutions of family, church, school, business, and government in order to effect the vitally needed cultural transformation in the American society. These resolutions are designed for urgent positive implementation of actions and change for the gift of humanity.

FATHER TO SON
BE A MAN BOY, BE A MAN

You may be born in the hood, and misunderstood,
But be a man boy, be a man.

You may be low rated, and failed in school, but you don't
Must be a fool. Be a man boy.
Be a man.

You may be criticized and scandalized. You may be
Marginalized and ostracized,
But be a man boy, be a man.

You may be neglected and rejected, and sometimes Harshly
corrected. Be a man.
Some day you will be
Respected. Be a man boy, be a man.

Doors have been shut in your face. You have been
Denied and deprived in life's competitive race.
Be a man boy, be a man.

Sometimes, you may feel unwanted; you may be
Cheated and mistreated, be a man, you won't be defeated.
Be a man boy, be a man.

You listen to me boy!
You think like a man. You look like a man.
You talk like a man. You walk like a man.
You work like a man. You stand like a man.
God made you a man.
Be a man boy, be a man!

(Anonymous)

CHAPTER 6
THEOLOGICAL LEADERSHIP EDUCATIONAL THEOLOGICAL LEADERSHIP IMPER ATIVES

FOUNDATIONS FOR LEADERSHIP

1. Know the Truth. Learn Relevant Knowledge. Be Wise, Reasonable, Rational, understanding and Focused.
2. Embrace Truth, Justice, Goodness, Beauty, Hope and Mercy.
3. Follow Pathways of Righteousness and the Light of Enlightenment.
4. Obey God. Oppose Evil, Hatred and Wickedness.

LEADERSHIP REQUIREMETS

1. Obedience to the Divine Imperatives: COME, TARRY AND GO: Come to yourself, Come to Jesus. Tarry for the Education, Regeneration, Identification, Mission, and Empowerment. GO to your own people with the Gospel. Go to other people with this Gospel. Go to the whole world with this Gospel.
2. Education and training program of Certified, Degreed, Licensed, Ordained Intellectual Competence. This is a part of the whole armor of God that is required.
3. The Optimum Scientific, Artistic, Legalistic, Theistic Educational Achievement of Recognized Bodies of Knowledge and Educational Institutions.
4. Endowed with a Solid Moral Character of Human Dignity, Reverence and Integrity Based on A Specific Belief

System that is rooted in Biblical Authority and Established by God.

5. Educated through a Qualified Certification of Biblical Literacy and Knowledge-based Competent Documented Study.

6. The Endowment of the New Birth and the New Creature in Jesus Christ following the Admonition of Jesus to Nicodemus: "You Must be Born Again." You must be able to Discern and Engage in the Spiritual Domain of God.

7. Endowed with the ability to Discern Spirits whether they be of God. Must be able to Discern False Spirits and False Prophets and Anti-Christ Spirits. Jesus admonished his Disciples to be Wise as Serpents. Know the God Spirit that Confesses that Jesus has Come in the Flesh.

8. Must be Grounded in Universal Principles of Love, Goodness, Equality, Freedom, Justice, Hope and Faith; and not be Captivated by Cultism, Sectarianism, Racism, Partisan Divisions, Genderism, and other Divisive ISMS. Embrace Universal Values and Principles.

9. Must understand the Skills to Disclose: COST BENEFIT ANALYSIS, VALUES CLARIFICATION, CONFLICT RESOLUTION, SUCCESS IDENTITY, FUTURE ORIENTATION FOCUS, MENTAL STATE AND STATUS ORIENTATION.

10. THE POSITIVE TRANSFORMATION OF HATRED, RAGE, AND ANGER INTO USEFUL SERVICES AND CONTRIBUTIONS. UTILIZE THE ENERGY OF RAGE FOR USEFUL WORK AND OTHER POSITIVE FOCUS.

11. CREATE A TRANSITION FROM WHAT IS TO WHAT OUGT TO BE ACCORDING TO THE BIBLICAL STANDARDS OF GOD. FROM DOUBT TO FAITH, FROM HATE TO LOVE....

12. INSTILL A SIGNIFICANT PURPOSE IN LIFE WORTHY OF ABONDONING ALL TO FOLLOW. ADD TO THIS PURPOSE THE SIGNIFICANT BEING CREATED IN THE IMAGE OF GOD.

The Christian Institute of Public Theology

SPECIALIZED TRAINING
RECOMMENDED
FOR
AMERICAN PUBLIC OFFICE
AND POLITICAL LEADERSHIP

The seriousness and intricacies of public office and political leadership requires specialized political training and sufficient standards of professional qualifications. The Civil Rights and human rights of Americans, as well as the security of the Nation must not be subjected to incompetent, unethical, unprofessional, unpatriotic, and otherwise unfit public and political representatives. This is an impending priority that must be addressed and appropriately legislated.

The standards for qualifying for public office in the United States are for the most part, are outdated. The standards for qualifying for public office in the United States have not kept pace with the great momentous social, cultural, demographic, technological and global changes that have taken place in the past 60 years (beginning around 1954). In addition to the impact of integration and the Civil Rights movement in the 1960's, over 50 million cultural and religious diverse immigrants have come to America. Substantial social, political, and economic changes are being created to accommodate the transformed heterogeneous society in America. America nor Americans were prepared for these dramatic changes. Simplistic answers and solutions are not sufficient to meet the demands and challenges of the complexities of the American society and institutions in this twenty First Century. Standards for leadership and political representation must be raised. The present incompetence and confusion are not just unsustainable, they jeopardize the lives of citizens and the security of the whole Nation.

A specialized contextual curriculum for the education and training of public officials and political leaders must be developed to meet the vast human needs, critical challenges, and the acute cultural crisis that America faces in this 21st Century. Fit-For duty standards for public officials must be legislated now. They are long overdue. This legislation must require minimum standards of educational, experiential, professional, patriotic and fitness competence commensurate with the public job responsibilities and compatibility with the U. S. Constitution. The curriculum must be so contextualized that it will recognize equity and justice for the diverse populations who have suffered historically and presently due to no fault of their own. The Black African Americans (off springs of American slaves) is a case in point. There are ways to approximate and objectify justice for all people respectively.

This curriculum must reflect basic understanding of science, art, law, and theology as they relate to and embrace justice, truth, and righteousness of the whole gospel for the whole person and for the whole

The prospective public official must be able to distinguish between
Divine law, natural law, and statutory law
The Christian Institute of Public Theology Atlanta, Georgia

CORE VALUES OF AMERICA

These core values have served America well. They have made America the most prosperous and the most powerful country on earth. These values have afforded the citizens and inhabitants of America more freedom and opportunities than any other country on earth. These values must be asserted by all people of goodwill who value freedom and God's gift of human life:

1. One Nation under God.
2. Judeo-Christian Holy Bible.
3. The Declaration of Independence.
4. Representative government by the people, for the people and of the people.
5. The Church of Christ.
6. The common language of English.
7. The Apostles' Creed.
8. The United States Constitution.
9. U.S. Motto - "In God We Trust."
10. The Pledge of Allegiance.
11. Individual freedom.
12. Freedom of speech, religion, press, assembly.
13. Due process of law for life, liberty, and property.
14. The equal protection of the law.
15. Self defense
16. Freedom from unreasonable searches and seizures.
17. Respect for the dignity and sacredness of human life.
18. Freedom from involuntary servitude.
19. The institution of family and marriage between a man and a woman.
20. Compulsory school attendance for children

21. Equal education and equal employment opportunities.
22. The free enterprise system.
23. Separation of governmental powers - Executive, Legislative and Judicial.
24. Redress of grievances.

This is not intended to be an exhaustive list of core American values. However, it is important for every American to be knowledgeable of their core values to appreciate the historical sacrifices and the importance of their perpetuation for generations to come.

(Christian Institute of Public Theology)
May 25, 2010

SOME OBJECTIVES OF CLERGY TRAINING AND EDUCATION

1. Provide a valid theological credential for the practice of pastoral care, public theology, and parish ministry. The professional, ethical, and effective practice of ministry requires valid certifications, licensure, and/or ordination by the church or other religious institution.
2. Provide valid and relevant foundational biblical/theological knowledge for professional ministerial practice in a diverse, heterogeneous, and pluralistic culture.
3. Learn pastoral care counseling skills for individual, group, family, crisis intervention, forensic and mentoring services.
4. Learn how to provide alcohol and other drug education, evaluations, diagnostic assessments, community referrals, case management and other treatment recovery counseling services for the alcohol and other drug abuse clients.
5. Assist clergy and laity to obtain professional respect and credibility along with other allied professionals in the government and other political, social, and human services arenas.
6. Develop the appropriate training, knowledge, and skills to have a credible prophetic voice and the input of values and ideas to influence public opinion, public policy, and corporate decision-making for the common good of society.
7. To become a knowledgeable, enlightened member and guardian of the vanguard for truth, freedom, social justice, human and Civil Rights.

8. Be involved in the organized effort to provide credible support for the promotion of ethical, moral, and spiritual values, sound principles and doctrine, academic achievement, economic development so that truth, social justice, and freedom will prevail throughout the earth.

9. To provide and advocate for responsible, accountable, effective, productive, benevolent, and redemptive leadership based on the whole gospel for the whole person and for the whole world.

10. Stop the literary trend of distorting and misrepresenting historical facts, established traditions, sound doctrines and validated truths of history. Focusing on a specific issue of misrepresentation, the Church must demand cessation and eradication of the false literary use of B.C.E (Before Common Era) as a substitute for B.C. (Before Christ); and C.E. (Common Era) as a substitute for A.D. (Anno Domini - In the Year of Our Lord).

GOALS AND THEMES FOR PUBLIC THEOLOGY

Theological Approaches for Cultural Transformation
Foundations for Biblical Exposition
(Christian Institute of Public Theology)

1. Biblical Truth Dissemination	25. The Universality of Justice
2. Artistic Creations	26. Righteousness of God
3. Exemplification of Love	27. Refinement of Humanity
4. Earth Replenishment	28. Valid Universal Principles
5. Ethical Codes Development	29. God's Spirit and Truth
6. Environmental Protection	30. Man Made in God's Image
7. Environmental Safety	31. Purpose of Human Life
8. Ethical Actions	32. Universal Biblical Truths
9. Ethical Reformation	33. The Bible and Human Nature
10. Esthetics of Beauty	34. Biblical Salvation Knowledge
11. Equity of Justice	35. The Spiritual Domain
12. Cultured Sociality	36. Cultural Transformation
13. Civilized Expressions	37. Kingdom of Righteousness
14. Characterization of Goodness	38. The Nature of Love
15. Health and Wholeness	39. The Gift of Life
16. Humanitarian Innovations	40. The Gift of Jesus Christ
17. Cultural Refinement	41. The Household of Faith
18. Decency and Order	42. Universal Christian Values
19. Revelations of Excellence	43. The Armor of God
20. Reality of Truth	44. Transcending Power
21. Spiritual Discernment	45. God's Ultimate Authority
22. Redemptive Human Services	46. God's Sovereign
23. Humanization of Technology	47. New Creature in Christ
24. God's Ethical Standards for Humanity	48. Salvation in Jesus Christ

LET US BEGIN THIS NOBLE MISSION OF GOD

The above-enumerated goals and themes apply to all humanity on earth. They represent the love of God for humanity and the gift of God to save humanity God provides these goals and themes to collaborate with humanity and enlighten humanity; to enrich, sustain, enhance, and show the way to abundant life and eternal salvation through Jesus Christ. These goals for humanity and themes for love and living have the potential to build God's Kingdom on earth, where all mankind can live as brothers and sisters. The Bible is the blueprint for life and human survival. These goals and themes for a living can heal sick nations, transform corrupt cultures, and establish God's Kingdom of Righteousness on the earth. LET US WORK TOWARDS THESE GOALS AND SPREAD THIS GOOD NEWS OF GOD THROUGHOUT THE EARTH!

TO HELP AMERICANS
REQUIREMENT PRIORITIES FOR THE NATION

One:

Responsible and accountable stewardship and leadership of the citizens and the resources of God to create and sustain a prosperous economy that affords equitable needs and opportunities, as a free people, for a quality livelihood and a quality life for all persons in the Nation.

Two:

In addition to the requirement of a high school education, all applicable able-bodied persons shall be required to receive appropriate training and education for socio-economic readiness for a job, vocation, career, or constructive volunteerism to earn a livelihood and be a productive and law-abiding citizen.

Three:

The requirement of a healthy lifestyle course for all students from kindergarten through high school that includes healthy diet, hygiene, grooming, thinking, relationships, leisure, recreation, activities, habits, family, school, community, and environment.

Four:

All relevant individuals must receive functional, technological, and educational literacy training. There are millions of Americans being deprived of entitled benefits and services due to educational and technological deficiencies and deprivations. Millions of citizens do not have the technological capabilities to access available benefits and services.

Five:

Require the establishment of protective facilities for the eventualities of natural and manmade disasters, along with the appropriate personnel, education, and training. Legislate building codes that require the home building and construction industries to build safer homes and other buildings and structures in every community. Most Americans are "sitting ducks" for disasters.

Six:

Require and enforce professional ethics in all government and business agencies to protect the citizens and the public. Professional ethics require validated true knowledge, optimum competence, a benevolent code of ethics, and investment in the common good of society.

Seven:

Require and enforce the practice of JUSTICE, COMPETENCE, PROFESSIONALISM, ETHICS, EFFICIENCY, AND REVERENCE in all branches of government and business. Require and enforce these practices in the LEGISLATIVE, JUDICIAL and EXECUTIVE branches of all Federal and Local Governments throughout all jurisdictions of the UNITED STATES OF AMERICA.

Eight:

Require a Course of Study on U.S. Constitutional Literacy for all Americans. This significant Document and Law of the United States of America is ignored and unknown by most Americans. (We perish for lack of knowledge).

Nine:

Require JUSTICE, RIGHTEOUSNESS, EQUITY, FREEDOM, LIBERTY, CIVILITY, HUMANENESS, HUMAN HEALTH, WHOLENESS, TRUTH, RESPECT FOR HUMAN LIFE, AND REVERENCE FOR GOD according to the HOLY BIBLE, Sacred Literature, The U. S. Founding Principles, and the U.S. Constitution. (SEEK THE KINGDOM OF GOD FIRST).

Ten:

Require policies, education, training, and procedures to promote healthy living and illness prevention to maximize the quality of human life and to minimize the morbidity and preoccupation with the pathologies associated with illness and death.

Eleven:

Establish sound doctrines and ethical principles congruent with truth and verifiable quantitative knowledge for safeguarding HUMAN RIGHTS, HUMAN FREEDOM, and HUMAN LIFE

Twelve:

Require the teaching and the availability of true Biblical Theological Salvation Knowledge and Character Education in all public schools and educational facilities. Humanity is perishing for lack of God's SALVATION KNOWLEDGE the soul is lost, and all is lost.

CHRISTIAN ASSOCIATION OF PUBLIC THEOLOGIANS
(CBC Clergy Training Committee Report)

This is a proposal for clergy leadership and Church involvement in the establishment of educational training, pastoral care, human liberation, and developmental service centers. This proposal is in response to the unprecedented American cultural crisis, which is accompanied by the disproportionate deterioration and human destruction in the Black community.

Recommendations for Clergy and Faith Leaders:

1. Establish priorities with a focus on Black American educational, economic, social, political, cultural, and spiritual development and empowerment.
2. Increase the budget for advanced education, skilled training, information technological expertise, pastoral care, and redemptive theological community involvement. Substantial economic investment must be made to salvage the values and the means for human and national survival.
3. Recruit, train, certify, license, and qualify skilled and competent theologically guided community chaplains, teachers, counselors, advocates, and other human services providers for the motivation, inspiration, restoration, and liberation for the downtrodden and victimized Americans.
4. Establish libraries, reading rooms, classrooms, study halls, educational forums, counseling, treatment services and fellowship centers. Committed ministers and designated places are needed to provide human restoration and

growth services for human health and human survival with dignity.

5. Establish case management, crisis intervention, community referral and advocacy for the deprived, traumatized, and victimized persons in need of pastoral care and human services for stabilization, remediation, and ongoing human support systems.

6. Increase the quality (competently trained), relevance and volume of Bible study (voluntary) in the Church, schools (after school day) and in other community facilities.

7. Form cooperative alliances with other churches, clergy, faith groups, and community groups for joint education, training, ministries, and services. People in need want to know WHERE to go for help - THE TIME AND PLACE and WHO is providing the helpful services.

THIS PROPOSAL CAN BE INITIATED BY INTERESTED INDIVIDUALS AND CORPORATE GROUPS

Rev. W. J. Webb,
Chair, Clergy Training Committee of Concerned Black Clergy

Rev. Frank Cornelius Brown
President, Concerned Black Clergy

CHRISTIAN ASSOCIATION OF PUBLIC THEOLOGIANS, INC.

A Caœes wPaxys wæoGzȷcar bdȷr yȷ dPzaφb Svza wd

Hdq zxyȷ s œ ϙvϙ ys yȷ dxz wd Ws vœ ax yazi j y, xs yȷ ayȷ dq aã adaaœdys i ȷàdȷr xyvɛbyȷsr ȷr xs zr c cs byyȷr dar c ys bsr ɛzyd yȷ sxdá j s bsr ywacȷbyȷy. Tȷyzx 1:9.

A Plea to My Colleagues - Your Wisdom and Guidance are Requested:

As founder and CEO of the Christian Association of Public Theologians (CAPT), I am seeking your participation in a unifying program - The Public Square - which we have launched to address, in a more holistic and expansive way, the spiritual uplift of our communities. The Public Square is an online magazine that facilitates our goal of reawakening and expanding the ministry of Jesus.

This is a call for pastoral writings and thoughts from you, on the issues confronting our communities and the Biblically based guidance available to address those issues. As critical matters press upon your hearts and minds, in your day-to-day ministry, we hope to receive from you, a one-to three-page discourse on a particular issue, that includes what you have witnessed, your educated and observational analysis of the problem, and references to the Biblically based guidance that address the problem. What we seek are "ground-level" insights - that you, as ministers of the Church, are seeing among your congregates and in your communities; what troubles you about what you are seeing; and your knowledge and thoughts, based on Biblical doctrine, that frame a perspective to address those situations. This can be painlessly accomplished as you go about preparing your regular weekly sermons and lessons; or you may find that in approaching this task, you may become even more inspired in identifying the focus of those sermons and lessons.

We now face what is perhaps the most challenging time in the history of the United States and in our communities. We are, indeed, witnessing a serious spiritual crisis as never before. The evidence is rapidly increasing that social, political, and economic problems are getting out of hand and, worse, that human to human interactions have seriously degenerated. Thus, The Public Square has been established to assemble and put before the public as much knowledge as possible about the capacity of human beings to control themselves and, thus, their society, by capturing God's combined powerful consensus, understandings, and guidance from the wider community of clergy.

People all around us are hurting. Interactions between people are absent the element of redemptive love. So many have simply lost their way and are relying on secular-based, popular, faddish, and entertainment-based messages to guide them. We are seeing this manifested by:

- a decline in Biblical and Spiritual Belief.
- the abandonment of Character, Integrity, and Values; laissez-faire morality
- family neglect, disintegration, and child abuse;
- substandard schooling that fails to prepare young people for life;
- the confusion and chaos resulting from gender hostilities:
- more extensive male and female juvenile delinquency:
- alcohol and substance addictions:
- marital disregard and abandonment:
- workplace offenses and decline in professionalism:

- massive gentrification, leading to displacement of worthy citizens;
- inadequate, unaffordable housing and homelessness;
- a decline in food and water quality, the corporatization of agricultural and water resources, and corporate concealment; and
- a significant expansion of eroticism and pornography.

These are but a few of the disturbing developments we are witnessing. I am certain you can add to the list.

Many people may have material wealth, and may be polite and industrious, and yet they are hovering on the brink of spiritual and moral ruin, as Jesus admonished the Pharisees. So many are living only for themselves and with no goal to their living but self-pleasure. Many, many more are becoming chronically poor, being rapidly dehumanized and cast aside.

Each of you can prevent such a fate from overtaking our communities, for NOW is the time to expand the delivery of the powerful and life-sustaining messages of God, as we have most certainly witnessed them. As the flock's doctrinal guardians and overseers of the church's life, each of you has the privilege of sitting during our communities, equipped by and accountable to God for feeding and care. And ministry of the people. God has called upon us to shepherd the people to His Word-the proven principles for living to which we have committed ourselves.

It cannot be understated that the answers to what we face take shape out of the values we hold, and the extent to which we are able to influence those values, as well as the urgency we attach to them, will govern what is to become of our communities. The stability of our communities and our nation depends upon the collective soul of the people.

Without integrity of character in the individual, a nation can have no real strength or soundness.

Public theology is the result of the growing need for theology to interact with published issues of contemporary society. It seeks to engage in dialogue with different academic disciplines such as politics, economics, cultural studies, and religious studies, as well as with spirituality, globalization, and society in general.

We ask that you join us in this most important endeavor. Help us to educate, instruct, and re-direct our community to Life, by submitting your written insights and guidance for publication in the online Public Square magazine.

THE MISSION OF THE GOSPEL
THROUGH THE MINISTRY OF JESUS CHRIST

1. Feed and Nurture: John 21:15-17; Matthew 25:31-46
2. Love & Evangelize: John 13:34, 4:16; Mark 12:30-31; 1Cor. 13
3. Teach, Preach & Witness: Matthew 28:19; Mark 16:15
4. Heal & Restore: Luke 4:18-19; John 11:25
5. Liberate & Elevate: Luke 4:18-19; 1John 4:1-2; John 8:32
6. Build & Establish: Matthew 6:33, Matthew 16:18; Rev. 11:15
7. Comfort & Encourage: John 14:16-18; Matthew 5:1-12
8. Warn & Prophesy: Ezekiel 3:17-21; Amos 4:12; Matthew 3:3; Col 1:28
9. Defend & Comfort: Psalm 82:3-4; Matthew 18:8-9; Ephesians 6:11-17
10. Have Dominion: Genesis 1:28; Matthew 24:14; Romans 13:1
11. Witness Truth 8i Light: Matthew 5:16, 33; John 14:6
12. Follow Jesus Christ: John 14:6; Acts 4:12; Isaiah 45:23; Phil 2:9-11

There is a place and a duty for all believers in Jesus Christ to participate in the mission and ministry of Jesus Christ in whatever position or calling you may be involved regardless to your title. There is plenty of room in the Kingdom of God as Expressed in (Matthew 9:37-38) and (Luke 10:2). The harvest is great and the laborers are few.

The Christian Institute of Public Theology, Inc.
Atlanta, Georgia

DEMOCRATIC PUBLIC POLICY PREFERENCES
FOR
A JUST, HEALTHY AND PROSPEROUS
AMERICA

1. Pro-Human Life as Sacred from God the Creator.
2. Patriotism for America as a Nation under God.
3. Acknowledge America and all Nations as Nations under God.
4. Acknowledge the Truth of the Holy Bible as Validated by History.
5. Acknowledge the Historical Truths of Jesus Christ as Savior Sent by God.
6. Uphold the Truths of the Bible and the Laws of the U.S. Constitution.
7. Support Judicial Equal Justice under Just Laws, God, and the U.S. Constitution.
8. Support Individual and religious Liberty under God and the U.S. Constitution.
9. Acknowledge and Respect the Sacredness of Christmas, the Cross and other Validated Religious Celebrations and Historical Monumental Symbols.
10. Establish and Utilize Just Merit-Based Administrative and Judicial Systems for Fairness, Justice, and Equality.
11. Respect, Support, Teach and Encourage the True, Sound, Ethical and Moral Traditional Social Values Based on Historical Precedents, Scientific Knowledge, and Biblical Truth.
12. Provide the Utmost Support for Public Education as Standard Education Designed for the Public Good as Paid for by Public Funds. Accommodate Charter Schools and other Private Bono-Fide Educational Institutions with Private Funding.

13. As Mandated by Law in Georgia, Teach Comprehensive Character Education from Kindergarten through Twelfth Grade. THE SERIOUS LETHAL MORAL VIOLENT CRISIS IN AMERICA DEMANDS MAJORING IN CHARACTER EDUCATION UNDERGIRDED BY CHRISTIAN EDUCATION.

14. As Mandated by Georgia Law, TEACH THE OLD TESTAMENT AND NEW TESTAMENT AS HISTORY, LITERATURE AND BIBLICAL KNOWLEDGE. THE DESTRUCTION OF THESE CHILDREN FOR LACK OF BIBLICAL (THEOLOGICAL KNOWLEDGE IS DESTROYING AMERICA AND THE BLESSINGS OF GOD UPON AMERICA.

15. Support Israel and Its Democracy and All God-Fearing Nations. AMERICA HAS BEEN BLESSED TO BE A BLESSING TO THE WORLD. CHRISTIANITY WAS BORN OUT OF ISRAEL (Judaism). AMERICA HAS BEEN KNOWN AS A CHRISTIAN NATION. USA IS IN THE MIDDLE OF JERUSALEM. THE UNITED STATES OF AMERICA HAS A CONNECTION WITH ISRAEL AND JERUSALEM. AMERICA MUST NOT FORFEIT THE BLESSINGS OF GOD!

16. Establish Appropriate Educational, Ethical, Moral, Patriotic, Professional, and Otherwise Competent and Fit for duty. Responsibility and Accountability Standards for All Elective and Public Officials Who Represent the People.

The Christian Institute of Public Theology

CHRISTIAN ASSOCIATION OF PUBLIC THEOLOGIANS, INC.
CHRISTIAN INSTITUTE OF PUBLIC THEOLOGY, INC.

Willie J. Webb
President and CEO
P.O. Box 3148
Atlanta, GA 30302

THE GUIDE FOR GOD'S INTERVENTION

1. Reverently and fervently, pray-
2. Cry out to God for His Mercy-
3. Trust in His power-
4. Rely and depend on His mercy-
5. Stand on the promises of God-
6. Believe in God's goodness-
7. Believe that He cares-
8. Believe that He is able-
9. Believe in the Exalted Name of Jesus Christ-
10. Accept God's Love Gift to the world in Jesus Christ-
11. Lift up your eyes, your head, and your heart to God-
12. Ask in all humility-
13. Seek God with all your mind, heart, soul, and strength-
14. Resolve-That love never fails-
15. Persevere in hope-
16. Keep knocking until the door opens-
17. Patiently, wait on God-
18. Pray for God's healing and wholeness-
19. Join God's Kingdom work-
20. Hold on and hold out-
21. Overcome through the power of faith-
22. Be assured that God will not leave you nor forsake you-
23. Continue to reach up with hope-
24. Continue to reach out with love-

FOUNDATIONS FOR CULTURAL AND HUMAN RESTORATION
Through
The Cultivation of Productive Civilized Social Processes &
The Enhancement of Positive Human Relationship Roles

The Christian Institute of Public Theology

The following social processes can be used and managed to identify, transmit and sustain ethical values, positive human relationships, and a healthy civilized culture:

1. Avoidance		7. Association	
2. Antagonism		8. Reconciliation	
3. Competition		9. Cooperation	
4. Conflict		10. Affirmation	
5. Affiliation		11. Restoration	
6. Accommodation		12. Assimilation	

It is the duty of the Church, government, and democratic institutions to protect the God given unalienable divine and natural rights of all people through social justice and human rights based on the self-evidentiary truths that all people are created equal and are endowed by the Creator of certain unalienable rights; among them, are life, liberty, justice and the pursuit of wellbeing and happiness. These unalienable rights and protections can be significantly enhanced and nurtured through the following institutionalized human and civilized relationships:

1. Kinship		7. Courtship	
2. Friendship		8. Guardships	
3. Partnership		9. Citizenship	
4. Companionship		10. Leadership	
5. Fellowship		11. Sportsmanship	
6. Membership		12. Championship	

The goal is to include everyone in human relationships and enhance these relationships to enrich the culture and the lives of each person and build God's Kingdom of righteousness, love, justice, goodness, and beauty on earth with peace and goodwill to all people of God.

GOD CENTERED WORSHIP
(THE CHRISTIAN INSTITUTE OF PUBLIC
THEOLOGY)

God-centered worship focuses on a reverent and solemn spiritual atmosphere and the presence of the Holy Spirit in the Body of Christ. This spiritual atmosphere includes sacred reverence, adoration, and glory to God. Thoughts and ideas are elevated to the heavenly realm. This is precious communion time with God.

This focus on the reverence, adoration and glorification of God rises above and beyond the distractions of the world. This meditation and concentration on the presence of God minimizes the distractions of the world and worldly things. This spiritual and sacred atmosphere allows and facilitates the minds, hearts, spirits, and souls of the worshippers to concentrate, focus and meditate on the adoration and worship of God.

This God-centered spiritual worship atmosphere is accomplished through the worshippers being assembled with reverence and in decency and order to worship God in truth and in spirit. This God-centered worship is enhanced by worship leaders who allow themselves to be used as vessels of God to meditate, to sing praises of glory and honor to God; to recite and exhort God's Word; to teach and preach the Word and the Gospel of salvation in Jesus Christ. The God-centered worship diminishes self-pride and exalts God, highly and lifted.

The welcome and the announcements in the church bulletin section allows for references to worldly matters, business matters, human, personal and community concerns. This section of the bulletin is a break from the God centered spiritual worship to attend church, personal and business matters during the church service.

The God centered worship service resumes when the tithes, gifts and offerings are announced. Songs of praise and prayers begin, as minds, hearts, spirits, and souls are elevated in great expectation and anticipation to hear the preached message of God; invitation to discipleship, followed by the benediction, the fellowship, and departures - until we meet again.

Pastor W. J. Webb, Foundation Baptist Church

THE SKILLED THEOLOGICAL HELPER
ESSENTIALS FOR HEALING AND WHOLENESS
THE CHRISTIAN INSTITUTE OF PUBLIC
THEOLOGY

The following generic helpers must be trained with certain knowledge and skills to maximize the effectiveness of the needed help they propose to provide. The human helping skills must be undergirded by biblical knowledge, Christian education, and professional ethics. The first prerequisite and obligation of the skilled theological helper is to do no harm. "First, do no harm," comes from the Hippocratic Oath as a code of ethics used by medical doctors. First, do no harm, is a fundamental ethical code for the skilled theological practitioner, as well as other human service providers. Love and wisdom must be employed in the human helping process.

The "do no harm" ethical code is required by the following theological skilled helpers as well as for the medical physician:

1. Teachers for their students	7. Physicians for their patients
2. Mentors for their mentees.	8. Healers for the sick.
3. Educators for the unlearned.	9. Ministers for those in bondage.
4. Guardians for children and minors.	10. Pastors for their congregations
5. Counselors for their clients	11. Priests for their parishioners.
6. Therapists for addicted and depressed.	12. Prophets for the wayward and lost.

The skilled theological helpers are in superordinate positions over those who are in subordinate positions. It is unethical and a violation of a sacred trust and an abuse of professional authority to do harm to those who are vulnerable and entrusted to be helped. The skilled theological helper is a servant and a vessel of God. Their service and effectiveness represent nor just what they do, but also who they are in the Kingdom of God. The mission of God's servants becomes the mission of God.

It must be noted that many skilled theological helpers do not have specific titles. Special titles do not always provide helpful services. The "Good Samaritan who helped the wounded man on the Jericho Road did not have a special title as did the priest and the Levite. The priest and the Levite failed to help the wounded man. It was a man with no specific title who provided the needed help.

Jesus Christ sets the ethical tone for the theological skilled helpers in Luke 4:18-19:

THE SPIRIT OF THE LORD IS UPON ME, BECAUSE HE HATH ANOINTED ME TO PREACH THE GOSPEL TO THE POOR; HE HATH SENT ME TO HEAL THE BROKENHEARTED, TO PREACH DELIVERANCE TO THE CAPTIVES, AND RECOVERING OF SIGHT TO THE BLIND, TO SET AT LIBERTY THEM THAT ARE BRUISED, TO PREACH THE ACCEPTABLE YEAR OF THE LORD.

The Christian Institute of Public Theology

CHAPTER 7
LETTERS OF ADVOCACY AND APPEAL
God's Hierarchy of Order and Authority
For
Human Governance
"Let every soul be subject unto the higher powers. For there is no power but of God: the powers that be are ordained of God." (Romans 13:1). "Render therefore to all their dues... ...Owe no man anything." Romans 13:7-8)

The Triune God
The Holy Bible

Justice, Truth, Righteousness, Equality,
Freedom, Goodness, Peace
Judeo-Christian Doctrines and Principles
The Governing Authorities of the United States of America In God We Trust Under God The Declaration of Independence The United States Constitution Democratic Form of Government Of the People, for the People, by the People Democracy Equal Rights, Equal Opportunity, Equal Treatment
Pledge of Allegiance
- One Nation Under God –

All human beings and Americans, as well as their identity characteristic groups of RACES, SEX, AGE, COLOR, GENDER, LANGUAGE, NATIONALITY, RELIGION,

BELIEF SYSTEM, ETHICITY, MARITAL STATUS, SOCIAL CLASS, ECONOMIC STATUS, and EDUCATIONAL OR PROFESSIONAL STATUS, are subject to the universal Divine, Natural, and congruent Statute Laws.

The Christian Association of Public Theologians
Atlanta, Georgia

MOREHOUSE COLLEGE GOLDEN TIGERS' 50TH YEAR REUNION REFLECTIONS BY ALUMNUS WILLIE JAMES WEBB, MAY 13, 2011

Fellow Morehouse Classmates of 1961:

We are certainly numbered among those who are blessed by God to be alive and able to contemplate and celebrate our class reunion after 50 years. Despite our narrow escapes from the "fire, dungeon and sword," we are still vertically positioned on our feet, clothed, sustained, and in our right mind. Thanks be to God for His countless blessings and tender mercies. Let us pause for a moment of silence in memory of those classmates who have transitioned and those who are not able to be with us at this 50th Reunion.

Thanks to Richard Hope and the 1961 Class Coordinating Committee for requesting me to share some reflections on the sojourn of this unique and special class at Morehouse College from 1957 to 1961. The significance behind the providential circumstances that caused our pathways to converge at Morehouse College may yet to be determined at some future time. I believe strongly that our unique educational experiences and exposures at Morehouse College have an extraordinary significance of a magnitude that will have a benevolent impact on the world for years to come.

I must admit that when we arrived at Morehouse in the fall of 1957, 1 was not impressed by the physical plant of Morehouse College or the AU Center. I had graduated as president of my senior class at Tuskegee Institute High School which was located adjacent to the campus of the renowned Tuskegee University founded by Booker T.

Washington in Alabama in 1881. I am certain that I had been overly influenced by Tuskegee University. However, after spending a few days on the campus of Morehouse College, the "sacred and spiritual mystique" of Morehouse convinced me that Morehouse was the college where I was supposed to be. I was highly impressed and fascinated by the lofty goals, noble ambitions, extraordinary motivations, and elevated expectations the freshman year of this 1961 Class. I had never been in the company of such a high number of young Black men who aspired so highly for academic excellence and career success. It seems that each of you were aiming for MD's, PhD's, and other terminal degrees. I was excited and felt challenged to be among students who demonstrated a commitment to climb the academic ladder to the very top.

Many of the Morehouse faculty members were to me, educational gurus. They were the most accomplished and scholarly academicians anywhere in the world. They were the most informed and thoroughly prepared teachers that I could ever imagine. It seems that they were especially made and commissioned by the Higher Power to teach the men of Morehouse College.

However, the rigorous demands of this well-prepared faculty at Morehouse screened out many of our classmates into early departures and caused many others to change their majors and rethink their careers. Professors McBay, Birney, Mapp, Houston, and Dansby dissuaded the medical and similar ambitions of several students. Professors Sam Williams and Lucius Tobin caused some students to drop out of the ministry and Morehouse as well. Many of the students had difficulty in reconciling their Sunday school lessons back home with advanced and different critical theological concepts and opinions. Overall, this 1961 Class was not guilty of "low aim" prognosticated by Dr. Mays.

I had heard about Dr. Benjamin E. Mays before I heard about Morehouse College. As a student in high school at Tuskegee Institute, I had read with great interest, Dr. Mays' articles, entitled, "My View" in the Pittsburgh Courier and the Chicago Defender. Dr. Mays was the first example that I recognized as a public theologian. However, I did not know it by that name at the time. I saw Dr. Mays as a most unusual minister of the Gospel who could write such in depth critical analyses and interpretations of social and political issues and events in the South during the racial segregation era. When I heard that he was the president of Morehouse College, it provided additional incentive for me to come to Morehouse. Because of my call to the ministry, Chaplain Wynn of Tuskegee University and my high school principal, R. W. Stone, encouraged me to go to Morehouse. It would be an interesting subject within itself to learn why each of you came to Morehouse.

While at Morehouse, I received three honors of which I am still very proud. In our junior year, I, along with Clyde James, received the Benjamin E. Mays Debating Prize. In our senior year, I was selected as the "Most Outstanding Student in Religion." Because of this honor, I was also selected to preach the Senior Sermon to the Morehouse Student Body in the Sunday Sale Hall Chapel Service. By the tutelage of Rev. Tobin and the grace of God my sermon was well received. I want to assure you that what I am sharing with you is not just about me, but it is headed for a bigger and more inclusive about all of us.

We, the Class of 1961, received a unique educational legacy at a critical time in American and world history. In 1954, the U.S Supreme Court ruled that segregation in the public schools was unconstitutional. In 1955 Rosa Parks refused to give up her seat to a white passenger on a city bus in Montgomery, Alabama. Her actions resulted in a bus boycott and gave rise to SCLC and the advent of Dr. Martin Luther King, Jr. as a national Civil Rights leader. On October 4, 1957, the Russians launched Sputnik, a spacecraft satellite into orbit around the Earth. These were among the momentous events that fermented and precipitated the most dramatic social and political changes ever to occur in American society. It was the time when Black Southern Americans decided to challenge nonviolently the social injustices of racial segregation and discrimination predominantly in the South.

We are the Morehouse men who were at the pivot of this turbulent transition from the engrained traditions of segregation, discrimination, and fear to the daunting challenge of desegregation, social equality, and hope. Many of the students in this Class participated in Civil Rights marches and sit-ins. Students in this Class, including Julian Bond, participated in the writing of the Student Civil Rights Manifesto of the Atlanta University Center. The Class of 1961 rose to the occasion to make difficult decisions, commitments and sacrifices for freedom, social justice, and the unalienable rights of life, liberty, and the pursuit of happiness. We were prepared for these radical changes from a long list of downtrodden people who were the off springs of slaves. They continued to work even when their strivings seemed futile. They continued to hope when hope seemed hopeless. We thank God for the long list of men and women who paved the way, such as Dr. Mays of Morehouse, Booker T. Washington of Tuskegee Institute, Roy Wilkins of the NAACP, A. Philip Randolph, Rev. William H, Borders of Wheat Street Baptist Church, Thurgood Marshall of U. S. Supreme Court to name a few. These intellectual and spiritual giants passed on to us an invaluable educational curriculum, along with an infallible ethical value system, with faith in God designed to insure our survival in a hostile, competitive and unjust society.

It was during the 1960's when the Negro, colored, Afro-Americans consolidated their identity as being Black Americans. The racial and national identity of Black Americans came out of the Civil Rights movement. It was the time when Black Americans embraced "blackness" as a positive terminology. Black Beauty', Black Pride and Black Power became slogans and themes in the Black Community. The concept of "Blackness" transcended color and took on connotations of racial pride, strong moral character, spiritual resilience, qualities of sacredness and dignity' of human life. The negative connotations and perceptions of racial blackness was transformed and redeemed into a peculiar quality and force of the soul, rooted in the historical, spiritual, intellectual, and emotional depths of a people who had been tried and tested in the hot flames of injustice and oppression and who came forth as gold.

Let me briefly summarize some synchronizations and the significance of the Class of 1961. This is the class that had a public theologian, Dr. Benjamin E. Mays, as President of the College. Dr. Mays, a public theologian, mentored Dr. Martin Luther King, Jr. who became the premier public theologian. Dr. King with this Black soul power and faith in God, led the most successful nonviolent revolution in history. The 1961 Class returns to Morehouse College after 50 years and is greeted by a President who encourages ministers to become public theologians. I was completing my Master of Divinity at ITC in 2000 when Dr. Franklin was President of ITC and that is when I embraced the concept of public theology. Had I nor been at ITC at this time, I could have very easily missed out on the concept that connected my religious education regarding the "culture crisis," 'and the "Social Gospel," that Rev. Lucius Tobin taught me at Morehouse. Dr. Franklin's advocacy for the role of the public theologian helped me to make that significant connection. As a result of making that connection, I have incorporated two organizations with the State of Georgia in 2002. One is the Christian Association of Public Theologians and the other one is the Christian Institute of Public Theology. Based on the concept of public theology and the two incorporated organizations, I have published a book entitled, The Way Out of Darkness: Vital Public Theology). The concepts of public theology, the two incorporated organizations and the Way Out of Darkness is what is needed at this critical time in history to resurrect, incorporate and complete the missions started by NAACP and SCLC. The success of Dr. King as a premier public theologian is the key. He embraced and practiced the concepts of public theology. Public theology has the vertical dimension up to the will of God. Our problems are too serious and dangerous now to depend on political, secular, and horizontal dimensional solutions.

I have not begun to scratch the surface on the significance of the 1961 Class. This is a class that produced a president of Morehouse College in the class member of Leroy Keith. This is the class that has a son of a president of Morehouse College, Richard Hope. Had Richard not asked me to share reflections for the 1961 Class, most of this information would have been dormant. Thanks to George Grant who has made a great effort to increase our communication and sharing. I believe that it is critical that we make every effort to share and publish our experiences that were conceived through our exposures at Morehouse College.

Morehouse men of 1961, 1 am proud to be one of you. Yourself actualization and personal accomplishments compel me to respect you and cherish our friendships and fellowships. Our academic challenges, intellectual debates, athletic competition, moral struggles, successes and failures, joys and sorrows and our mutual companionship has been our inspiration and our propelling incentive for the future.

May God bless us and keep us and our families in his care. May God bless Morehouse College. May the Class of 1961 pass on this legacy. May the legacy of Morehouse College live forever.

In the service of our Lord,

Willie James Webb, Class of 1961
May 13, 2011, 50th Class Reunion

CHRISTIAN INSTITUTE OF PUBLIC THEOLOGY, INC.
WILLIE J. WEBB-PRESIDENT & CEO

Dear Friend:

The Christian Institute of Public Theology (CIPT, Inc.) was incorporated through the State of Georgia in 2002 as a non-profit corporation, to provide theologically based skilled human services, education, training and treatment services to ameliorate human deprivations and other social and culture crisis-related problems. The services rendered by CIPT are based on sound ethical, professional, scientific and theological principles. The mission is to provide redemptive human services to individuals, community groups, families, agencies, and institutions, along with equipping them with marketable skills and certified credentials. This mission is designed to provide intellectual competence, professional standards, moral values, ethical behavior, economic foundations, positive and effective leadership, and optimum human health for personal well-being and for the good of society.

The services that CIPT is proposing and providing are critical and urgent for the homeless, helpless, and hopeless. The American culture crisis along with the deterioration of survival values is escalating at an alarming rate. The indices of human failures, deprivations, helplessness, and hopelessness are increasing at a staggering rate. The public theological services provided by CIPT can make a critical positive difference. The health and well-being of millions of Americans and the Nation, itself, are at stake. WE NEED YOUR HELP AND SUPPORT. The Christian Institute of Public Theology (CIPT) has a 501 © (3) IRS tax-exempt status.

On behalf of the Christian Institute of Public Theology, we are appealing to you as an individual, church, institution, business, foundation, or any other American corporate entity, to provide your tax-exempt contribution to the Christian Institute of Public Theology. Please make your check or money order payable to CIPT, Inc. and mall to CIPT, Inc. P. 0. Box 3148 Atlanta, Georgia 30302. Since CIPT Is biblically based and theologically guided, we need a center of operation, administration, education, treatment, and consultation to accommodate facilities for ongoing benevolent and redemptive public engagement. We anticipate the growth and development of CIPT into a premier educational, training and treatment center to combat the forces that would destroy survival values and the gift of God of a free, prosperous, peaceful, and qualitative way of living. Therefore, we need buildings, office space, equipment, supplies, paid personnel and human resource workers and a core of trained volunteers. We propose to use the best of science, art, law, and religion to accomplish the mission of CIPT.

CIPT has been educating public theologians, community chaplains, ministers, and Christian and drug addiction counselors for over ten years. The founder of CIPT published a book entitled, The Way Out of Darkness in 2007. This book explains the significance, role, principles, and practice of public theology in a culturally diverse and religious pluralistic society. CIPT is involved in tutorial services and educational advocacy. The CIPT president is also the Chair of the Clergy Training Committee with Concerned Black Clergy of Atlanta. CIPT is teaching the use of various community groups, including fellowship groups and music therapy. CIPT has participated with CAPT (Christian Association of Public Theologians) for seven years in the production of the Annual

Conference of Public Theologians. Websites and online magazines are being developed to educate the public and influence public policy.

You are invited to be an ongoing partner in this visionary theological initiative regardless to your religious affiliation or geographical location. There is no cause more worthy and no service more relevant. We solicit your support and prayers for our people, our community, and our Nation.

May the richest blessings of God be yours.

Serving for love, peace, and prosperity
Willie J. Webb, MDIv, MS, MA, CCS
President
Christian Institute of Public Theology

CAPT. Inc.
P. O. Box 3148
Atlanta. GA 30302
July 4, 2021

Dear Citizen,

This is an urgent appeal for your help to get these significant laws of Georgia on Character Education and Old and New Testament History and Literature implemented in the public schools of Georgia and publicized throughout the Nation.

Enclosed, please find a copy of the Character Education Law, (House Bill 605) and the Elective Course in Old and New Testament History and Literature (O.C.G.A., 20-2-148). These two laws are not implemented consistently, not well known nor publicized. Cobb County School District appears to have done more with these two laws than other Georgia School Districts.

Also, please find enclosed some documented efforts on the part of the Christian Association of Public Theologians, the Christian Institute of Public Theology, and the Concerned Black Clergy of Metropolitan Atlanta to prioritize the implementation and publication of these two significant laws of Georgia. There appears to be an inexplicable silence and disregard concerning these two significant and very relevant laws in the educational system, the society and news media. These laws are more relevant now than they were when enacted in 1999 and 2007 respectively.

The consistent implementation and publication of these two Georgia laws are urgent and vital for the education of our children, culture, and Nation. It is sad and tragic the

Character Education Law was enacted in 1999 and the Old and New Testament History and Literature Law were approved by the State Board of Education in 2007 and very few people are aware of the existence and significance of these two Georgia laws. The unprecedented escalation of crime, conflicts, confusion, and cultural crisis in America demands serious and urgent implementation, education, and publication of these rio significant and relevant Georgia Laws. THESE LAWS ARE MEANT TO BE BLESSINGS FOR OUR CHILDREN AND NATION. PLEASE BE PROACTIVE, INNOVATIVE AND CREATIVE IN THIS ENDEAVOR!

THANK YOU!

Pastor W. J. Webb, CEO, CAPT, Inc.
Foundation Baptist Church

CHRISTIAN ASSOCIATION OF PUBLIC THEOLOGIANS
PO Box 3148
Atlanta. Georgia 30302

Mr. Harold L. Martin, Jr., Interim President
Morehouse College
830 Westview Drive, SW
Atlanta, GA 30314

Dear President Martin:

Congratulations for your leadership initiatives as Interim President of Morehouse College. Increasing the enrollment and graduation rates at Morehouse are worthy goals. Graduating students with strong foundations in science, technology, engineering, and math are mandatory in the high technological world in which we live. They are certainly essential for efficient operation in almost every human and business endeavor. I am also pleased that you are attempting to take a more serious approach in the engagement of the Morehouse Alumnus. Morehouse is forfeiting many benefits and opportunities for its failure to seriously engage its alumni. I am encouraged by your leadership.

The challenging times in which we live compels me to share some reflections on some of the traditions and values of Morehouse College that I feel must be retained or revived if it is to remain true to its mission. These traditions and core values have been articulated and demonstrated by several persons, but especially by Dr. Benjamin E. Mays, Booker T. Washington, WEB Dubois and Dr. Martin Luther King, Jr.

These men and others demonstrated and advocated the following:

1. The survival values of the American Negro slaves and their offsprings who lived resiliently with faith in God as demonstrated in their Negro Spirituals, their educational and religious institutions contributed significantly to the values and traditions of Morehouse College's core knowledge and mission.

2. Morehouse College has a foundation of strong validated ethical, moral, and spiritual values. Dr. Mays required daily chapel attendance of all Morehouse students during his twenty-seven years at Morehouse College. Chapel was very significant.

3. The traditional leadership of Morehouse was based on a valid universal moral compass. It was not based on moral relativity. It was not based on ethical neutrality. It was not based on arbitrary decisions. It was based on validated true directions.

4. Morehouse encouraged and demanded intellectual competence, moral solidity, cultural enrichment, and spiritual values. Morehouse leadership and faculty invested significant time and energy in undergirding its education with honesty and truth. Interim President, Mr. Harold L. Martin, Morehouse College, 9-12-2017

5. The Foundation of Morehouse College was based on human dignity, moral integrity, and a universal benevolent code of ethics. These are foundations for all education.

6. Morehouse has an educational duty through its curriculum to the legacy of Black Americans and America to realize some vindication for the suffering

and the sacrifice Of the African American slaves and their offspring to memorialize their faith, perseverance, vigilance, and will to live and survive to the world.

7. It is incorporated and built into the soul of Morehouse College to be excellent and duty-bound to teach the best of science, art, law, and theology to educate and enlighten the world of the precious gift and possibilities of human life; so that human injustice will be eliminated and man will never again impose the barbaric evil of human enslavement. It is the duty of Morehouse to eliminate injustice, ignorance and evil.

The substantial emphasis on educating students in science, technology, engineering, and math is very important. However, it is even more important to teach students how the STEM education must be used for the protection, enhancement, sanctity, and salvation of human life. Therefore, Morehouse must not fail to teach the men of Morehouse the harmony, balance, refinement, and elevation of the arts for congruence and synchronization. We must not fail to educate the heart and spirit of the man of Morehouse in terms of character education, ethics, morals, and the revelatory knowledge of God in the Holy Bible and in Jesus Christ, the Savior.

The survival values salvaged through African American enslavement and human deprivations played out on the stage of American history are redemptive human treasures for the freedom and dignity of all mankind. Morehouse College is a repository of those human survival values. Those survival values that brought freedom to Black Americans and prosperity to America are not just for Black

Americans. These human survival values are for all Americans and the world.

Morehouse College has a significant duty and responsibility for the world. remember that Dr. Benjamin E. Mays stated that God has a special job and purpose for every person and Institution. And he said further, "If you don't do it, it may never get done."

Thanks again for your leadership initiatives on behalf of Morehouse College

Rev. Willie James Webb, CEO
Public Theologian
Class of 1961

August 20, 2010
Dr. Lawrence Carter, Dean International M. L.
King Chapel Morehouse College
830 Westview Drive, SW
Atlanta, Georgia 30314-3773

Dear Dean Carter:

Thank you for returning my call after your return from out of the Country travel. However, for the past couple of weeks, I have been unable to reach you by telephone. As you recall I conferred with you near the close of the last semester 2010 regarding a proposal to establish a public theology association for students at Morehouse College on a voluntary basis as the other College organizations operate.

I am aware of the Chaplain Assistance Program designed primarily for the PR seminarian students. The proposed public theology association is designed to include all students who wish to participate on a voluntary basis regardless of their respective academic concentration of study. This theological exposure and availability would be very beneficial to interested students. It has become unwise and even dangerous for educational institutions to neglect the theological exposure and fellowship of their students.

The educational genius of Dr. Benjamin E. Mays was based on his consistent inclusion of the generic undergirding of theological exposures of the students at Morehouse. The daily chapel services during the presidency of Dr. Mays served as a public theology association and fellowship for the students during that time. Since Morehouse no longer has daily chapel services, the proposed public theology association could help to bridge that significant theological/biblical knowledge vacuum.

Dr. Mays' literary public theology influenced me to attend Morehouse College as a high school student at Tuskegee Institute in Alabama. 1 often read his article entitled "My View," in the Pittsburgh Courier and the Chicago Defender newspapers. I benefited significantly from the daily chapel experience at Morehouse from 1957 to 1961. During my Senior year, I was selected the most outstanding student in Religion, preached the Senior Sermon, and won the Benjamin E. Mays Debating Prize.

The rich theological exposure at Morehouse impacted thousands of Morehouse men for good; the most prominent was Dr. Martin Luther King, Jr. It must be remembered that Dr. King was a public theologian. His mentor, Dr. Mays, was also a public theologian. It was the public theology component that elevated and sustained the leadership stature of Dr. Mays and propelled Dr. King into global Civil Rights leadership recognition.

Dr. Lawrence Carter, Dean, MLK International Chapel, August 20, 2010

I wrote a letter to Dr. Franklin dated September 05, 2008, proposing the public theology association. He made references to you and the Chapel Assistance Program for preseminarian students. This is a continuing follow-up to the initiative that I took in 2008 to get the Public Theology Association started.

Based on the concepts of public theology that I learned at Morehouse College and the Morehouse School of Religion at ITC, I have incorporated two organizations through the State of Georgia. They are The Christian Institute of Public Theology and The Christian Association of Public Theologians. Additionally, I have published a book entitled, "The Way Out of Darkness: Vital Public Theology-Actions to Turn the Lethal Tide." I also teach courses in public theology. I have spent considerable time and expense for the past four years attempting to get the Church and educational institutions involved in public theology. I must confess that I am disappointed. I am disappointed that the Church is ignoring public theology and indulging in private religion while satanic forces and antichrist spirits are busy transforming the American culture into pathological illnesses and Godless forces of destruction.

Morehouse College cannot afford to forfeit the blessings of God, the legend of Dr. Mays, the legacy of Dr. King, and the thousands of Morehouse men and other persons who have suffered and sacrificed for human dignity, survival, and freedom. There is an unprecedented crisis in American and global culture that demands serious theological involvement, commitment, and leadership. The dire predicament that humanity is currently in history requires direction and rescue from above. The genuine believers in the vertical and horizontal dimensions must rise and provide leadership. God's prophets and messengers were public theologians. Jesus, his disciples, and apostles were public theologians. The succession appears to have been broken. Who will begin to make the connection?

Willie J. Webb 1961
CC: Dr. Robert Franklin

February 3, 2016

The Honorable John Conyers, Jr. U. S. Congressman
2426 Rayburn HOB
Washington, D. C. 20515

Subject: The American Atonement and Black African
American Restoration Act of 2016

Dear Congressman Conyers:

Thank you for your many years of leadership and honorable service to the American people and the world. Thank you for your persistent efforts for decades to get your Reparation Legislation passed. Those accumulative deficits for four hundred years have taken such a detrimental toll on the Black Americans, it is critical that the U.S. Government make restoration in the interest of Black Americans as well as America. Therefore, I am submitting to you a supplemental proposed resolution for legislative restoration.

I am using the word, RESTORATION, because this great human need warrants and merits immediate humane attention by the National Government, irrespective to the past contributing causes. On its face, it is self-evident that the Black Americans have sustained and endured more discrimination, deprivations, abuse, violations, human sufferings, and casualties than any other group in America. America is known for helping other people within its borders and people in foreign nations. The Black Americans have been a part of all these rescue and war efforts of America. Since America is perpetually involved in helping people of other nations and other human descriptions, it cannot afford the hypocritical contradictions of being false to its own values, constitution, and traditions by refusing to restore its own people.

The most just, righteous, and noble thing that America can do at this time in history, is to restore its own longest-suffering and most severely abused loyal American people and citizens. There is no greater priority than to restore Black Americans and their American institutions of schools, churches, neighborhoods, businesses, and birthright entitlements. Black American history is American history. No other people have paid more, contributed more, or sacrificed more than the Black Americans (The offspring of American slaves).

Enclosed, please find my resolution for the above restoration legislation.

Thank you, Congressman Conyers.

Rev. Willie J. Webb, U.S. citizen, Atlanta, Georgia 30311

May 16, 2015

Honorable Congressman John Lewis
The Equitable Building
100 Peachtree Street, N.W. #1920
Atlanta, Georgia 30303

Dear Congressman Lewis:

Thank you for all the sacrificial services you have rendered to Black African Americans, America, humanity, and the world. May God continue to bless you for God's services to humanity.

Come this November 2019, Black African Americans will have been in America for 400 years. I am sad to say that after all these years, Black African Americans are still not treated as equal U.S. Citizens. Black African Americans are suffering despite all the sacrifices and legislation that have been accomplished. From your vantage point, you know more about the inequities and injustices than I do. It would be so tragic for America and all of humanity if the oppression of Black African Americans had not been lifted Within this 400-year period. I cannot think of an American priority that is more important than for America to invest in its own loyal Black African Americans, who have been disadvantaged for 400 years.

Congressman Lewis, the piecemeal approaches to correcting these 400-year systemic wrongs against a loyal Christian American people have not worked sufficiently to correct these destructive wrongs. Therefore, I am requesting that you and other U.S. Public Officials and National Leaders to introduce and pursue the enactment of the enclosed Resolution of this proposed Legislation, known as The

American Atonement and Black African American Restoration Act of 2015. Black African Americans (offsprings of slaves) have stood shoulder to shoulder with White Americans in supporting and sacrificing lives and treasure for people around the world. It is right for America to fulfill its long-overdue moral obligation and national duty of extending a charitable heart and a helping hand to its own unprecedentedly loyal people, the longsuffering Black African Americans.

This Act of acknowledging a wrong against an indigenous people and restoring those people is the greatest thing America can do for America. This is needed for America's healing, prosperity, and survival as a great Nation.

(Enclosure)

Rev. Willie J. Webb, CEO, CAPT, INC

August 24, 2015

Dean Lawrence Edward Carter, Sr.,
Martin Luther King, Jr. International Chapel
Morehouse College
830 Westview Drive, SW
Atlanta, Georgia, 30314

Dear Dean Carter:

Thank you for your invitation to attend the 2015 Parliament of the World's Religions, to be held on October 15, 2015, in Salt Lake City, Utah. The Parliament's agenda reflects my core beliefs and sentiments. However, I must, with regret, decline due to prior commitments on the same dates. However, I would welcome the opportunity for very relevant input.

Dean Carter, I am submitting to you, as well as to President John S. Wilson of Morehouse College, the core human rights priority of the 21st Century. The enclosed proposal to enact legislation known as the American Atonement and Black African American Restoration Act addresses this critical human rights priority. This Proposal has been submitted to the Concerned Black Clergy of Metropolitan Atlanta and to Congressmen John Lewis and Hank Johnson.

This proposed legislation is the essential critical piece needed for the spiritual, social, cultural, economic, political, racial, and religious healing for America and the world. The resurrection of the extraordinary faith, mercy of God, and survival values of the oppressed Black African Americans for four hundred years is the key to America's survival. There is a correlation between the oppressive destruction of Black

African Americans and the downfall of America, itself. After four hundred years, isn't it time for atonement, restoration, and justice?

Your serious attention, reflection and response is petitioned in the name and under the universal authority and the universal Savior of the World, Jesus Christ. (In remembrance of Benjamin E. Mays, Martin Luther King, Jr., and Julian Bond)

Rev. Willie James Webb'61
CC: President John Silvanus Wilson Enclosures

May 23, 2013

Honorable Governor Nathan Deal
Office of the Governor
240 State Capitol
Atlanta, Georgia 30334

Dear Governor Deal:

Thank you very much for your intervention and authorizing the return of the Bibles to the lodges and cabins of the State Parks. I feel that your courageous and decisive actions expressed the sentiment of most Georgia citizens.

I do believe that if you encourage the adoption of Character Education (GA. Law, 1999) and the Biblical Curriculum (GA. Law, 2007) by the Local Boards of Education in Georgia, a significant positive educational impact is quite possible. The consistent practice and incorporation of the twenty-seven-character traits in the Character Education Law will certainly help the students of Georgia to develop good character and moral, ethical, professional, and disciplinarian values.

The approved Georgia Biblical Curriculum Law provides for teaching the Old Testament and the New Testament in high schools in Georgia. The Courses are electives and they are to be taught objectively as history and literature by certified history and literature teachers. The Bible Curriculum complies with Federal Constitutional Law and by the National Council on Bible Curriculum in Public Schools. Judeo-Christianity is historical and is the religious and philosophical foundation of the American Creeds. It is the oldest and best-known classical literature in the annals of history and the greatest story ever told. The Georgia Law does not force any student to take these courses. However, the courses ought to be available for any high school student who elects to take them in Georgia.

Governor Deal, I applaud you for your intervention on behalf of the legality of the Bible being in the lodges and cabins of the State Parks. I request your intervention for character education and the Bible Curriculum in the public schools in Georgia.

Thank you very much.

Pastor Willie J. Webb, MDiv, MS, MA, CCS

February 12, 2015

Mr. Richard Woods
State School Superintendent
205 Jesse Hill Drive,
SE Atlanta, Georgia 30334

Dear Superintendent Woods:

This is to express thanks for your appearance and presentation of your educational vision for the State of Georgia and the Nation. I was favorably impressed with the rich and significant information that you provided on each subject that you addressed. You spoke as a well-informed and realistic educator. You articulated practical, common-sense kind of values based on the sound doctrines of American democratic values. I was impressed with your spontaneous expressions from the heart. You gave hope for higher academic standards. You inspired us Georgians to be creative, innovative, and limitless in order to achieve standards beyond the constraints of Common Core curriculums. I know that you will be challenged to conform to those unsound policies and principles that stand in the way of true educational progress for our children. I and others pray that you will stay the course.

Please find enclosed Georgia Law (House Bill 605) and the Elective course in History and Literature of the Old and New Testaments Eras.

Also, this is the centennial year of the death of Booker T. Washington who encouraged through the Four H Clubs (Education of Head, Hands, Heart, and Health). You alluded to the practical education and the healthy development of our youth and it reminded me of Booker T. Washington.

Thanks again for your educational vision for Georgia. You have great support! Stay the course!

Rev. Willie J. Webb

October 22, 2019

Mr. Jason Esteves, President, and Members of the Atlanta Board of Education

Thank you for the opportunity to provide input on the desirable qualifications for the next Superintendent of the Atlanta Public Schools.

The Atlanta Public School System needs a Superintendent who models traditional family values of responsible, moral, ethical, and spiritual parental American values, in addition to rigorous academic qualifications and demonstrated professional experience. These values include respect, reverence and knowledge of the Bible and the religious community institutions of Atlanta. In addition to Biblical knowledge, the prospective Superintendent must be respectful and knowledgeable of the United States Constitution, the Declaration of Independence, the Pledge of Allegiance to the Flag as a Nation under God and the American Motto, In God We Trust. Atheism, along with the other isms is unacceptable for any other public leaders and public administrators who influence the lives of children.

The prospective Superintendent of APS must be familiar with Gender Dysphoria, the mental disorder as described on pages (451-459) in the Diagnostic and Statistical Manual of Mental Disorders (5th edition) by the American Psychiatric Association. The prospective Superintendent must be capable of writing and implementing a policy and procedure that will safeguard the protection of the person, rights, property and dignity of all APS personnel and students and those under the jurisdiction of APS as they utilize bathroom facilities, other school accommodations and facilities. The validity of all values can be tested and determined by science, art, divine/natural laws, and theology.

APS needs a consummate ethical, moral, and spiritually guided Superintendent. It must be a person dedicated to PUBLIC SCHOOL EDUCATION.

W. J. Webb, CEO
Public Theologian

Note:
APS must have a Superintendent who will implement Georgia Law, House Bill 605 From K-12.

CHRISTIAN ASSOCIATION OF PUBLIC THEOLOGIANS
PO Box 3148
Atlanta, Georgia 30302

January 22, 2018

Mr. Jason Esteves, President
Atlanta Board of Education
130 Trinity Avenue, SW
Atlanta, GA 30303

Dear Mr. Esteves, Board Members and Superintendent:

As a U. S citizen, resident and voter of Atlanta, Fulton County, Georgia since 1961,1 greet you as a minister of God through Jesus Christ, the Savior. This is information for you and an appeal to you as you represent the citizens of Atlanta and the Atlanta Public Schools, the students, teachers, and staff.

Since my ministerial and civic involvement with Atlanta Public Schools since the year 1999, under the Beverly Hall Administration; I am familiar with your operations and administrative record. For whatever reason, your record indicates that you do not listen to the citizens of Atlanta and subsequently, do not respect or represent them in your decisions. Unfortunately, your decisions and actions have been more about your personal ambitions, greed, identity politics, and self-promotion than the educational achievement of students.

Your record has been administered by intimidation against teachers and staff through non merit-based personnel actions and the denial of due process of law. You have placed APS and former APS employees' names on damaging, "No Hire Lists" arbitrarily, capriciously, illegally, and without any due process of law and without any accountability for your violations and administrative abuse. Additionally, you hire lawyers at taxpayers' expense to attempt to cover up your wrongdoings and obstruct justice.

It is my hope and appeal as you enter the year 2018, that you will make amends for your wrongdoings, and unlawful damages, obey the U. S. Constitution, observe ethical professionalism, respect the human dignity of every person, listen to - hear - understand - weigh - consider the voices and messages of the Atlanta community and make your decision based on a moral compass. Do not allow your personal biases, arrogance, pride, privileges, favoritism, fears, conflicts of interest, belief system, vanities, or lack of knowledge to hinder the optimum educational potential of teachers and the maximum quality education for all children.

Depriving Children in the American public schools the knowledge of the Bible and faith in God is a very recent development in American public schools and education. It began in the 1960s after the US Supreme Court outlawed segregation in public schools in 1954 via the Brown vs Board of Education Decision. The serious educators must reflect on this important history regarding the Church and school relationship before the 1954 Supreme Court decision.

It is interesting and insightful to learn that the knowledge of the Bible and faith in God were not denied the Black African American slaves, nor the subsequent segregated and discriminated against descendants of slaves. Black Americans survived the destructive dehumanization of slavery because they embraced the available knowledge of the Bible, God, and Jesus Christ. Their knowledge of the Bible and their faith in God kept them spiritually, mentally, psychologically, emotionally, and socially alive. The public schools in America came out of the Judeo-Christian Church for White and Black Americans. Depriving Children of knowledge and faith in God is a dangerous civilization-threatening flaw in the current American educational system.

When the prophet Hosea made the following proclamation in the 8th Century before the birth of Jesus Christ, STEM (science, technology, and mathematics), had not been envisioned two thousand eight hundred years ago: MY PEOPLE ARE DESTROYED FOR LACK OF KNOWLEDGE: BECAUSE THOU HAST REJECTED KNOWLEDGE, I WILL ALSO REJECT THEE, THAT THOU SHALL BE NO PRIEST TO ME: SEEING THOU HAST FORGOTTEN THE LAW OF THY GOD, I WILL ALSO FORGET THY CHILDREN. (Hosea 4:6)

The knowledge that Hosea is referring to is not STEM or STEAM knowledge. The knowledge that Hosea is referring to does not minimize the significance of STEAM. God is the creator of all knowledge. Hosea is referring to theological knowledge. Theological knowledge is about God and God's moral, ethical, and spiritual commandments and requirements for all humans. If STEAM knowledge is not undergirded by theological/ Biblical knowledge, education and civilization will deteriorate into utter chaos and destruction. This lethal trend is already in motion and gaining momentum every day all over this Nation.

It is an urgent priority that you put at the top of your agenda and in the curriculum of the Atlanta Public Schools the already approved Comprehensive Character Education (House Bill, 605) and the Elective Course of the Old and New Testaments Eras as History and Literature. This law was approved by the Georgia Department of Education in 2007. Character Education was mandated April 23,1999. If for any reasons, you cannot follow the vital mandates of these laws of Georgia for the vital education and living armor of our children, it will be in the vital interest of Atlanta Children, citizens, state, and nation for you to resign your positions. Without character education and Biblical/theological knowledge in Atlanta Public Schools, the APS students are being set up for failure and destruction. Those are not the wishes of the parents for their/our children in Atlanta. The slave masters did not deprive the slaves of the knowledge of God. You, as representatives, must not deprive these vulnerable at-risk young people of knowledge that has the potential to save and preserve their dignity, lives, freedom, and souls. CAPT (Christian Association of Public Theologians) is in the business of using science, art, law, and religion to solve human problems.

Rev. W. J. Webb
CEO Theologist, CAPT, INC.

Atlanta Board of Education/Atlanta Public Schools
130 Trinity Avenue, SW
Atlanta, GA 30303

TO: Mr. Courtney English, Chair of ABE

Board Members:

> Leslie Grant, Byron Amos, Matt Westmoreland,
> Nancy Meister, Steven Lee, Eshe Collins,
> Cynthia Briscoe-Brown and Jason Estes
> Superintendent:
> Dr. Meria Carstarphen

FROM: Rev. W. J. Webb, Public Theologian
       Voter, Taxpayer, U.S. Citizen of Atlanta, Georgia
RE: Implement Character Education Program, K-12,
Georgia Law (House Bill 605), 4-23-1999

DATE: January 18, 2016

This is a request for the ABE (Atlanta Board of Education) according to Georgia Law, House Bill 605 (April 23, 1999) to implement the Character Education Program K-12, with a substantive course of study, that includes the students' development of the 27-character traits enumerated in the law. Since the need for character education is so dire at APS, it is requested that this Character Education Program be implemented from K-12 with content and quality comparable to other regular academic courses.
There are volumes of character education information to encompass the 27-character traits.

True and valid history teaches that individuals, agencies, institutions, and nations perish when they become arrogant and Godless. God has given individuals the autonomy to choose their fate and the gods or God they serve. However, God, nor the U.S. Constitution, has given any person the right or the authority to make that choice for others. When you deprive students of available theological knowledge and character education, you have violated an inalienable right of the students to choose their own fate.

The Code of Secrecy and the Code of Silence have been unlocked. It explains why the news media, political, educational, corporate, and religious leaders have ignored the Character Education Law of 1999 and the Elective Course of History and Literature of the Old and New Testaments Eras of 2007 of Georgia. The Code of Secrecy and the Code of Silence is designed to continue the cycle of educational and socioeconomic failure pattern of Black American students and Black Americans in general. They are predatory engineered failures by design.

THE KEY TO BLACK AMERICAN STUDENTS (AND BLACK AMERICANS) ACHIEVEMENTS AND SUCCESS HAVE BEEN BASED PRIMARILY ON THEIR FAITH IN GOD. THIS FAITH HAS BEEN NURTURED BY THE BLACK CHRISTIAN CHURCH AND THE BLACK SCHOOLS. (Yes, Black Americans have had allies from certain White Americans and other groups.). Depriving Black American students of character education, biblical knowledge, moral, ethical, and spiritual education will deprive them of the incentive, motivation, inspiration, purpose and meaning of achievement and success. The deprivation of character education and other moral, ethical, and spiritual values, significantly minimizes educational incentive and opportunity for the Black American student to be a successful academic achiever in school.

The school failures are characterized as major failures. These major failures result in disciplinary problems, mental, emotional, juvenile, criminal justice, drug abuse and a host of other socioeconomic problems. The Code of Secrecy and the Code of Silence are designed to perpetuate this cruel cycle of failure and destruction of the children of APS and the broader community.

Historically and traditionally, the true strength of the Black Americans has been related to their faith in God. The destruction of their faith destroys their strength. Faith in God has been a necessary transcendent power to counterbalance and compensate for the racial injustice and socioeconomic inequality, constant and pervasive in American society. Those who participate in the Code of Secrecy and the Code of Silence in the denial of biblical knowledge, character education, and the inalienable right of religious freedom to any people, and especially to Black American students, are participating in ungodliness and genocide. The reality and the judgement of God are inevitable and inescapable.

NOTHING CAN BE HIDDEN FROM THE OMNIPOTENT AND OMNISCIENT GOD WHO NEVER

SLUMBERS NOR SLEEP!

The Christian Association of Public Theologians, INC.

TO: Mr. Courtney English, Chair of ABE
        Board Members:
        Leslie Grant, Byron Amos, Matt Westmoreland,
        Nancy Meister, Seven Lee, Eshe Collins, Cynthia
        Briscoe-Brown, and Jason Estes Superintendent: Dr.
        Meria Carstarphen

FROM: Rev. W. J. Webb, U. S. Citizen of Atlanta, Ga., and CEO
        of CAPT, INC.

RE: Notice of APS/ABE Educational Deprivation Legal
        Liabilities
RE: Notice of APS/ABE Educational Deprivation Legal
        Liabilities

This is to put Mr. Courtney English, Chairman, and other members of ABE (Atlanta Board of Education), and Dr. Meria Carstarphen, Superintendent of APS (Atlanta Public Schools) on Notice for Legal Liability in Denying the Students of APS the Legally Mandated Comprehensive Character Education Program, House Bill 605 (April 23, 1999) from K-12. Additionally, Atlanta Public Schools and in conjunction with the Atlanta Board of Education are Put on Notice for Legal Liability in Denying All Eligible High School Students who have been enrolled in APS since 2007, the Opportunity and the Right to take the Elective Courses of the Old and New Testament Eras, as History and Literature pursuant to Georgia Law (O.C.G.A. 20-2-148, 2007).

The Atlanta Public Schools Superintendents, Beverly Hall (deceased), Errol Davis, Meria Carstarphen, along and in conjunction with the respective corresponding Atlanta Board of Education Members, have refused and failed to adopt the (State Department Approved Curriculum) Elective Courses of the New and Old Testament Eras of History and Literature, pursuant to Georgia Law (O.C.G.A. 20-2-148,2006, 2007) after repeated formal requests since 2007.

The arbitrary, intentional denials of implementing the Comprehensive Character Education Program as mandated by House Bill 605 (April 23, 1999) K-12, by APS in conjunction with failure to adopt Georgia Law (O.C.G.A. 20-2-148, 2007), have created and continue to create damaging educational deficits and harmful consequences for the thousands of deprived and impacted students of APS. The APS students are being denied arbitrarily and intentionally the most significant, universally recognized, traditionally and historically authenticated, moral, ethical, and spiritual educational values that are indispensably foundational for all other education and for the students' personal, social, and human wellbeing.

March 3, 2022

Ms. Dawn Stastny, President
Georgia Parent Teachers Association
114 Baker Street, N.E
Atlanta, GA 30308

Dear President Stastny:

On behalf of the parents of Georgia and the public theologians, we are urgently requesting your help in getting the full implementation of the Character Education Law and the Elective Course in History and Literature of the Old and New Testaments Eras in all Georgia Schools. It is also requested that the Elective course in History and Literature of the Old and New Testament Eras be amended to be required from Kindergarten through twelfth grades. These two Georgia laws are excellent laws that do not violate the U.S. Constitution or any other credible civilized law. THIS KNOWLEDGE IS VITAL.

OUR CHILDREN, OUR SOCIETY, OUR NATION, AND CIVILIZATION ARE BEING DESTROYED FOR THE LACK OF THIS KNOWLEDGE.

Please find copies of these two Georgia Laws enclosed along with other supplementary information.

Thank you for your human services and educational leadership.

Pastor W. J. Webb, CEO
CAPT, INC

ESSENTIAL QUALIFICATIONS FOR SUPERINTENDENT OF AN AMERICAN SOUTHERN METROPOLITAN PUBLIC SCHOOL SYSTEM

1. An American citizen, at least thirty-five years of age, who has been socialized and acclimated to the core American values and the Black American historical ethnocentric traditions must be familiar with the historical founding principles, laws, belief systems, and creeds of America.
2. The applicant must have a minimum of three years of credible classroom teaching experience, a broad liberal arts education, and a graduate degree in educational administration or the equivalent from an accredited educational institution of higher learning. Must understand the principles of behavior modification, reality therapy, and the individual hierarchy of needs.
3. The applicant must have a sound religious and ideological philosophy that is compatible with the religious and ideological philosophy of the predominant population of students being served. It is preferable to have a biblically based spiritual identity that is rooted in a sound theological tradition.
4. The applicant must be able to demonstrate cultural diversity competence in a multicultural, religiously pluralistic, and heterogeneous society. Must have an acceptable understanding of the concepts of Dr. Maria Montessori in The Absorbent Mind, and Schools Without Failure by Dr. William Glasser.
5. The applicant must understand the administrative components of management: Organization, Planning, Coordinating, Supervising, Staffing, Decision-making, Strategy, Policy Formulation, Evaluation, Monitoring,

Grievance Procedures, Staff Development, EAP (Employee Assistance Programs), Adverse Actions, EEO/Equal Employment Opportunity.

6. The applicant must be able to demonstrate an understanding of cultural diversity competence in a culturally diverse and religious pluralistic and heterogeneous society. How does one lead, manage, enrich, and bring about equitable accommodations in a diverse learning population?

7. The applicant must be able to demonstrate an understanding of the existential holistic relationship between science, art, religion, and law. And how can these disciplines be used educationally to ameliorate the deepening culture crisis? The applicant must be able to demonstrate the possession of exemplary moral, ethical, and spiritual values.

The Christian Institute of Public Theology
PO Box 3148 Atlanta, Ga. 30302

CHRISTIAN INSTITUTE OF PUBLIC THEOLOGY

CHRISTIAN ASSOCIATION OF PUBLIC THEOLOGIANS

The following are the proposed activities, objectives, goals, and mission of the Christian Association of Public Theologians:

1. Provide education and training for interested individuals to become trained and certified Public Theologians.
2. Train and educate the laity of the church to become more knowledgeable Christians, effective witnesses, teachers, and servants of the Christian Faith.
3. Give ministers, officers, heads of departments, assistants, and teachers of the church more training in Christian leadership that is tailored to their specific situations.
4. Provide educational foundations for the vital necessity of ethical, moral, and character training and education for all interested persons to protect, enhance freedom, democracy, civilization, and the common good of humanity.
5. Give people the education they need to grow culturally, spiritually, artistically, scientifically, and in terms of helping others.
6. Establish institutional ministries for worship, education, re-habilitation, counseling, support services, training, development, and growth.
7. Create theological mentoring programs to inspire positive attitudes, elevated self-respect, self-pride, self-esteem, respect and reverence for life, productive behavior, educational achievement, career success, and

being a benevolent contributor to the community and the common good of society.

8. Provide Christian worship services, inspirational, educational, motivational, consultation, counseling, training, and other needed Christian services in and outside of institutional group settings. such as schools, Boys/Girls Clubs, YMCA/YWCAs, group homes, detention centers, prisons, homeless shelters, nursing/assisted living homes, hospitals, businesses, and other support and self-help groups.

9. Write, publish, and distribute Christian/theological educational materials for the general health, security, safety, and welfare of individuals and the social and spiritual salvation of members of the community and society at large.

10. Establish, train, educate, recruit, and nurture a fellowship and a networking association of Public Theologians to carry out the Christian/theological mission of the Christian Church.

W. J. Webb, MDiv, MS, MA, CCS, CACII
Pastoral Care Counselor
Public Theology Instructor

THE PUBLIC THEOLOGY ASSOCIATION

This is a generic proposal for the establishment of a student organization on the campuses of colleges and other educational institutions (and under their respective jurisdictions) known as The Public Theology Association.

PURPOSE OF ORGANIZATION

The purpose of this voluntary student organization is to learn about public theology and to promote its precepts of academic excellence/achievement, religious/spiritual/ethical values, human health, social advancement, cultural enrichment, and economic, and leadership development. The purpose is to provide an opportunity for students to learn about the most noble values and ideals known to humanity and a means to summon the faith and the courage to practice them for the public and the common good.

SOME CORE OBJECTIVES

1. Explore the role and values of public theology based on sound biblical and religious doctrines.
2. Reflections on biblical foundations for improving the quality of life, security of civilization and guidance for the success and triumph of humanity.
3. Learn how to apply religious creeds, ethical and spiritual values to motivate positive attitudes, ethical behavior, and responsible living for the common good.
4. Learn how to incorporate the spiritual (biblical)domain of learning in education along with the cognitive, affective & psychomotor learning domains.

5. To explore ethical and moral foundations for cooperative and constructive living in a culturally diverse, heterogeneous, and religiously pluralistic society.
6. Develop an appreciation for the historical, social, cultural, and universal role of the Judeo-Christian religion in America and the world.
7. Explore the role of public theology in American history, Black American history, the Civil Rights movement and as the guardian of truth, social justice, liberty, freedom, Democracy, the way, and the witness of God in earth and the Universe.

In respectful submission:

Willie James Webb
The Christian Institute of Public Theology, Inc.

May 23, 2013

Honorable Governor Nathan Deal
Office of the Governor
240 State Capitol
Atlanta, Georgia 30334

Dear Governor Deal:

Thank you very much for your intervention and authorizing the return of the Bibles to the lodges and cabins of the State Parks. I think that by being brave and taking action, you spoke for most people in Georgia.

I do believe that if you encourage the adoption of Character Education (GA. Law, 1999) and the Biblical Curriculum (GA. Law, 2007) by the Local Boards of Education in Georgia, a significant positive educational impact is quite possible. The consistent practice and incorporation of the twenty-seven-character traits in the Character Education Law will certainly help the students of Georgia develop good character and moral, ethical, professional, and disciplinarian values.

The approved Georgia Biblical Curriculum Law provides for the teaching of the Old Testament and the New Testament in high schools in Georgia. The Courses are electives, and they are to be taught objectively as history and literature by certified history and literature teachers. The Bible Curriculum complies with Federal Constitutional Law and the National Council on Bible Curriculum in Public Schools. Judeo-Christianity is historical and is the religious and philosophical foundation of the American Creeds. It is the oldest and best-known classical literature in the annals of history and the greatest story ever told. The Georgia Law does not force any student to take these courses. However, the courses ought to be available for any high school student who elects to take them in Georgia.

Governor Deal, I applaud you for your intervention on behalf of the legality of the Bible being in the lodges and cabins of the State Parks. I request your intervention for character education and the Bible Curriculum in the public schools in Georgia.

Thank you very much.

Pastor Willie J. Webb
MDiv, MS, MA, CCS

THE DETRIMENTAL INCURSION
OF THE ATLANTA BELTLINE
"A Trojan Horse"

The Atlanta Beltline is a hazardous public intrusion into private neighborhoods without their consent and without official public disclosure of the harmful effects and detrimental personal and community impact. The Beltline's adjacent neighborhoods and residents face significant risks of invasion of privacy, diminished quality of life, and criminal victimization. The Atlanta Beltline is an open invitation to the world to unknown persons to come trespass, invade, plunder, and occupy private neighborhoods. It is an invitation to accommodate potential derelicts and conceal illicit and criminal behavior and other detrimental behavior. It also creates a dangerous environment for the innocent and vulnerable people who use and are associated with the Beltline. Many citizens and residents are very disturbed by these detrimental prospects for the Atlanta Beltline.

The engendered political divisions, identities, diversities, chaos, confusion, violence, and rising crime rates is a loud message that the Beltline will exacerbate and accentuate more turmoil, crime, confusion, destabilization, and destruction. These prospective detrimental consequences raise serious unanswered questions. When will the ARC (Atlanta Regional Commission) share its Atlanta Beltline Impact Study with the Southwest Atlanta Community? What is the plan of the Atlanta Beltline to provide 24-hour security and protection for the citizens, participants, and the impacted communities by the Beltline? What are the specific laws, policies, guidelines, and personnel to protect and safeguard the rights, persons and property of all persons impacted by the Atlanta Beltline?

It appears that a massive and expensive police force is required to adequately protect and safeguard all the people and communities impacted by the Atlanta Beltline. It appears that this leisure and recreational adventure of the Atlanta Beltline initiative has overlooked the pragmatic, real priority needs of the residents, citizens, and the common good of the City of Atlanta. Considering the drastic changes resulting from the COVID-19 Pandemic and political divisions in the United States of America, an urgent re-evaluation of the Atlanta Beltline is warranted. It is mandatory that the City of Atlanta and the State of Georgia major in majors.

CONCERNED CITIZENS OF ATLANTA AND GEORGIA

THE CHRISTIAN ASSOCIATION OF PUBLIC THEOLOGIANS

Table Topics, Issues and Questions
CAPT Conference
10/20/2018

1. How can children receive the optimum character education, including ethical, moral, and spiritual values? Please be as specific as possible.
2. What are some good models for teaching children and youth good character, morals, ethics, and spiritual values between the ages of five and ten and between the ages of eleven and seventeen? Please enumerate specific teachings, activities, and exposures that could enhance these ethical, moral, and spiritual developments.
3. How can the parents be more effective and intentional about the ethical, moral, and spiritual development of their children and youth? List recommendations.
4. Describe some specific ways and methods by which the church could improve its influence and the development of children's optimal mental, moral, and spiritual health, as well as their physical health. Please make recommendations.
5. Make a list of community resources that specialize in various aspects of child and youth development. How can more youth development services be initiated in the various communities?
6. List some ways and methods the Church could assist parents and the schools in the teaching of morals, ethics, spirituality, and successful living for children and youth. What are some recommendations that CAPT could make

to initiate more Church involvement in youth, family, and community development?

7. How can many deprived children and youth, particularly in Black American communities, be provided with biblical knowledge and Christian education on a consistent and deliberate basis? (Take into consideration competent and ethical teachers.)

8. List specific ways, methods, and means to enhance the physical, mental, social, and spiritual health of youth from birth to 17 years of age. Consider needed legislation, public policies, and private, and volunteer initiatives. (Adequate laws must be considered to protect and safeguard the mental, spiritual, and physical health of our youth. The delinquency, failure in school, drug abuse, crime, and other illnesses in our society are, in part, manifestations of mental and spiritual illnesses.

9. What specific programs and services do you recommend for the Church and clergy for the wholesome and healthy development of the spiritual and mental health of its members, especially its youth? Draft recommendations suitable for transmitting to the churches and clergy.

10. What messages must the public theologians send to church pastors and clergy to solicit their help in the promotion of mental and spiritual health in families, schools, businesses, government, community, and Nation? Our culture is permeated with pathological social and spiritual illness. This pathology has also infected the Church. How can we get the Church to see this illness and become an ally against it?

11. How must the public theologians get involved in revitalizing, promoting, and providing Guidance for the PTAs in the redemption and salvation of our children? What education must CAPT provide to the parents to get

their involvement in looking at the great spiritual, moral, and ethical needs of our children as well as the needs of the whole society?

12. What must CAPT do to free teachers from intimidatory administrations? Ungodly Educational administrations are hindering the teaching of character education, ethics, morality, biblical knowledge, and spiritual values. What legislative, political, social, and theological strategies must be implemented to remove the barriers that prevent our children from learning survival values?

IT IS HOPEFUL THAT WE CAN GET SUBSTANTIAL CONCRETE RECOMMENDATIONS AND SOLUTIONS THAT CAN BE PUT IN A TRANSMITTABLE FORM TO ANSWER THE QUESTIONS RAISED AND provide RESOLUTIONS TO THE ISSUES DISCUSSED. IT IS IMPERATIVE THAT THE TABLE TOPICS BE TRANSMITTED TO THE APPROPRIATE AUTHORITIES AND CONSTITUENCIES TO BRING ABOUT THE SOLUTIONS WE SEEK.

The Christian Association of Public Theologians
Atlanta, Georgia

FOUNDATIONS FOR SPIRITUAL RECOVERY

The pastoral addiction counselor must be aware of and knowledgeable about certain information, procedures, sequences, and resources to be effective in the recovery process. The following is a general guideline for that effort:

1. Must have basic pharmacological knowledge of drug use, abuse, dependence, and addiction. Must understand the concepts of drug use, abuse, dependence, and addiction.
2. Must be knowledgeable of the predictable consequences of drug abuse and addiction in the following areas:

    A. Medical (physical and psychological)
    B. Personal and social
    C. Ethical and spiritual

3. Learn how to evaluate, assess, and provide the appropriate DSMIV diagnosis and number. Learn how to write a plan for prevention, treatment, and recovery.
4. Learn the dynamics of alcohol and other drug withdrawal syndrome. Learn the distinction and rationale for ambulatory and inpatient detoxification.
5. Be knowledgeable of the community resources for help in the appropriate areas of need, such as medical, social, economic, housing, employment, ethical and spiritual, etc.
6. Learn the clinical skills of providing individual, group, family, crisis, and intervention counseling, appropriate referral, and case management services.

7. Learn the skills for providing motivation, inspiration, community support systems, and a sustained commitment to spiritual recovery.
8. The pastoral must have a resource of educational and spiritually sound principles and doctrines for teaching and guidance. The pastoral counselor must be an advocate for social justice and educational and economic opportunities.

W.J. Webb, Instructor

PARABLE OF PRODIGAL SON
ST. LUKE 15:11-32

Assignment:

Write out your answers to the following questions and be prepared to discuss them in class:

1. Identify the various social processes, feelings, and attitudes expressed in the social interactions and in the relationship between the Prodigal Son and his father.
2. Explain some of the problems involved in the experience of the Prodigal Son's leaving home. What possible mistake did he make in the process?
3. What are some problems involved in the experience of the Prodigal Son's leaving home? What possible mistakes did he make in the process?
4. What are some key factors that brought about a change in the Prodigal Son's attitude and actions?
5. How do you explain the older brother's reaction to his brother's return home?
6. How does this parable relate to addictive attitudes, thinking, and behavior?
7. What are some important lessons we can learn from this story that could help us avoid making bad choices, living without discipline, and getting into bad relationships?

W. J. Webb, Instructor

THE STRUGGLE FOR SPIRITUALITY

Assignment:

Read and study the following scriptural references, provide written answers to the questions, and be prepared to discuss them in class:

Carnality and Spirituality
Romans 7:15-25

For we know that the law is spiritual: but 1 am carnal, sold under sin. For that which I do I allow not; for what I would, that do I not; but what I hate, that do I. If then I do that which I would not, I consent unto the law that it is good. Now then it is no more I that do it, but sin that dwelleth in me. For I know that in me (that is, in my flesh,) dwelleth no good thing: for to will is present with me; but how to perform that which is good 1 find not. For the good that I would I do not: but the evil which I would not, that I do.

(Romans 7:14-19, KJV)

Assigned Questions for Discussion:

1. Describe the spiritual dilemma of Paul and the conflicting roles of the body, the mind, and the spirit.
2. How does an individual arrive at such a conflict and dilemma in his or her life? Explain the emotional, psychological, and spiritual dynamics of this human tug of war.

3. Can you draw a parallel or see a correlation between Paul's dilemma and the dilemma of a chemically addicted person?
4. What are some consequences when carnality (flesh) wins the battle over the spirit?
5. What was Paul's answer and resolution to this problem? (Read Romans 7:24-25.)

W.J. Webb, Instructor

**FOUNDATIONS FOR RE-EDUCATING
AMERICA EDUCATING AMERICA FOR
GREATNESS
PRESENTS**

A Town Hall Forum on Human Relations
(Health and Humanitarian Services Prerequisites)
THE SEARCH FOR HUMAN JUSTICE
Some Dynamic Exploratory Questions:

1. What is human injustice?
2. What are some effects of human injustice?
3. What are some root causes of human injustice?
4. Who benefits from human injustice?
5. When benefits for some create detriments for others, is the benefit bona fide?

WHAT ARE SOME PRIMARY BARRIERS TO HUMAN JUSTICE?

WHAT METHODS MUST BE EMPLOYED TO REMOVE THE BARRIERS TO HUMAN JUSTICE?

HOW CAN THE FOLLOWING VALUES, INSTITUTIONS, AGENCIES ASSIST HUMAN JUSTICE?

1. Families, neighborhoods, and communities.
2. Kindergarten, Primary, Middle, and High Schools, Public and Private Schools.
3. Educational Institutions such as Colleges, Universities, Trade Schools, Businesses, and others.
4. Churches, Seminaries, other Religious Organizations, and institutions.

5. Government, Health, Legal, Social, and other Professional Agencies.
6. Professional, Moral, Ethical, Scientific, Artistic, and Spiritual Values.

SOME FORUM TAKEAWAYS FOR RE-EDUCATING AMERICA

(Specify your commitment regarding what YOU WILL DO, WHERE WHEN and HOW)

1. A commitment to re-educate members of my organization and other individuals.
2. A commitment to work in specific ways to serve individuals and other Americans in order to improve the core American values of civility and abundance of life.
3. A Commitment to strengthen the institution of the family to nurture and educate children and other family members more effectively for successful living.
4. Commitment to teach true knowledge, sound doctrines, and noble values to family members, friends, neighbors, and all Americans.
5. Commitment to support quality and excellence in education at all levels; in the home, schools, colleges, universities, and community forums.
6. Commitment to practicing and encouraging others to practice the democratic form of government outlined in the United States Constitution and Declaration of Independence.
7. The commitment to be a model American citizen by obeying the Just Laws of America and the Supreme Laws of God.
8. Commitment to be positive, fruitful, enhance life, respect, and replenish the earth, serve humankind, and be a responsible guardian of the resources provided by God.
9. Commitment to respect the dignity and integrity of all human beings as belonging to one human family and being made in the image and likeness of God.

10. Commitment to assisting each individual and humanity in establishing peace in human hearts, peace on earth, and goodwill toward all humanity.
11. Commitment to create a world where each person will have an optimum opportunity to actualize his or her God-given potential to the fullest to serve humankind and glorify God, the Creator.
12. Commitment to make specific plans to be a vital part of the Re-Education of America and make America a Great Nation Under God.

The Christian Institute of Public Theology, INC.

EDUCATIONAL DEFICIENCY OF CRITICAL RACE THEORY
Readiness & Relevance for Learning are Critical
CI PT, Inc

It is self-evident that a child must have a series of readiness, development, and maturational levels to comprehend certain concepts, ideas, and realizations. The educational Gradations of kindergarten, early and advanced elementary, middle school, and four years of high school exist to accommodate the child's educational readiness from childhood, adolescence, to young adulthood. These series of developmental stages involve the child involve physical, mental, emotional, and social growth of the child.

Human beings, unlike lower forms of life, require years of developmental growth and learning that correspond with their overall maturational and developmental processes and learning readiness. These developmental and growth stages involve the physical, mental, emotional, social, moral, and ethical components of the human individual. Although this process evolves naturally and is very fascinating, it is also very delicate and complex. The failure to recognize this delicacy and complexity in the growth, development, and education of children can be very detrimental to their health, lives, and well-being.

The primary flaw of Critical Race Theory supporters is their failure to recognize the delicate and complex nature of human development. This totally dependent child must learn to crawl on its hands and knees before it can walk or stand on its legs and feet. This totally dependent child must be compassionately cared for and nurtured for a long period of time. During this process, a child must consciously discover and recognize itself and its own self-consciousness. The child must learn its name, identity, and the identities of others in relation to itself and the world around it. A child must learn words and speech before it can communicate ideas in an intelligible language. It usually takes about five years before a child is ready to begin kindergarten. The child must learn to read before it can read to learn. The child must learn the alphabet, how to recognize and spell words, and the art and skills of communicating orally and in writing.

This lengthy elementary indulgence in childhood development is a solicitous plea on behalf of children to all who are entrusted to work with them. This plea is especially for educators to be extra compassionate and sensitive to the natural limitations of each child's respective developmental stages. The imposition of tasks and complexities beyond the child's comprehension readiness is detrimental, abusive, and cruel. The imposition of Critical Race Theory on children is a blatantly detrimental example of abuse and cruelty to innocent, and mistreated children. American students from kindergarten through twelfth grade do not have the historical nor the educational developmental foundations to understand the historical, cultural, political, and sociological implications of Critical Race Theory. Most college students are not equipped to fully understand the complexities and multiplicity of variables involved in the analysis of Critical Race Theory.

PREREQUISITES FOR OBJECTIVE TEACHING

An objective merit-based and needs-based teaching and learning of Critical Race Theory would require graduate-level competence in Public Education, American History, Black American History, Sociology, Psychology, Cultural Competence, Political Science, Christian Ethics, Constitution of the United States, Declaration of Independence, and the Pledge of One Nation Under God. There is no evidence to suggest that such prerequisites exist with the current administration of Critical Race Theory.

The current administration of Critical Race Theory in American Educational School Systems ignores the readiness and competence of the students to understand the contextuality of such teaching. No known publicized credible educational needs for Critical Race Theory have been established. Critical Race Theory ignores the primary cognitive domain of learning. The cognitive domain of learning takes precedence over the216ffective and emotional domains of learning. This imbalanced emphasis on the emotional domain aspect of learning jeopardizes the mental, emotional, and social health of all students involved. This also highlights the detriment of SEL (Social Emotional Learning) that is spreading in American Schools and American Educational Institutions. The primary domain of learning, cognitive (intellectual), is being neglected and hijacked by the SEL (social-emotional learning) that is prevalent in many American educational school districts.

This is not the time in history to minimize and neglect the cognitive domain of learning. The technological, global, and space ages require more objective, scientific, artistic, legalistic, and theistic objectivity than at any other time in human history. America and humanity cannot afford the superficial, counterproductive indulgence of misguided, miseducation, unsound doctrines, deceptive ideologies, and blind emotionalism for leadership and guidance. Humanity must be guided by validated truth, justice, and righteousness already established by God. The margin of error has become too narrow and the cost too high to gamble with naive and infantile incompetence.

HISTORICAL REALITIES OF RACIAL INJUSTICE

Let it be known that Black Americans lived with, dealt with, and survived the tragic reality of 250 years of racial slavery and another hundred years of racial segregation and discrimination in America. During all these atrocities, Black Americans contributed to the building of the greatest and most blessed nation on the earth, One Nation Under God. America is an exceptional nation. The Black Americans are significant contributors to this exceptionalism. It is difficult to imagine America becoming a great nation without the presence and contributions of Black Americans. The documented presence of Black people has been in America since 1619. America is the national home of Black Americans. After 1619 Black Americans were born, lived, worked, and died in America. They helped to build the country. They have fought and died in all of America's wars and international conflicts, unlike any other ethnic group.

Despite enslavement, segregation, discrimination, and degradation, Black Americans remained more loyal to America than any other American group. Marcus Garvey, a Black Jamaican, came to America in 1916 for the purpose of meeting with Booker T. Washington of Tuskegee. However, Booker T. Washington died in 1915, before Garvey's arrival. Garvey started the "Back to Africa Movement" in America in 1916. Garvey had an estimated two million followers among Black Americans. However, the majority of Black Americans considered America their home. Garvey was released from prison in 1927 and returned to Jamaica. Most Black Americans, like Booker T. Washington, accepted America as their home and refused to accept invitations and enticements to claim citizenship or a homeland in Africa. Most indigenous Black Americans, the offsprings of slaves, and especially those who believe in the Bible and Jesus Christ, have resisted the alien influences to hate America and White Americans. Psalmist 24 says, "The earth is the Lord's, and the fullness thereof; the world, and they that dwell therein." This makes people aware that no person or nation has a monopoly on the blessings of God. America was exceptionally blessed because of its founding documents were based on Biblical Judeo-Christianity. The prosperous blessings of America were and are not based on geography or the color or race of its inhabitants. It was based on their faith in God and biblical belief systems. Those who are familiar with Black American history know that their faith in God was fundamental for their survival, progress, and accomplishment in a horrible environment. America is the official and God ordained national home of Black Americans. Those who would deny the equal rights and privileges of this homeland to Black Americans are in violation of all of America's founding documents. governing laws, and the Biblical Mandates of God.

THE SIGNIFICANCE OF BLACK AMERICAN HISTORY

The failure to teach Black American History seriously and broadly is an indictment against American educational, theological, and governmental institutions Black American History has universal and significant lessons and values for America and the world. It is an integral part of the sacred Judeo-Christian redemptive American history as "One Nation Under God. Biblical Ethics and the Spirit of God are at the center of Black American History. The American Civil War, the Emancipation Proclamation, and the freedom of the Negro slaves were acts of God in answer to over two hundred fifty years of prayers and supplications. This was an extraordinary epoch played out on the stage of American History.

To highlight this extraordinary history of epic proportions, consider that God sent Moses to Egypt to lead the children of Israel out of captivity and bondage. This intervention on the part of God required the opening of a pathway through the Red Sea. As related in the Bible, Pharoah's army chased them, and they drowned in the sea. In America, the Negro slaves had nowhere to go and no weapons to fight with. HOWEVER, GOD PERFORMED A MIRACLE BY FREEING THE NEGRO SLAVES IN THE MIDST OF THEIR CAPTORS. Booker T. Washington, in his book, UP From Slavery, witnessed this miracle as a child on a Virginia plantation of slaves.

THE EMANCIPATION PROCLAMATION

Booker T. Washington stated that all the slaves were summoned to the Plantation Big House. He said that a White man rode up on a horse at the gathering of the plantation slaves and read the Emancipation Proclamation to the gathered slaves. After the man finished reading, he cold the slaves that they were free and that they were free to leave the plantation. They left in jubilation and celebration. After 244 years of slavery, they left the plantation as free men, women, and children. This was a miracle of God. The White Americans could no longer reconcile slavery with the truths of the Bible and the Gospel of Christ. This sacred redemptive Black American History is ennobling and significant, with lessons for America and the world. All American educational, social, and theological institutions have a duty to teach American Black American History.

THE AVAILABILITY OF BLACK AMERICAN HISTORY

The libraries, museums, colleges, universities, churches, state capitols, the Capitol of Washington D. C. and other historical places are replete with the annals and archives of Black American History. Great lessons and blessings for the Nation and the world are enshrined in Black American History. The bountiful sharing of this vital knowledge has the potential to enlighten, enrich, and elevate America to more noble and celestial civil and moral heights. When this dynamic evolutionary history is judged in its totality, all true Americans will be repentant and humbled, but also grateful and proud to be an American of ONE NATION UNDER GOD.

A very comprehensive Afro-American History of Selected Bibliography has been put together by Monroe Fordham. This extensive bibliography covers topics ranging from West African origins and the Atlantic Slave Trade to the current era of the Black American Civil Rights Movement. It is recommended that all American public schools, colleges, and universities utilize this comprehensive, rich bibliography to develop an ongoing Black American History curriculum and courses. The rich content of this scholarly and professionally written authentic Black American history will provide enlightening knowledge, pride, and appreciation. It is recognized that many of the advocates of Critical Race Theory are sincere and have good intentions. It is hoped that they will embrace this more enlightened and constructive means of educating our youth and all Americans about Black American History and its significance for America and the world.

The Christian Institute of Public Theology

EDUCATION PROHIBITED BY RELIGIOUS DEFINITION
The Bible Defies Constitutional Religion Clause
The Christian Institute of Public Theology

The nebulous definitions, meanings, and connotations of religion as used in the First Amendment of the United States Constitution, arbitrarily mischaracterize the Bible as a part of the nebulous meaning of religion; and subsequently prohibit the unique, inexhaustible, educational, cultural, historical, social, legal, and theological values of the Bible. The Bible is not ordinary, general, or nebulous in its description. The Bible is not synonymous with religion as presumed in the First Amendment of the United States Constitution's "religion establishment clause."

The Bible Is a distinct, unique, and specific historical, legal, ethical, and theological composition of sixty-six specifically named books, combining the Old and New Testament Eras of Jewish History. It covers the whole spectrum of life from Genesis to Revelation in the New Testament. The Old Testament contains 39 books; five books of law; twelve books of history; five books of wisdom and poetry; five books of major prophets; and twelve books of minor prophets. The New Testament contains 27 books: four books of Gospels, one book of history, twenty-one letters, and one book of Revelation.

It must be acknowledged that the Bible is not a book of sectarianism, cultism, or any other ism that is less than monotheism. It is not a book of fiction, mythology, or perceptual creations of the imagination. The Bible is a one-of-a-kind historical book that reveals and historically represents one monotheistic God, one humanity, and one Savior. It teaches only the existence of one God who is omnipotent, omnipresent, omniscient, infinite, immortal, and eternal. The Bible teaches further that the worship of any entity or being less than God is idolatry. According to the bible, there is only one God with a capital G. The polytheistic gods with the small g are idols and are not the monotheistic God of Abraham, Isaac, and Jacob. This God resurrected Jesus Christ from the dead. The Bible teaches against religious idolatry. The God of the Bible is the God of love and truth.

DEFINITIONS OF RELIGIONS:

The World Book Dictionary (1998, World Book, Inc.) provides four credible definitions of religion as follows: (1) Belief in God or gods. (2) Worship of God or gods. (3) A particular system of religious belief. (4) Anything done or followed with reverence and devotion. These described academic and professional definitions of religion from the World Book Dictionary illustrate the expansive, general, and broad definitions of religion. These general and nebulous definitions of religion clearly raise the question as to how the specificity of the Bible and its criticisms of idolatry and dishonesty can be considered as any part of a false and idolatrous religion. The Bible is not synonymous with God. It is not a book to be worshipped. It is not a being that worships. It is not a being that follows. The Bible is not a being that devotes or reveres. The Bible is not a religion. It is a book of history, knowledge, education, truth, God's love, historical acts, and instructions for the salvation of mankind.

THE NATURE OF RELIGION MERITS SERIOUS STUDY:

The World Book Dictionary's four definitions of religion are linked and related to personal and individual beliefs, worship, reverence preferences, and devotions by individual decisions and choices from a universe of things, objects, and beings. The core meaning of religion seems to reside in the personal feelings, belief systems and choices of the respective individuals or groups. Based on the limited information provided, a rational analysis must conclude that the Bible is not a religion. Contrarily, anything can be considered religious. Therefore, the government cannot be isolated from the definition and concept of religion. According to the nebulous definition of religion, the United States Constitution and the American Government could be considered religions.

The Bible itself proclaims that the worship of anything less than God is idolatry. Human beings adore, reverence, and worship a variety of things, objects, and beings. Religion appears to originate and reside in the minds, hearts, spirits, souls, and wills of individuals and groups as they focus on objects of devotion, reverence, and worship. These objects, things, or beings are not necessarily specifically limited or defined. The conglomerate complexities of religion and the associated consequences must not be taken lightly. Serious attention is needed.

REVISITING THE RELIGION ESTABLISHMENT CLAUSE:

The Religion Establishment Clause derives from the First Amendment to the United States Constitution. The

Religion Establishment Clause is used as the legal basis to prohibit the Bible from being taught in the government's public schools in America. This law is used to justify the prohibition of Bibles and use of Bibles in government agencies and other places of public accommodations, such as hotels and motels. The words, quotations, and references to the Bible are often censured, discouraged, and disparaged. Some candidates who are being sworn in for American public office refuse to place their hand on the Bible for the administration of the oath of office. The legal restrictions and public prohibitions against the Bible and the use and content of the Bible are being done without sufficient competent legal investigation and study. A serious revisit of this "Religion Establishment Clause" is urgently needed. In addition to reviewing the legality of the "Religion Establishment Clause," a competent social, national, political, economic, cultural, health, educational, and theological impact study would be of great service to America and the world. The heterogeneous and technological complexities of the world have critically narrowed the margins of error. This error is unaffordable.

THE READING AND LANGUAGE OF THE FIRST AMENDMENT OF THE U.S. CONSTITUTION:

"Congress shall make no law respecting an establishment of religion or prohibiting the free exercise thereof; or abridging the freedom of speech or of the press; of the right of the people peaceably to assemble and to petition the government for a redress of grievances."

THE CONSTITUTION OF THE UNITED STATES OF AMERICA

RELATIONSHIP OF THE BIBLE TO AMERICAN LAW:

The influence of the Bible predates the 13 American Colonies that began about 1607 AD. Christian ministers and other Christians spread the teachings of the Bible throughout the Thirteen Colonies in America. The spread of the teachings of the Bible and the salvation news of Jesus Christ eventually brought about what is called the "Great Awakening" in the American Colonies. The great spiritual awakening resulted from a massive Christian-led movement of evangelistic teachings, revivals, conversions, and dedication to freedom to live, work, and worship without government restrictions and hindrance. It must be noted that Black Africans (Negro slaves) were first brought to the Colony at Jamestown, Virginia, in 1619, and they were not considered as fully equal or equally human as their White counterparts. However, they became a part of this vibrant social and political movement in the new colonial world.

The culture of the Colonies became saturated with the ethical teachings, enlightening knowledge, and liberating spirit of the biblical knowledge of the Bible and the soul salvation knowledge of Jesus Christ. The Colonists were inspired and motivated to build communities, churches, and schools and to engage in free enterprise endeavors. This new beginning was inspired and sustained by Christians and Bible believers. The Bible was their primary reading and teaching book. Many could not read or write, but they learned through the oral quotations of Scripture in the Bible. The Bible became a motivator to learn to read, write, and get an education. Many schools were established during this colonial period. Many African American slaves were motivated to read and get an education so that they could read the Bible. The American Negro slaves never considered the Bible a "White man's religion."

It was the influence of the Bible that initiated the Declaration of Independence in 1776 and the Constitution of the United States in 1787. The Bible influenced the ratification of the Bill of Rights in 1791, the recognition of a democratic form of government described by President Abraham Lincoln in 1863 as "a government of the people, by the people, and for the people," and the issuance of the Emancipation Proclamation in 1863 that freed the Negro American slaves in 1863. In subsequent years, the Bible influenced the Pledge of Allegiance to the U.S. Flag as "One Nation Under God" and the American Motto on American currency, "In God We Trust." The influence of the Bible is deeply embedded deeply in American culture, education, social, economic, and political institutions.

The single most important document that has made the greatest difference for good in America and the world, has been and is the Holy Bible. This magnificent, unfathomable, and extraordinary gift to humanity must be respected, re-examined, revisited, reconsidered, reunited, reclaimed, replenished, renewed, and revitalized. Generations, civilizations, and nations have been enlightened, guided, nurtured, and strengthened by the knowledge, understanding, wisdom, spiritual concern, and love contained in and radiating from the Bible.

EXPLORING THE BIBLICAL AND LEGAL PARADOX:

Considering the massive enlightening and constructive influence of the Bible on American culture and its founding documents, as well as Western Civilization as a whole, this paradoxical irony must be emphatically noted and explored. It is an egregious ironical paradox that the Religion Establishment Clause of the First Amendment of the U.S. Constitution is used (paradoxically) to prohibit the Bible from being taught in the public government schools, along with disparaging attempts to build a wall of separation between the Bible and the government; cloaked as "separation of government and religion," and "separation of "Church and State," How is this rational, legitimate and reconcilable when the unique Bible has been influencing cultures, civilization and nations for civility and good for over five thousand years? Biblical knowledge and the foundation and guidance for the governing documents, the Constitution and the democracy of America are based on biblical influence. The Bible is the foundation for America's Constitution, Democracy, and civilization's humanizing influence.

The disparagement, marginalization, and misrepresentation of the Bible, in reference to the "Religion Establishment Clause" is based on dogmatic ignorance of the Bible's manifested significant truths and pro-life human values for over five thousand years of world history. The expansive disparagement and prohibitions against the Bible are also based on the false premises and presumptions that the Bible is a religion (undefined). The disparagement and subservient relegated status of the Bible in the American Government and general society, has and continues to cause tragic human deprivations, cultural damages, political corruption and national calamities beyond description and calculations.

APPEAL, REQUEST, AND RECOMMENDATION:

THE DULY INCORPORATED CHRISTIAN INSTITUTE OF PUBLIC THEOLOGY OF THE STATE OF GEORGIA, USA, HEREBY APPEALS, REQUESTS, AND RECOMMENDS IT.

TO: THE PRESIDENT OF THE UNITED STATES; UNITED STATES CONGRESS; THE UNITED STATES SUPREME COURT

IT IS RESPECTFULLY REQUESTED THAT THE APPROPRIATE AGENCIES OF THE AMERICAN GOVERNMENT:

1. DEFINE THE MEANING AND ROLE OF RELIGION IN THE FIRST AMENDMENT OF THE CONSTITUTION OF THE UNITED STATES.
2. CLARIFY THE LEGAL PLACE, PUBLIC ROLE, EDUCATIONAL, CLASSIFICATION, AND RELATIONSHIP OF THE GOVERNMENT TO THE BIBLE AS RELATED TO THE FIRST AMENDMENT TO THE CONSTITUTION OF THE UNITED STATES OF AMERICA.

THE CHRISTIAN INSTITUTE OF PUBLIC THEOLOGY, INC

PUBLIC THEOLOGIAN ORIENTATION
THROUGH
QUALITY CIRCLE FELLOWSHIP GROUPS

1. Spiritual Growth Group
2. Black American Heritage Group
3. Message of Negro Spirituals
4. Political Awareness Group
5. Education Success Group
6. Self-Respect and Pride Group
7. Career Planning Group
8. Personal Awareness Group
9. Music Appreciation Group
10. Career Development Group
11. Government Financial Assistance Group
12. Scholarships and Educational Group
13. Success Focus Group
14. Creative Writing Group
15. Bible Study Focus Group
16. Grants and Charitable Foundation Group
17. Booker T. Washington Legacy Group
18. George Washington Legacy Group
19. Martin Luther King, Jr. Legacy Group
20. Negro Spirituals Listening Group
21. U. S. Constitution and Bill of Rights Group
22. Business Letter Writing Group
23. Tutorial Services Group
24. Recreation Group
25. Cultural Enrichment Group
26. Cultural Diversity Education Group
27. Religious Pluralism Education Group

These groups may be conducted in the church facility or community facilities.

PUBLIC THEOLOGIAN MINISTRIES

1. Prison and Jail Ministry	Group Leader	
2. Homeless Ministry	Group Leader	
3. Sick Visitation Ministry	Group Leader	
4. Nursing Home Ministry	Group Leader	
5. Alcohol and Drug Rehabilitation Ministry	Group Leader	
6. School Success Ministry	Group Leader	
7. Employment/Job Development	Group Leader	
8. School Dropout/Tutorial Services	Group Leader	
9. Government Assistance Ministry	Group Leader	
10. Allied Health Services/Education Ministry	Group Leader	
11. Indigent Transportation Ministry	Group Leader	
12. Single Parent and Family Support Services Ministry	Group Leader	

It is recommended that each group select someone to take notes and also someone to present to the group at large.

CHRISTIAN INSTITUTE OF PUBLIC THEOLOGY (CIPT) EDUCATION AND TRAINING FOR PUBLIC THEOLOGIANS CERTIFIED EDUCATION AND TRAINING

1. Certified Christian Counselor CCC I
2. Certified Christian Counselor CCC II
3. Certified Christian Public Theologian
4. Certified Christian Group Counselor
5. Certified Bible Class Teacher
6. Certified Christian Group Leader I
7. Certified Christian Group Leader II
8. Certificate in Children Ministry
9. Certificate in Youth Ministry
10. Single Parent Ministry Certificate
11. Certificate in Jail/Prison Ministry
12. Certificate in Nursing Home Ministry
13. Certificate of Sick Visitation
14. Certificate in Homeless Ministry
15. Certificate in Alcohol and Drug Education
16. Certificate in Allied Health Education
17. Job, Economic, and Career Development
18. Investment and Management of Money
19. Certificate in Civil Rights Ministry
20. Consumer Protection Ministry
21. Certificate in Public Policy Formulation
22. Government Services and Community Resources
23. Certificate in Advocacy for the Poor
24. Business Management Principles
25. Effective Christian Leadership Principles
26. Effective Public Speaking Skills
27. Writing Wills and Transfer of Property

28. Certificate in Character Education
29. Music Appreciation and Spiritual Growth
30. Certificate in Christian Ethics
31. Certified Community Chaplain
32. Certificate in Pastoral Hospice

Place of training and instructors to be designated later.

CHAPTER 8
SALVATION INITIATIVES FOR HUMANITY

GOD'S WILL TO RESTORATION

One of the great themes that runs through the Bible is restoration.

God wants those who are enslaved to be free. He wants the wicked to cease from their torment. He wants the weary to be at rest. He wants the lost to be found. He wants those in bondage set free.

He wants those who are stumbling in the darkness to come to the light.

He wants the ignorant to get knowledge, the foolish to get wisdom, and the simple to get understanding.

God wants harmony where there is conflict. He wants peace where there is war. He wants clean hearts, clear minds, and spirits of righteousness. He wants justice to run down as water and righteousness as a mighty stream.

God wants the hungry to be fed, the naked to be clothed, and the thirsty to be filled with living water. He wants the homeless to be sheltered. He wants those who are in prison to be visited.

He wants those who are lonely to have companions. He wants those who are in despair to find hope. He wants the depressed to have joy and happiness. God wants to heal the brokenhearted and renew the Spirits of those who are disappointed.

God wants the poor to be rich and the weak to be strong. He wants the deaf to hear and the blind to see. God wants prosperity for the poor and respect for the downtrodden. He wants a family of brotherhood and sisterhood of goodwill.

God wants to make all things new. God wants to give you a new life. He wants Everyone to be new creatures in Christ. God's will was to create a New Heaven and a New Earth. Glory be to the God of Restoration!

(Pastor W. J. Webb)

SOME ISMS THAT BLIND, LIMIT, EXCLUDE, CIRCUMSCRIBE AND CAUSE HARM
(A Diagnostic Evaluation Instrument for Human Heterogeneous Fitness and Leadership Capability)
The ISM Rating

Classification	The ISM	Severity	Totals
1.	Racism	0 1 2 3 4	
2.	Classism	0 1 2 3 4	
3.	Ethnocentrism	0 1 2 3 4	
4.	Elitism	0 1 2 3 4	
5.	Masochism	0 1 2 3 4	
6.	Sectarianism	0 1 2 3 4	
7.	Cultism	0 1 2 3 4	
8.	Partisanism	0 1 2 3 4	
9.	Asceticism	0 1 2 3 4	
10.	Narcissism	0 1 2 3 4	
11.	Nationalism	0 1 2 3 4	
12.	Secularism	0 1 2 3 4	
13.	Materialism	0 1 2 3 4	
14.	Agnosticism	0 1 2 3 4	
15.	Nihilism	0 1 2 3 4	
16.	Atheism	0 1 2 3 4	
17.	Egotism	0 1 2 3 4	
18.	Sadism	0 1 2 3 4	
19.	Chauvinism	0 1 2 3 4	
20.	Heathenism	0 1 2 3 4	
21.	Stoicism	0 1 2 3 4	
22.	Epicureanism	0 1 2 3 4	
23.	Infantilism	0 1 2 3 4	

Total Severity

0=none	1=mild	2=moderate	3=severe	4=extreme

Summary of the ISM Rating Scale:

Human nature is susceptible to all the isms listed above. There can be serious problems associated with each one of them. Many persons are influenced adversely by many of the isms listed above. Individuals may have these biases and subjective perceptions to the extent that their judgement, decision-making and leadership ability may be seriously and detrimentally impaired. It is unfortunate and, in many instances, tragic, that most people do not evolve beyond or transcend the above listed isms. This poses a serious problem and challenges for education and leadership in our global society. What are the qualifications for competent teachers, ministers, public servants, and leaders in a global and heterogeneous society?

In addition to ISM rating scales, it is now necessary to develop more instruments to evaluate, assess and determine the spiritual and ideological identities of individuals who are in the society with a potential of doing harm due to their spiritual and ideological ismatisms.

The Christian Institute of Public Theology, Inc.

THE CHRISTIAN INSTITUTE OF PUBLIC THEOLOGY
Educational Themes to Save Humanity & Enrich Civilization

(The Following Themes are Vital Mandates to Respond to the Global Culture Crisis)

1. Education to Lead Humanity
2. Education to Build & Enrich Civilization
3. Education to Build Nations
4. Education to Establish Just Societies
5. Education for Liberation and Salvation
6. Education for Values Clarification
7. Education for Establishing Equitable Priorities
8. Education to Preserve Survival Values
9. Education to Acknowledge the God of Creation
10. Education to Serve and Glorify God
11. Education for God's Kingdom Building
12. Universalizing Biblical Education
13. The Salvation Use of Knowledge as a Priority
14. Defining the Role of Biblical Knowledge in Human Affairs
15. Knowledge for Truth, Guidance, Light and Life
16. God's Role in Biblical Knowledge for Humanity
17. The Educator's Role for a Civil and Humane Society
18. Establishing Priorities for Biblical Education
19. Establishing Goals and Objectives for Theological Knowledge
20. Defining the Established Authority for Human Governance
21. Defining the Role and Authority for Theological Knowledge
22. Establishing Universal Ethics for All Humanity

23. Public Theologians as Guardians of True Knowledge
24. The Synchronization of Science, Art, Law, and Theology
25. Public Theology as the Guardian of Sound Doctrines
26. Public Theologians as the Vanguard for Truth
27. Establishing Salvation Values for Public Education
28. Instituting Core Survival Values for Public Education
29. Exploring the Vertical and Horizontal Dimensions of God's Will
30. The Ethical Balance of the Sacred and Secular Values of Society

HOW DOES JESUS CHRIST RELATE TO THESE THEMES:

The Christian Institute of Public Theology

GOD'S SPIRITUAL GUIDANCE AND BLESSINGS FOR MANKIND

1. Fear God and keep his commandments: for this is the whole duty of man. (Eccles. 2:13)
2. Let this mind be in you which was also in Christ Jesus. (Philippians 2:5)
3. Thou shall love the Lord thy God with all thy heart, and with all soul, and with all thy Mind. (Matthew 22:37)
4. Thou shall love thy neighbor as thyself. (Matthew 22:39)
5. Be fruitful, and multiply, and replenish the earth, and subdue it: and have dominion over the fish of the sea, and over the fowl of the air, and over every living thing that moves upon the earth. (Genesis 1:28)
6. But seek ye first the kingdom of God, and his righteousness; and all these things shall be added unto you. (Matthew 6:33)
7. Except a man be born again, he cannot see the kingdom of God. (John 3:3). Marvel not That I said unto thee, you must be born again. (John 3:7)
8. But be ye transformed by the renewing of your mind, that ye may prove what is that Good, and acceptable, and perfect, will of God. (Romans 12:2)
9. Fight the good fight of faith, lay hold on eternal life. (1Timothy).
10. Be strong in the grace that is in Christ Jesus. (2Timothy 2:1)
11. Preach the word; be instant in season, out of season; reprove, rebuke, exhort with all long suffering and doctrine. (2Timothy 4:2)

12. But watch thou in all things, endure afflictions, do the work of an evangelist, make full Proof of thy ministry. (2Timothy 4:5)
13. I have fought a good fight, I have finished my course, and I have kept the faith. (2Tim. 4-7)
14. Son of man, I have made thee a watchman unto the house of Israel: Therefore, hear the word at my mouth, and give them warning from me. (Ezekiel 3:17)
15. Warn the wicked. (Ezekiel 3:18-19). Warn the righteous. (Ezekiel 3:20-21)
16. Therefore, let us not sleep, as do others, but let us watch and be sober. (Thessalonians 5:6)
17. Rejoice evermore. Pray without ceasing. In everything give thanks. (Thessalonians 5:16-18)
18. I press toward the mark for the prize of the high calling of God in Christ Jesus. (Philippians 3:14)
19. But let judgment run down as waters, and righteousness as a mighty stream. (Amos 5:24)
20. Draw nigh unto God, and he will draw nigh unto you. James

The Christian Institute of Public Theology

THE BIBLE IS THE ULTIMATE UNIVERSAL AUTHORITY ON
HUMAN LIFE AND HEALTH
THE BIBLE IS INCLUSIVE OF ALL VALUES ESSENTIAL FOR
MANKIND'S SALVATION
THE BIBLE HAS THE MESSAGE TO TRANSFORM HUMAN INSTITUTIONS

THE BIBLE'S TRANSFORMING POWER

1. The Bible Transforms Minds, Hearts, and Spirits.
2. The Bible Transforms the Lives of Men, Women and Children.
3. The Bible Transforms Lives, Social Relationships and Families.
4. The Bible Transforms Educational, Ideological and Spiritual Institutions.
5. The Bible Transforms Religious and Philosophical Institutions.
6. The Bible Transforms Governmental and Political Institutions.
7. The Bible Transforms Economic and Business Enterprises.
8. The Bible Transforms Cities, States and Nations.
9. The Bible Transforms Cultures, Cults and Corruption.
10. The Bible Transforms the Degeneration of Civilizations.
11. The Bible Transforms the Ethics and Morals of Humanity.
12. The Bible Transforms the Secular Cities of Men to the Sacred Kingdom of God.

FOUR THOUSAND-PLUS YEARS OF HISTORY HAVE CONFIRMED THE VALIDITY OF THE TRANSFORMING POWER OF GOD'S BIBLICAL WORD. HUMANITY AND CIVILIZATION ARE AT A DANGEROUS JUNCTURE IN THE TWENTY FIRST CENTURY THAT REQUIRES THE TRANSFORMING POWER OF GOD'S WORD. THEREFORE, ALL OF AMERICA'S RELIGIOUS, EDUCATIONAL, POLITICAL, ECONOMIC AND SOCIAL INSTITUTIONS MUST BEGIN TO PRIORITIZE THE TEACHING, PREACHING, WITNESSING AND DISSEMINATING OF GOD'S BIBLICAL WORD IN THE CULTURE OF AMERICA AS NEVER BEFORE. THE CHURCH, AMERICANS AND THE BELIEVERS IN THE BIBLE AND JESUS CHRIST CAN NO LONGER IGNORE THE TRUTH OF THE WORD OF GOD.

"HOW SHALL WE ESCAPE, IF WE NEGLECT SO GREAT SALVATION?" (Hebrews 2:3)

The Christian Institute of Public Theology

THE MISSION OF THE GOSPEL
THROUGH THE MINISTRY OF JESUS CHRIST

1. Feed and Nurture: John 21:15-17; Matthew 25:31-46
2. Love & Evangelize: John 13:34,4:16; Mark 12:30-31; 1Cor. 13
3. Teach, Preach & Witness: Matthew 28:19; Mark 16:15
4. Heal & Restore: Luke 4:18-19; John 11:25
5. Liberate & Elevate: Luke 4:18-19; 1John 4:1-2; John 8:32
6. Build & Establish: Matthew 6:33, Matthew 16:18; Rev. 11:15
7. Comfort & Encourage: John 14:16-18; Matthew 5:1-12
8. Warn & Prophesy: Ezekiel 3:17-21; Amos 4:12; Matthew 3:3; Col 1:28
9. Defend & Comfort: Psalm 82:3-4; Matthew 18:8-9; Ephesians 6:11-17
10. Have Dominion: Genesis 1:28; Matthew 24:14; Romans 13:1
11. Witness Truth & Light: Matthew 5:16, 33; John 14:6
12. Follow Jesus Christ: John 14:6; Acts 4:12; Isaiah 45:23; Phil 2:9-11

There is a place and a duty for all believers in Jesus Christ to participate in the mission and ministry of Jesus Christ in whatever position or calling you may be involved regardless to your title. There is plenty of room in the Kingdom of God as Expressed in (Matthew 9:37-38) and (Luke 10:2). The harvest is great, and the laborers are few.

The Christian Institute of Public Theology, Inc.
Atlanta, Georgia

CLERGY LEAD GROUPS
FOR EDUCATIONAL ACHIEVEMENT AND
SCHOOL SUCCESS
FOCUS GROUPS

1. Character Education Groups
2. School Dropout Prevention Groups
3. Study and Academic Improvement Groups
4. Self Esteem and Success Identity Groups
5. Values Clarification Group and Life Purpose Groups
6. Academic Subjects Tutorial Groups
7. Biblical Literature and Wisdom Groups
8. Biblical History and Cultural Variety Groups
9. Messages of Inspiration and Motivation Assemblies
10. Drug Abuse Prevention, Health, and Education Groups
11. Lessons and Values from Black American Heroes and History
12. Promotion of Health, Wholeness and Excellence Groups

Concerned Black Clergy: Clergy Training and Education
Committee

Rev. Willie J. Webb, Chairperson
Christian Institute of Public Theology, Inc.
(February 2013)

CHRISTIAN INSTITUTE OF PUBLIC THEOLOGY
AN URGENT SERVICE CHALLENGE FOR CLERGY AND THE BLACK CHURCH

The following human service areas offer challenges as well as opportunities for theologically guided churches and institutions to get redemptively involved in the education, healing, restoration and salvation of the victimized people of this Nation. The challenge is to reform and transform disordered persons & nations.

Consultation Services:

1. Legal and Judicial
2. Business Management Concerns
3. Organizational Administration
4. Domestic Relations & Child Development
5. Public Relations & Social
6. Educational Concerns
7. Religious (Spiritual)
8. Mental Health & Human
9. Alcohol and Drug Related
10. Criminal and Civil Justice Issues

"Call upon me in the day of trouble: I will deliver thee."

Counseling Services
(Individual, Group, Family, Career, Guidance)

1. Employment, Civil Rights, Social Justice
2. Marital, Premarital Separations, Divorce
3. Alcohol, Drugs, Dependence, Addiction
4. Crisis, Intervention, Trauma, Stabilization
5. Government Assistance Programs
6. Mental Depression, Demoralization
7. Stress and Anger Management
8. Values Clarification, Priority Focus
9. Conflict Resolution, Guilt Relief
10. Sexual Dysfunction and Concerns

"Ask, and it shall be given you; Seek and ye shall find; Knock and it shall be opened."

Ethical and Legalistic Training to Protect Life, Liberty, and Human Rights:

1. Constitutional Rights
2. Civil Rights and Human Rights
3. Equal Employment Opportunity
4. Consumer Protection Laws
5. Contractual Agreements, Business Law
6. US Labor Relations Board
7. Health Laws, EPA, OSHA, FDA
8. Complaint & Grievance Procedure
9. Administrative, Judicial & DOJ Remedies
10. Equal Educational Opportunity

"My people are destroyed for lack of knowledge"

Developmental Training for Personal Growth & Productive Living:

1. Communication, Information Techn.
2. Leadership Training Skills
3. Group Leadership Interaction Skills
4. Composition Writing Skills
5. Assertiveness Training
6. Drug Addiction Recovery Education
7. Responsible Business Transactions
8. Success Identity Through Reality Training
9. Activity Therapy and Spiritual Growth
10. Motivation & Self Actualization

Rev. W. J. Webb, MDIV, MS, MA, CACH, CCS, CPE

November 15, 2015

Dear Clergy, Pastors, and Community Leaders:

The Concerned Black Clergy, through its Clergy Training Committee, is strongly recommending that individual churches and other clergy alliances establish ongoing weekly fellowship group meetings. Fellowship groups have great potential for needed enlightenment, inspiration, motivation, healing, and restoration of our people. These groups, when spiritually led, can have a significant positive impact on the alleviation of depravity, hatred, violence, and crime in our communities.

In the interest of restoring and sustaining the health and wellbeing of massive numbers of Black African American citizens and families, the establishment of fellowship groups is recommended as an ongoing initiative of the Black Church. The fellowship group provides an opportunity to find faith, grow faith, share faith, and apply faith. The restoration of the homeless, helpless, and hopeless is also the restoration of America.

The establishment of the following fellowship groups are recommended:

1. Bible Study Group - for, "Learning Foundational Truths for Life and Living."
2. Spiritual Growth Group - for, "Building Character, Self-worth and Self-esteem."
3. Conflict Resolution Group - for, "Positive Problem Solving and Conciliation."
4. Values Clarification Group - for, "Learning Prioritization of What is Important."

5. Socio-Economic-Political Awareness Group - for, "Discovering What is Going On."

(There are many other groups that offer infinite benefits and possibilities.)

The Concerned Black Clergy, through the Clergy Training Committee, is available to provide training and technical assistance in the establishment and effective leadership and operation of fellowship groups. It is urgent and critical that we get started with this God inspired, self-help initiative without delay. The unique role, experience, and history of the Black African American Church make it the largest, most capable, and most resourceful American Institution to lead and nurture the restoration of Black African Americans in America.

We look forward to hearing about your urgently needed fellowship group initiatives.

Rev. Willie James Webb, CEO, CAPT, INC
CBC Clergy Training Committee Chair

CASE MANAGEMENT EMPOWERMENT

Remedial, Preventive and Growth Service Needs:

1. Food, Shelter, Clothing
2. A Living Environment of Safety and Security
3. Health Services and Personal Care
4. Employment and Financial Security
5. Human Support Services and Fellowship
6. Education and Training Opportunities
7. Transportation
8. Computer and Internet Access
9. Religious and Fellowship Experience
10. Recreational and Peaceful Leisure Time

Some Barriers to Human Services:

1. Physical Barriers
2. Psychological Barriers
3. Socioeconomic Barriers
4. Educational and Technological Barriers
5. Racial, Class and Ethnic Barriers
6. Age, Religious and Sex Barriers
7. Geographical, Language and cultural Barriers
8. Legal, Political, and discriminatory Barriers
9. Unethical, Immoral, Unprofessional and Criminal Barriers
10. Negligence, Passive, Uncaring and Indifference Barriers

Case Management Services:

1. Link the Client's needs to the available services
2. Remove barriers that prevent service and resources to clients
3. Identify and create needed support services for the disadvantaged clients
4. Be aggressive in cutting through administrative and bureaucratic red tape for clients
5. Create Support systems for the helpless, homeless, hungry, and hopeless
6. Become A Bold and Consistent Advocate for the Disadvantaged Clients/Persons
7. Create Policies and Systems to Motivate, Inspire and Empower the Disadvantaged
8. Create Directories of Community Resources and Referral Agencies for the Disadvantaged.
9. Connect Clients to Community Agencies and Fellowship Groups of Spiritual Growth
10. Connect Clients with Agencies that Educate and Nurture the Human Spirit for Growth, Success, Self-Reliance and Resilience.

The Christian Institute of Public Theology, Inc.
Atlanta, Georgia

CHRISTIAN ASSOCIATION OF PUBLIC THEOLOGIANS

The following legislative and administrative recommendations will serve the causes of justice, peace, goodwill, health, and prosperity in our government and society. It will enhance trust and confidence in the government and create an atmosphere of respect and hope for the future.

Recommendations:

1. PUBLIC OFFICIAL ACCOUNTABILITY - Adopt legislation requiring all public officials, local, state, and federal, to provide quarterly constituent meetings and quarterly written political updates to be made available to constituent communities.
2. FIT FOR DUTY STANDARDS - Adopt legislation requiring a minimum standard of educational, ethical citizenship, and patriotic competence for all public officials, compatible with the laws of the U.S. Constitution.
3. BIBLICAL LITERACY AND THEOLOGICAL COMPETENCE. Adopt legislation requiring Biblical literacy and theological competence courses in the curriculum of all law schools. Statutory laws cannot ignore the divine laws and natural laws of God and be valid in the administration of human and social justice.
4. BIBLICAL JUDEO-CHRISTIAN EDUCATION - Adopt Legislation requiring courses of the Old Testament and the New Testament to be taught as history and literature in all public schools. Based on ecological studies (which are scientific and objective),

the Judeo-Christian Bible has been validated by history to be inclusive (but not coercive) of all people. It has been validated by rigorous scholarship to be progressively revelatory, historical, redemptive, comprehensive, wholistic, universal, and foundational for democratic, ethical, moral, and spiritual values that are compatible with the disciplines of human nature, law, art, science, and religion.

5. THEOLOGICAL REPRESENTATION IN PUBUC POLICY - The Church and the faith community must insist on credible theological representation at the local, state, and federal levels about the formulation and implementation of public policy for the American people. It is dangerous for the Nation to make decisions for the people without being theologically informed.

6. ESTABLISH IMPARTIAL GOVERNMENT MERIT SYSTEMS - Establish through legislation, impartial merit systems with explicit fair employment policies, practices, and procedures. The government must set an example for fairness and justice in its employment practices, contractual agreements, and other transactions involving the rights of citizens and the equitable allocation of taxpayer's money. The subversion of fairness undermines trust in government. True merit systems reinforce trust in government and democracy and contribute to peace and goodwill.

7. PERSONAL LIABILITIES FOR RIGHTS VIOLATIONS-Institute legislation for personal liability for any government employee or government agent in the course of their employment, who violate the Civil Rights of a subordinate or another employee

during their employment with the respective agency. This prohibits the violating employee from claiming administrative Immunity from prosecution.

8. EMPLOYMENT GRIEVANCE PROCEDURE-Enact legislation requiring a fair, clear, and understandable grievance policy and procedure that complies with the 14th Amendment's due process of law, with reasonable time limits for resolution that do not exceed 180 days.

9. PROHIBIT NO HIRE LISTS-Institute legislation that prohibits any government or private agency from placing the name of an employee, former employee, or prospective employee on a designated no-hire list without the due process of law. In the event a person's name is placed on a no-hire list after a due process hearing has been granted, specify the full nature of the no-hire list, including its jurisdiction, effects, duration, removal, and appeal procedure.

10. CONFLICT OF INTEREST DISCLOSURE-Institute legislation that requires legal penalties for an attorney or other legal representative to agree to represent a client for consideration and fail to disclose a known conflict of interest when entering into the contractual agreement with the client or fail to make disclosure after the agreement.

11. CIVIL RIGHTS SEMINARS - It is recommended that human rights and Civil Rights seminars be held in each government agency monthly at a convenient time and place to keep employees and citizens informed of the laws and the education about the Civil Rights of U.S. Citizens. Such meetings are also recommended for the Church and other faith organizations.

12. PROFESSIONAL CODE OF ETHICS - It is recommended that each government employee be required to subscribe to a designated code of professional ethics with explicit required conduct and behavior. Each employee is entitled to know with specificity what conduct, mannerisms and expectations are required of them. It is recommended that professional codes of ethics be instituted in all agencies where people are served, including the clergy and faith-based organizations.

Rev. W.J. Webb, CEO, CAPT, INC

GOD INSPIRED ARTISTIC EXPRESSIONS
Theological Values for Human Redemption

1. Acculturation
2. Assimilation
3. Balance
4. Beauty
5. Civility
6. Compatibility
7. Complementary
8. Congruence
9. Continuity
10. Elevation
11. Elegance
12. Equality
13. Equilibrium
14. Goodness
15. Grace
16. Harmony
17. Humanitarianism
18. Joy
19. Justice
20. Kindness

21. Knowledge
22. Liberty
23. Love
24. Meditation
25. Order
26. Peace
27. Radiance
28. Reconciliation
29. Regeneration
30. Righteousness
31. Restoration
32. Resurrection
33. Serenity
34. Symmetry
35. Synchronization
36. Systemization
37. Transfiguration
38. Transformation
39. Transcendence
40. Truth

These elevating and transformative theological spiritual values can be expressed through human hearts, spirits, minds, personal service, families, agencies, institutions, culture, and nations. They can be illustrated, demonstrated, transmitted, and assimilated through the blessings of SCIENCE, ART, LAW, AND THEOLOGY. These values give a picture beyond the reality of WHAT IS - TO WHAT OUGHT TO BE, AND WHAT GOD HAS MADE POSSIBLE TO BE,

AND CAN BE. EVERY PERSON IS INVITED TO EMBRACE THESE TRANSFORMATIVE ARTISTIC VALUES.

The Public Theologian

November 15, 2015

Christian Association of Public Theologians
PO Box 3148
Atlanta, Georgia 30302

Dear Clergy, Pastors, and Community Leaders:

The Concerned Black Clergy, through its Clergy Training Committee, is strongly recommending that individual churches and other clergy alliances establish ongoing weekly fellowship group meetings. Fellowship groups have great potential for needed enlightenment, inspiration, motivation, healing, and restoration of our people. These groups, when spiritually led, can have a significant positive impact on the alleviation of depravity, hatred, violence, and crime in our communities.

In the Interest of restoration and sustaining the health and well-being of massive numbers of Black African American citizens and families, the establishment of fellowship groups Is recommended as an ongoing Initiative of the Black Church. The fellowship group provides an opportunity to find faith, grow faith, share faith, and apply faith. The restoration of the homeless, helpless, and hopeless Is also the restoration of America.

The establishment of the following fellowship groups is recommended:

1. Bible Study Group - for, "Learning Foundational Truths for Life and Living."
2. Spiritual Growth Group-for, "Building Character, Self-worth and Self-esteem."

3. Conflict Resolution Group - for, "Positive Problem Solving & Conciliation."
4. Values Clarification Group - for, "Learning Prioritization of What Is Important"
5. Sodo-Economic-Political Awareness Group - for, "Discovering What Is Going On."

(There are many other groups that offer infinite benefits and possibilities.)

The Concerned Black Clergy, through the Clergy Training Committee, is available to provide training and technical assistance In the establishment and effective leadership and operation of fellowship groups. It is urgent and critical that we get started with this God inspired and self-help Initiative without delay. The unique role, experience, and history of the Black African American Church, makes it the largest, most capable, and resourceful American Institution to lead and nurture the restoration of Black African Americans in America.

We look forward to hearing about your urgently needed fellowship group initiatives.

Rev. Willie James Webb, CEO CAPT, INC
CBC Clergy Training Committee Chair

Concerned Black Clergy of Metropolitan Atlanta, INC

ISSUES FOR PREMARITAL COUNSELING

- Is the prospect legally eligible?
- Is there a willingness to provide full disclosure?
- Is the prospect sufficiently mature and responsible?
- Is the Prospect morally and ethically fit for the union?
- Is there convincing potential for mature love and commitment?
- Is there convincing evidence of trustworthiness?
- What is the prospect's philosophy of life? (Core beliefs)
- Where is the prospect headed in life? (Is the direction clear?)
- What are the primary ambitions of the prospect?
- What are the specific religious beliefs? (Extent of compatibility?)
- Is there a criminal justice history? (Get the specifics) Is there a history of mental illness? (Get the specifics)
- What is the prospect's sexual orientation? (past and present)
- What is the prospect's health history and current health status?
- What is prospect's past and current substance use & abuse history?
- Has there been any treatment or associated problems?
- Is this prospect of good sound character? (Based on what?)
- What is prospect's past and current habits and obsessions?
- Does the prospect have a solid responsible history?
- What jobs, how many, how long respective tenures, benefits?
- What is prospect's educational qualifications & work experience?
- What marketable skills does prospect possess?

- What is prospect's financial status?
- How much cash on hand? (In banks & investments, etc.)
- How much or what is the value of prospect's personal Property?
- What are the locations, values, and unpaid balances on real property?
- Is the residence and the utilities in the name of the prospect?
- Has the prospect been successful in establishing independent living?
- Is there joint ownership of the property? (With whom and relationship)
- Get a summation of prospects' assets.
- Get a summation of prospects' debts and liabilities.
- In view of the circumstances, would a prenuptial agreement be appropriate?
- Get a list of past marriages, divorces, and current status.
- Are there significant residuals from past marriages and relationships?
- What is the prospect's responsibility and relationship to children as well as parents or other relatives or persons?
- What institutions, agencies, community organizations, groups, and individuals is the prospect is associated with?
- Assess the compatibilities and the incompatibilities.
- Has the prospect accepted Jesus Christ his Lord and personal Savior?

W. J. Webb, MDiv, MS, MA
Pastoral Counselor

EDUCATION AND TRAINING FOCUS FOR CLERGY TO MEET THE 21ST CENTURY SERVICE CHALLENGES

1. The public's theological leadership is significantly important and critical for the Welfare and advancement of human civilization. American history is replete with public theologians, especially black American theologians, who played critical roles in advancing civil rights and civilization. There have been many, with Martin Luther King, Jr. being the most prominent.
2. The clergy (public theologians) must be diligent as guardians of the truth and survival values and as faithful stewards of the blessings and resources of God.
3. The clergy must recognize in view of advanced technology that there is a very small margin for error in this 21st Century. One wrong or one bad decision can Result in irreversible catastrophic consequences. Random decisions, arbitrary Decisions, and partisan political decisions are dangerous decisions in the 21st Century. The clergy must insist on more informed precise, righteous, and just Decisions, actions from our leadership.
4. The clergy must invest significantly more money and resources in the training, Education, and skill building of its leaders and laity to meet the serious cultural Crisis challenges of the 21st Century.
5. The clergy must make its case for righteous and just leadership from its public officials and representatives as opposed to partisan, self-serving political Decisions. The only safe decisions are based on truth, justice, and righteousness.

6. The clergy must step away from private religion and accept the theological responsibility for public advocacy leadership.

7. To be relevant and responsive to the needs of these present times, the Clergy must tell the Story in a new updated way. The clergy must design the Prophetic gospel message to meet the needs of the present cultural crises, Technological and ideological challenges presently facing humanity.

8. The clergy must ger involved in the construction and formulation of redemptive social policies needed for the guidance, safety, and welfare of society from the Theological perspective.

9. The clergy must point the way to light, life, hope, social justice, freedom, redemption and salvation, as well as a community of love and human dignity.

10. The ultimate responsibility of the clergy is to guide humanity on the path of righteousness and justice, as well as to civilize the baseness and crudeness of human nature; to transform human culture and human hearts into the new nature in Jesus Christ.

11. The clergy must proclaim and practice to respond to the new needs as well as the new and old threats and challenges of the twenty-first century. The clergy must lead in the Transformation of the destructive threat of technology into a constructive ally for humanity.

12. The clergy must lead us from the conflicts of tribalism to the universality of brotherhood and sisterhood. The clergy must lead us from the bonds of sectarianism, cultism, secularism, materialism, greed, and the bonds of hatred and addictions.

13. The clergy must advocate for the inclusion of public theology in the curriculum of law schools, medical

schools, and business schools. Doctors, lawyers, judges, and business executives make critical decisions regarding human life. They must have prime exposure to the highest known ethical and moral principles.

14. Advocate for the establishment of public theology associations for students on a voluntary basis in colleges and universities. It is irresponsible and dangerous to educate students and leave them with theological knowledge that is void.

15. The clergy must provide more theological education in their churches and schools, along with the addition of libraries, study sanctuaries, educational Forums, training seminars, a fellowship network, growth groups, and Think tanks.

16. Encourage the already legally approved adoption of the Bible courses in public schools as history and literature. This was approved in Georgia in July 2007. Most local educational boards in Georgia have failed to adopt the Approved Bible course curriculum.

17. The clergy must get positively and proactively involved in the rearing, development, education, and educational institutions of our children.

18. The clergy must advocate for the institution of merit systems in education, employment, and other venues that allocate public resources to ensure equity, fairness, and justice to avoid the harmful effects of arbitrary decisions.

19. The clergy must focus prime time, attention, resources, and strategies on the Criminal Justice, civil justice, and judicial systems that impact massive numbers of black and brown men adversely and disproportionately.

20. The clergy must form supportive and redemptive alliances with our anchor institutions of families, schools,

churches, synagogues, mosques, businesses, and government agencies.

The Christian Institute of Public Theology
Atlanta, Georgia
June 28, 2010
Atlanta, Ga. 30302

THE PRINCIPAL IS KEY TO SCHOOL SUCCESS
Willie James Webb, MA. MS, MDiv

The key to a successful school is a competent, compassionate, and wise leader. A successful school is one that maximizes the teaching ability and resourcefulness of each teacher and the receptivity of each respective student. To elicit the optimal benefits from teachers and to maximize the optimal receptivity of students, the school leader must create the environmental conditions and the social atmosphere for the reciprocal effects of optimum teaching and learning.

The leader must have the qualifications, the care, and the understanding to create the conditions that will be conducive and promotional for optimizing and sustaining the highest possible educational achievement. To accomplish the creation and sustaining of this unique learning environment, the leader must know and practice the science, art, and professional ethics of effective administration.

There are many variables that impact the educational experience in public schools. These variables include the teacher, the student, the parents, the principal, the superintendent, the educational board, the PTSA (Parent Teacher Student Association), the church, and other community interest groups. Unfortunately, despite all of these variables, the classroom teacher bears the majority of the blame for low student academic achievement. By the same token, there is a lack of emphasis on the role of the principal as the primary key to educational achievement in the public schools.

Too often, principals who lack competence, compassion, wisdom, and the art of effective administrative skills resort to the intimidating force of their authoritative position. Administration by intimidation creates an anti-educational and anti-motivational learning environment. Authoritative intimidation is counterproductive to motivation, inspiration, innovation, and education.

The use of authoritative external pressures to force academic achievement usually has the opposite effect. External forces create resistance and resentment. The resistance and resentment become disruptive and obstructive to teaching and learning. Authoritative intimidation creates a hostile and negative environment that minimizes educational opportunity and effectiveness.

The ideal conditions for teaching and learning are a positive and non-threatening environment, motivated by inspiration instead of intimidation. Inspiration creates a desire within the student to want to learn. External intimidation creates internal resistance to learning and academic achievement Outside intimidation by an authoritative administrator forces the teacher into a self-protective and defensive posture. Such demoralization impairs teaching ability and effectiveness.

The principal, the onsite leader, is the key variable to setting the tone and creating the policies that create the conditions and positive environment for optimum learning and academic achievement. A principal who is competent, compassionate, ethical, and professional, with expertise in administrative skills, offers the greatest hope for student and school academic achievement and success.

The challenge and the duty of the principal are to create a healthy, familial, purpose-driven environment with significant and worthy goals. The principal must create a team spirit where each member feels like a significant part of the team with commensurately significant roles. Out of this team spirit, the school must develop a corporate identity of success based on high self-esteem and pride. Outstanding teaching and significant learning will occur when the school becomes a place where teachers and students enjoy being present and are proud to be a part of it.

A school that recognizes and reinforces the concept that each teacher, each student, and every person has inherent personal dignity and significance, will be permeated with sentiments of kindness, respect, fairness, and pride. A school environment that is enriched with a noble purpose, worthy goals, inspirational ideals, and an inspired, dedicated, and purpose driven staff, will create an atmosphere and conditions for maximum educational achievement. The quality of leadership is what makes a significant difference.

Willie J. Webb is Pastor of Foundation Baptist Church, Atlanta, Ga., and the Author of: The Way Out of Darkness- Vital Public Theology, Psychotrauma - The Human Injustice Crisis, and God's Spiritual Prescriptions. He is the founder and CEO of The Christian Association of Public Theologians, Inc. and The Christian Institute of Public Theology, Inc. He is an instructor of public theology and a certified clinical supervisor with GACA (Georgia Addiction Counselors Association). He is a graduate of Morehouse College, Clark Atlanta University, Georgia State University, and the Morehouse School of Religion at the Interdenominational Theological Center, Atlanta.

AMERICAN PRAYER
UNITED STATES DECLARATION
OF REPENTANCE

Lord, we have violated the self-evident truth that all men are created equal. We have violated the inalienable human rights of life, liberty, and the pursuit of happiness of our brothers and sisters.

Our executive, legislative, judicial, and corporate systems have denied equal rights and equal opportunities to certain citizens of the United States. We are guilty of enslaving and oppressing other selected human beings. We have denied truth, obstructed justice, violated goodness, and practiced unrighteousness. We have rejected your undisputable sovereign authority. We have turned our backs on the outstretched arms of your love and grace.

Lord, our heads are confused, our hearts are hateful, our purposes are vain, our bodies are abused, and our souls are lost. In lieu of growing up as enlightened men and women, we have chosen the naive prison house of childhood. You have created us as your children and given us your image, and yet we seek other identities that are alien, idolatrous, and contrary to your will. We have chosen sinful self-righteousness instead of your righteousness of truth.

Lord, forgive us for violating, selectively and arbitrarily, the laws of the U.S. Constitution and the Declaration of Independence. Forgive us for defaming your name on our currency, "In God We Trust." Forgive us for betraying the American Motto, "One Nation Under God." Forgive us for ignoring the Biblical Word of Truth and for rejecting the Way, the Truth, and the life in Jesus Christ.

Lord, give us the spirit of repentance, atonement, restitution, and restoration. Create in us, and in America, a clean heart, and renew a right spirit within us.

In the name of the only begotten son and Savior,
JESUS CHRIST, amen.
(Pastor W. J. Webb, U.S. Citizen)

BIBLIOGRAPHY/REFERENCES

Alcoholics Anonymous. Living Sober. New York: World Services, Inc., 1975.

American Psychiatric Association (1994), Diagnostic and Statistical Manual of Mental Disorders (4th ed.) Washington, DC: 1994.

American Psychiatric Association. Diagnostic and Statistical Manual of Mental Disorders (5th ed.). Washington, DC: 2013.

Barth, Roland S. Improving the Schools from Within. San Francisco: A Wiley Company, 1990.

Benne, Robert. The Paradoxical Vision. A Public Theology for the Twenty-First Century. Augsburg: Fortress Press, 1995.

Bettelheim, Bruno. The Informed Heart. New York: Avon Books, 1971.

Blanchard, Ken and Hodges, Phil. The Servant Leader. Nashville: Thomas Nelson, 2003.

Brick, John. Drugs, the Brain, and Behavior. New York: Harworth Medical Press, 1998.

Bright, John. A History of Israel. Philadelphia: Westminster Press, 1972.

Buttrick, George Arthur (ed.) The Interpreters Bible. New York: Abingdon Press, 1952

Clinebell, Howard. Basic Types of Pastoral Care and Counseling. Nashville,1984.

Corey, Gerald. Theory and Practice of Counseling and Psychotherapy. Pacific Grove, CA: Brooks Cole Publishing Co., 1977.

Cone, James H. Black Theology. A Documentary History, New York. Orbis Books, 1993

Cox, Harvey. The Secular City. New York, The MacMillan Co.,1965.

DuBois, W.E.B. Dark Water: Voices from Within the Veil. Mineola: NY: Dover Publication, 1999.

DuBois, W.E.B. The Souls of Black Folk. New York: Vintage Books, 1990.

Egan, Gerard. The Skilled Helper, Boston: Brooks/Cole Publishing Co. 1998.

Everly, George S. and Lating, Jeffrey. Psychotraumatology New York: Plenum Press, 1995.

Felder, Cain Hope. Stony The Road We Trod. Minneapolis: Fortress Press, 1991.

Fosdick, Harry Emerson. The Modern Use of the Bible. New York: McMillan Co., 1961.

Frazier, E. Franklin. On Race Relations Chicago: University Press,1968.

Friere, Paulo. Pedagogy of the Oppressed. New York: Continuum Publishing Co., 1997.

Grant, Joanne- Black Protest: History, Documents, and Analyses. New York: Fawcett Premier, 1968.

Gray, Fred D. The Tuskegee Syphilis Study, Montgomery Al. New South Books, 1998

Hanson, Rick. Buddhas Brain. Oakland CA: New Harbinger Publications, Inc., 2009.

Hodgson, Peter C., King, Robert H. Readings in Christian Theology Minneapolis: Fortress Press, 1985.

Hyders, O. Quentin. The Christian's Handbook of Psychiatry Old Tappan, New Jersey, 1973.

Jorg, Jeff. Ministry in the New Marriage Culture. Nashville: Publishing Group, 2015.

James, Muriel, Jongeward, Dorothy. Born to Win, Massachusetts; Perseus Books, 1996.

Jones, James H. Bad Blood: The Tuskegee Syphilis Experiment. New York: Macmillan Publishing Company, 1981.

Mark, Vernon H. Brain Power. Boston: Houghton Mifflin Co.1989.

Masters, Kim J. The Angry Child. Santa Monica, CA: Psychiatric Hospital Division, 1993.

Montessori, Maria. The Absorbent Mind. New York: Dell Publishing, 1967.

Quarles, Benjamin. The Negro in the Making of America. New York: MacMillan Publishing Co.,1987.

Roberts, Deotis J. The Prophethood of Black Believers. Louisville, KY: Knox Press, 1994.

Simeons, A.T.W. Man's Presumptuous Brain. New York: E.P. Dutton & Co.1962.

The Holy Bible (King James Version)

Tillman, William M. Understanding Christian Ethics. Nashville Broadman & Holman Publishers, 1988.

Twerski, Abraham. Addictive Thinking Center City, Minn: Hazelden, 1997.

Urschel, Harold C. Healing the Addicted Brain. Naperville, Illinois Sourcebooks Inc.,2009.

Walker, David. David Walker's Appeal. Baltimore, Md: Black Classie Press, 1993.

Washington, Booker T. Up From Slavery. Doubleday, Page & Co., 1901.

Webb, W.J. Psychotrauma: The Human Injustice Crisis. Lima, Atlanta GA

Webb, W.J. God's Spiritual Prescriptions. Atlanta GA, 2024

Webb, W.J. The Way Out of Darkness. Atlanta GA, 2024

Wright, Bobby E. Psychopathic Racial Personality. Chicago: Third World Press, 1984.

Yalom, Irvin D. The Gift of Therapy New York: Harper Collins Publishers,2002.

www.ingramcontent.com/pod-product-compliance
Lightning Source LLC
Chambersburg PA
CBHW060854120626
46553CB00001B/85